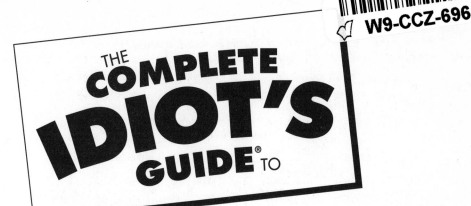

THE
COMPLETE IDIOT'S GUIDE® TO

Toltec Wisdom

by Sheri A. Rosenthal, DPM

ALPHA

A member of Penguin Group (USA) Inc.

I would like to dedicate this book to my father, Martin Rosenthal, and my grandmother, Ann Haber. These two dear and wonderful souls passed away during the writing of this book. They would have loved seeing this guide published!

ALPHA BOOKS

Published by the Penguin Group

Penguin Group (USA) Inc., 375 Hudson Street, New York, New York 10014, U.S.A.

Penguin Group (Canada), 10 Alcorn Avenue, Toronto, Ontario, Canada M4V 3B2 (a division of Pearson Penguin Canada Inc.)

Penguin Books Ltd, 80 Strand, London WC2R 0RL, England

Penguin Ireland, 25 St Stephen's Green, Dublin 2, Ireland (a division of Penguin Books Ltd)

Penguin Group (Australia), 250 Camberwell Road, Camberwell, Victoria 3124, Australia (a division of Pearson Australia Group Pty Ltd)

Penguin Books India Pvt Ltd, 11 Community Centre, Panchsheel Park, New Delhi—110 017, India

Penguin Group (NZ), cnr Airborne and Rosedale Roads, Albany, Auckland 1310, New Zealand (a division of Pearson New Zealand Ltd)

Penguin Books (South Africa) (Pty) Ltd, 24 Sturdee Avenue, Rosebank, Johannesburg 2196, South Africa

Penguin Books Ltd, Registered Offices: 80 Strand, London WC2R 0RL, England

Copyright © 2005 by Sheri A. Rosenthal, DPM

International Standard Book Number: 1-59257-392-4
Library of Congress Catalog Card Number: 2005926962

08 07 06   8 7 6 5 4 3 2

Interpretation of the printing code: The rightmost number of the first series of numbers is the year of the book's printing; the rightmost number of the second series of numbers is the number of the book's printing. For example, a printing code of 05-1 shows that the first printing occurred in 2005.

Printed in the United States of America

Note: This publication contains the opinions and ideas of its author. It is intended to provide helpful and informative material on the subject matter covered. It is sold with the understanding that the author and publisher are not engaged in rendering professional services in the book. If the reader requires personal assistance or advice, a competent professional should be consulted.

The author and publisher specifically disclaim any responsibility for any liability, loss, or risk, personal or otherwise, which is incurred as a consequence, directly or indirectly, of the use and application of any of the contents of this book.

This book relates anecdotes that illustrate the use of Toltec wisdom in practice. Although each anecdote portrays a real-life situation, each is comprised of factual elements derived from several different real incidents, with some aspects fictionalized as well. Likewise, the individuals depicted in these anecdotes are composites that may include fictional elements.

Most Alpha books are available at special quantity discounts for bulk purchases for sales promotions, premiums, fund-raising, or educational use. Special books, or book excerpts, can also be created to fit specific needs.

For details, write: Special Markets, Alpha Books, 375 Hudson Street, New York, NY 10014.

Publisher: *Marie Butler-Knight*
Product Manager: *Phil Kitchel*
Senior Managing Editor: *Jennifer Bowles*
Senior Acquisitions Editor: *Randy Ladenheim-Gil*
Development Editor: *Michael Thomas*
Senior Production Editor: *Billy Fields*

Copy Editor: *Jan Zoya*
Cartoonist: *Richard King*
Cover/Book Designer: *Trina Wurst*
Indexer: *Heather McNeil*
Layout: *Angela Calvert*
Proofreading: *John Etchison*

Contents at a Glance

This book belongs to
Tina Dreamweaver
dw_creations@yahoo.com

Contents

Foreword

by don Miguel Ruiz

In 1998, I had the privilege of meeting Dr. Sheri Rosenthal on a Power Journey to the pyramids of Teotihuacán, Mexico. In that first encounter, I immediately knew that I had met an angel who did not yet know herself. Sheri was searching for something, but she did not know what she was searching for. As a medical doctor, she functioned in a world where it was very important to be right and to be smarter than everyone else. Sheri's opinions and judgment were so strong, and she practiced the art of dominating with her firm point of view. She always had to find a way to be right, and by doing so, made everyone else wrong.

When I first accepted Sheri as an apprentice, I systematically challenged each one of her beliefs and her rational mind. So much insecurity and fear came into her life when she found out that she could not always be right. She felt threatened and had to face many of her emotional wounds. I kept challenging her until she was unable to defend any of her false beliefs, and the entire structure of her mind started falling apart. Sheri tried so hard to become "Dr. Rosenthal" again and to recover her point of view and beliefs. But finally she realized that she was not the person she always thought she was, and she started surrendering to the truth.

It wasn't until another Power Journey, years later in Guatemala, that the belief structure of Sheri's scientific mind finally crumbled and "Dr. Rosenthal" dissolved into pure love and wisdom. Sheri surrendered completely and let go of her entire belief system. In that moment, she became absolutely happy because she had found her authentic self. The false image of Dr. Rosenthal was finally "dead" and Sheri, an angel of love, was born. In that experience, she saw love coming from everywhere, from every flower, from every person, from everything around her. Most importantly, she felt all the love that was coming from inside her own heart. Sheri no longer cared about the past and no longer worried about the future. She was completely authentic and she no longer pretended to be what she was not.

After that experience, Sheri became my business manager and accompanied me on a speaking tour all over the country. She shared her joy wherever she went and made a big difference in the lives of all the people she met. After several years, Sheri was ready to go out on her own to write and teach. This book is the result of her challenging years of learning, growing, and transforming.

Sheri is a delightful teacher, and you will enjoy her gift of explaining the Toltec philosophy in a clear, concise, and understandable way. These teachings will help you to understand your nature as an angel of divine consciousness, and allow you to surrender to what you really are, rather than fight to be what you are not.

It is my great pleasure and privilege to present to you the mind, the work, and the teachings of Sheri Rosenthal, one of my best apprentices, and one of the greatest gifts to humankind.

With all my love and with all my blessings,
don Miguel Ruiz

Born into a family of healers in the Eagle Knight lineage, Miguel Ruiz was raised in rural Mexico by a curandera (healer) mother and a Nagual (shaman) grandfather. As the youngest of 13 children, he was chosen to carry forward his family's centuries-old legacy of healing and teaching. Instead, distracted by modern life, Miguel chose to attend medical school and become a surgeon.

Late one night in the early 1970s, a near-death experience changed his life. He awoke suddenly, having fallen asleep at the wheel of his car. At that instant the car careened into a wall of concrete. Miguel remembers that he was not in his physical body as he pulled his two friends to safety.

Stunned by this experience, he began an intensive practice of self-inquiry. He devoted himself to the mastery of the ancient ancestral wisdom, studying earnestly with his mother, and completing an apprenticeship with a powerful shaman in the Mexican desert.

For more than two decades, Miguel has worked to impart this wisdom to his students. His best-selling books, including The Four Agreements, The Mastery of Love, Prayers, *and* The Voice of Knowledge, *have sold over four million copies.*

Today, Miguel and his sons, Jose Luis and Miguel Jr., offer workshops, lectures, and journeys to sacred sites around the world.

Introduction

The Toltec philosophy is a fascinating esoteric tradition, what we fondly call a Warrior's path to personal freedom. We're not at war with anyone outside of ourselves, but instead with the domesticated programming of our rational mind. It is a path that encourages us to let go of our preconceived ideas, limiting beliefs, and rigid concepts to enable us to be free to express our spirit fully in our lives with an open heart.

I have been on this path for eight years now and it has been the most incredible opportunity, for which I have unending gratitude. And so I'd like to share a few things about my experience of this path with you. I was drawn to these teachings back when I was in college reading Carlos Castaneda's books (which some of you might be familiar with). Unfortunately, he never taught much publicly and so I put aside my dream of ever studying this path with a teacher. But years later when I was going through a challenging time in my life, I saw a book by another Toltec teacher, don Miguel Ruiz. I figured this was my chance, and I signed up for a spiritual journey he had scheduled, never having met the man. Oh boy, was I in for a surprise! Nothing could have prepared me for the experience I was to have on that journey. For the first time in my life, I had an encounter with the real me, the Spirit within, and I wanted more!

I fell in love with that intense and loving man (as did we all!), who always seemed to know exactly what was going on inside of me. He proceeded to slowly but surely tear my entire belief system apart until I could see who I really was. Looking at ourselves is *not* an easy task—it's truly a Warrior's challenge. For me it was harder than medical school or anything I had ever done in my life. Yet, it has rewarded me in ways that nothing in my life has come close to matching. I (my programmed mind) argued relentlessly with don Miguel about everything, constantly defending my personal point of view and my beliefs. (I was a most difficult and stubborn apprentice, but if I could accomplish this, anyone can!) And time after time he mirrored back to me what was true. My mind fought tooth and nail over the years, yet don Miguel never stopped encouraging me with his love and ruthlessness. Truly we are blind to ourselves and it is a blessing to have assistance on the path, so we can see what is.

There was a great war in my mind for many years until something shifted for me one day. Since then it has been an ongoing love affair with myself and life, and it is wonderful. I have thanked my teacher so many times and asked him even more times what I can do for him. But he wants for nothing and simply says, "Go out and share yourself with others. Love, enjoy your life, and be happy." (Of course he tells all of us the same thing!) So I am taking that very wise advice from my teacher and putting it into practice right here and right now with this book. I adore sharing this path and myself with others, and it is my Intent that you find it exciting, informative, encouraging, and challenging. I hope that you enjoy the Toltec teachings as much as I do. And perhaps you will come and join me on a spiritual journey sometime soon; I do look forward to meeting you and hearing about your experience with this book! (You can also contact me through my website at www.sherirosenthal.com or www.journeysofthespirit.com.)

How to Use This Book

We often find in esoteric traditions and religions a basic text or treatise written by the founder of that philosophy or by its disciples. (Examples of this would be the Old and New Testaments, the Koran, and so on.) Not so for the Toltecs! The only written work other than the pictures upon the walls of the ancient cities themselves are several sets of pictorial codices that originate from pre-Columbian times, and several sets of prose sources that are from post-Columbian times. There have been several interesting books written by scholars who have done their best to decode the intent behind these pictures, but that's all we have. As far as history is concerned, the Toltecs disappeared into obscurity long ago.

That was until Dr. Castaneda wrote his first book about his apprenticeship with don Juan Matus in 1968. He claimed he was apprenticing with a Yaqui Indian, the head (a Nagual) of a Toltec Warriors party who was training Castaneda to follow in his lineage. He revealed that the Toltecs were indeed still around, and created these Warriors parties to pass the teachings along secretly so that they would be preserved and kept safe over the centuries. Not just anyone could become an apprentice; they had to be pointed out to the Nagual of the party by Spirit itself. In general, then, these parties were made up of all different people and were not necessarily of familial origin or members of one race. In this way, the tradition survived until the time when it would be released to the general public, which, for all intents and purposes, is now! (Supposedly there is a prophecy that says that the teachings would be revealed publicly at the proper time.)

There was intense speculation around the stories Castaneda recounted in his books, and people wondered if there was even a don Juan, if anything he said was truth, or if, in fact, the Toltecs still existed. But other teachers started publishing books, too, stating they had met "don Juan," although they often called him by other names. More recently, other Toltec teachers have made their presence known (like don Miguel Ruiz and Theun Mares). They have *not* descended from Castaneda's lineage, and they state that they have studied with other Naguals.

As a result of these separate lineages and lack of written documentation, we cannot say that there is *one* definitive way of sharing this tradition or that one teacher is "right." In writing this book, I have endeavored to share with you a concise rendering of the most important aspects of this tradition. In doing so, I have shared them in language that is common to most of the Toltec teachers, so you should have no difficulty reading any of the books I listed in Appendix B. In other words, I did not write this book from any one point of view, but instead, it is inclusive of all—including my own experience of this path. If I missed some particular terms that you might be familiar with, I apologize, as it has been a challenge to include our entire tradition in one book!

Since the Toltec tradition is about freedom from the belief system of the mind (as well as from the need to be attached to any one point of view as "right"), I encourage you to approach this book from an open place, without judgment or the desire to make my methodology right or wrong. Instead, enjoy, learn, and have fun with the questions and exercises in the book. They are designed to make you think and question what you believe about everything. I do suggest that you follow the book in chapter order, since each set of concepts and teachings builds upon each other. If you jump around, you will miss important information that you will need to understand the exercises and questions.

Here's what's included in the seven parts of this book:

Part 1, "Toltec Mythology and Mystery," is where you will find a historical rendering of the Toltecs, some of the mythology of our tradition, basic esoteric concepts, and some of the popular Toltec teachers.

Part 2, "Comprehending the Human Mind," takes you into the workings of the human mind, how it creates the reality we function in, and the ways we get trapped by the concepts and beliefs we as humans have fashioned.

Part 3, "Living a Toltec Warrior's Life," briefs you on the principles that a Toltec Warrior lives by and how anyone can use these tenets to create a happy life for him- or herself.

Part 4, "Mastery of Awareness," looks at the strategies that our minds use to keep us invested in our way of creating our reality and the ways we justify and rationalize our words and actions.

Part 5, "Mastery of Transformation," introduces us to the Toltec practice of Stalking and all the techniques involved that assist us in increasing our awareness of the behaviors and beliefs that create limitation in our lives.

Part 6, "Mastery of Intent," is the place to go for the more complex facets of our traditions like losing the human form, understanding Intent, and the Toltec practice of Dreaming.

Part 7, "Living the Life of a Master," investigates how a Toltec master lives his or her life and the ways that we can adapt to help us create our own dream of heaven.

Extras

In my book, you'll encounter lots of little boxes that share powerful quotes, important definitions, wise words, and cautionary advice. Look for:

Warrior Warnings

In these boxes you'll find cautions, warnings, and pitfalls to watch for along your spiritual path.

Warrior Wisdom

These boxes contain sage Toltec advice and clever insights for everyday life.

Toltec Topography

These boxes define important Toltec terms.

Impeccable Words

These boxes contain quotes from famous Toltec teachers along with wise and pithy words from a range of sources.

Acknowledgments

Gratitude beyond human words and conceptual limitations goes to my teacher, Miguel Angel Ruiz, M.D. Thank you for giving me the minimal chance, and for showing me who I really am. Truly, when I look in your eyes I see the Infinite.

I would like to thank all of the lovely editors at Alpha Books for their wise and heartfelt contributions to this book, especially Randy Ladenheim-Gil, Michael Thomas, and Jan Zoya. Without them this book would not be a reality. Extreme gratitude goes to my personal editor, Shelly Hagen, who took my grammatical oddities and morphed them into clear, concise English. Deep appreciation to Kimberly Lionetti, the agent who co-created this wonderful opportunity with me.

Extreme love and appreciation goes to my parents Ilene and Steven Weinstein, who have made my life effortless during the writing of this book, and who support and love me unconditionally no matter what crazy adventure I dream up.

Special Thanks to the Technical Reviewer

The Complete Idiot's Guide to Toltec Wisdom was reviewed by an expert who double-checked the accuracy of what you'll learn here, to help us ensure that this book gives you everything you need to know about the Toltec philosophy. Special thanks are extended to Toltec angel Meghan McChesney Gilroy.

Meghan McChesney Gilroy is a practicing Toltec committed to living a life of love and happiness. She creates with passion and inspiration as an artist, author, editor, entrepreneur, and teacher. Named "a spiritual leader for the next generation" by don Miguel Ruiz, author of *The Four Agreements*, Meghan co-founded InLoveWithLife. com, FindYourTrueLoveNow.com, and LifeMastery.us to support others on their path of personal growth. She has been certified as a Four Agreements Facilitator, Teacher, and Mentor trained by don Miguel Ruiz. As the Executive Direc-tor of don Miguel's nonprofit organization, Sixth Sun Foundation, Meghan developed Living The Four Agreements Wisdom Groups to help individuals integrate Toltec teachings into their daily lives. She currently resides in the Boston area where she runs a suc-cessful consulting and coaching practice for small businesses and individuals. She and her husband, Jamie, share their love and wisdom around the world through private appointments, teleclasses, seminars, and journeys.

Trademarks

All terms mentioned in this book that are known to be or are suspected of being trademarks or service marks have been appropriately capitalized. Alpha Books and Penguin Group (USA) Inc. cannot attest to the accuracy of this information. Use of a term in this book should not be regarded as affecting the validity of any trademark or service mark.

Part 1

Toltec Mythology and Mystery

The Toltec path is an ancient and beautiful tradition developed with the purpose of personal freedom for humanity. Like most philosophies, it has both mystical and practical aspects. In Part 1, we will explore the historical and mystical framework of the Toltec teachings. I'll share with you some fascinating information about ancient ruins in Mexico, along with the reasons we call this a Warrior's path. In addition, we will discuss the esoteric parts of our tradition, like the Warrior's party and the ability of the Toltecs to shift levels of consciousness. I also provide you with a list of teachers who are involved in promoting this tradition.

Toltec History

In This Chapter

- ◆ A classic tale of good versus evil
- ◆ The thousand-year history of the Toltecs
- ◆ The story of Quetzalcoatl
- ◆ The Pyramids of Teotihuacán and the Atlanteans of Tula
- ◆ The mysterious circumstances of the end of the Toltecs

There certainly has been a lot of speculation, intrigue, and romanticism centered around the Toltec civilization. Stories of war and sacrifice, mysticism and shamanism, and the deeds of obsessive sorcerers and sorceresses abound. It's been said that the ancient Toltecs were masters of awareness and seeing, remarkable humans who learned to control the awareness of others. Rather than using their great gift and knowledge to reach their own personal freedom, it's said that they got lost in the intricacies of power, which ultimately led to their downfall.

The few people who were able to perceive that trap transcended those temptations and went on to create a philosophy based on freedom, unconditional love, and an appreciation of the mystery of life. I am not an archaeologist, but as a life student of the Toltec philosophy, I want to share some of the most intriguing parts of this wonderful tradition.

Who Were the Toltecs?

The name *Toltec* in the Aztec Nahuatl language means *artist*. The *Aztecs* probably chose this title in part because of the incredible abundance of beautiful creations such as carved figures, extremely detailed masks, jade carvings, and all kinds of obsidian blades and objects located at the ruins of the Toltec cities of Teotihuacán and Tula in central Mexico. (Archaeologists have no idea what Toltecs called themselves because their records were all in pictures or codices, so they have adopted the name the Aztecs used.) Personally, I like to think of the Toltecs as artists of the Spirit, experts at creating the most exquisite lives, filled with beauty and joy.

Toltec Topography

The **Toltecs** were Warriors of the Spirit, masters of awareness, and great artisans of anything they chose to create in their lives.

The **Aztecs** were a wandering Mexican-Indian tribe who founded the great city of Tenochtitlán (now Mexico City) in 1325 C.E.

Warrior Wisdom

Most modern Toltecs consider Teotihuacán and Tula to be Toltec cities, but according to archaeologists' theories, the inhabitants of Teotihuacán were not Toltecs and have chosen to call them Teotihuacános.

A City of Artisans

As far as archaeologists can figure, the Toltec were not a race, but a society of people. Their cities, like Teotihuacán and Tula, attracted artisans of all kinds from near and far. These people were textile artists, building trade experts, leather workers, jade designers, obsidian fashioners, stone workers, shell artisans, and feather work specialists.

There was a great marketplace in the center of these cities where artists sold goods to visitors from all over Meso-America. Many of these people ended up staying to work in the temples, workshops, and marketplaces. Teotihuacán became a powerful center of commerce and religious worship. Along with all the artisans were priests and other religious figures as well as governmental personnel.

Since this area of Mexico was rich in resources and had abundant obsidian mines, it became the place to be if you were skilled in the trades.

Warriors or Pacifists?

For years archaeologists have been trying to figure out whether the historical Toltecs were warlike or religious pacifists. When a series of human skeletons were unearthed in the Temple of *Quetzalcoatl* (pronounced Ket-sal-ko-a-tl) in the city of Teotihuacán, there was a lot of academic debate about this discovery. In the early 1920s, the first group of burials was found in the upper part of this monument. Then in 1925, four more skeletons were located in one of the corners of the temple. That discovery was followed in 1939 by an interesting group of offerings at the foot of the temple, objects that were carved into human and animal forms.

> **Toltec Topography**
>
> *Quetzalcoatl* was the god-man that the Toltecs worshipped in their mythology.

A number of years later another group of remains were found at the north and south facades of the building. In addition to all this, over 120 skeletons were found buried in groups of 1, 4, 8, 9, 18, and 20, and placed symmetrically in the north, east, and south sides of the building inside the pyramid's base and also alongside its outer wall. As research continues, more skeletons continue to be discovered.

What I find interesting is the type and number of objects that were found along with these skeletons, both on the Warriors themselves or placed purposefully around them. Some of the bodies were wearing rich attire and large necklaces of shell that looked like jaws; one even wore a necklace of dog's teeth. Lots of obsidian arrow points, knives, and blades were found, along with spool-shaped earrings, beads, and nose plugs (the height of fashion in those days). There were small conical objects that were carved from green stone, which archaeologists can't determine the use for. (My guess is that these items were meant to be held in one's hand and used as *power objects*.) One of the Warriors had a staff of carved wood with a feathered serpent on it that is representative of Quetzalcoatl.

> **Toltec Topography**
>
> **Power objects** are items that have no particular use or meaning other than the Intent which the Warrior imbues them with. Often plain objects were used to focus a Warrior's Intent, making the item dangerous *if* it was imbued with malevolent desire. A power object can be filled with beautiful Intent, too, like the wearing of a cross your grandma gave you to protect you from harm.

A Mesmerizing Mythology

There are people who have proposed that the Toltecs were an extremely ancient civilization that went through a multitude of transformations and political upheavals. Others say that even today there are Toltec groups all over the world that have developed in secret, with some *lineages* extending back tens of thousands of years. Let's start our journey at the beginning of the Toltecs' mythological creation of the world.

The Fifth Sun

As far as the Aztecs were concerned, time began in Teotihuacán when the Gods decided to re-create the world again for the fifth time. The city became the marker for the beginning of the Fifth Sun, the light for a new humanity. It is said that each of these ages of humanity concluded with cataclysmic disaster and rebirth as directed by the sun. When the Gods gathered in the city of Teotihuacán after the end of the Fourth Sun, Quetzalcoatl the man/god was appointed for a divine mission on Earth that he accepted. This first great king came from heaven and lived as a celibate, a sorcerer, and priest, and founded an empire that was the envy of all surrounding cities. He had many names: the Feathered Serpent, Lord of the Morning Star, God of the Wind, Precious Twin, and many other beneficent titles.

> **Toltec Topography**
>
> The purpose of these **lineages** was to pass down the knowledge of the Toltec teachings in secret, safe from corruption and misuse for generations to come, until they could be revealed again at the appropriate time. This knowledge was passed down over the ages from many different teachers, until recently when these lineages have been making themselves known.

> **Warrior Wisdom**
>
> The *Quetzal,* an extremely beautiful and precious bird, is found in Central America. *Coatl* can mean "serpent" or "twin." The best interpretation of Quetzalcoatl's name is said to be "one who emerges from the serpent."

A Dastardly Plot

Quetzalcoatl was supposedly a real man, but he had an enormous amount of myth created around him. Although the Toltec empire existed longer than one human's lifetime, it is said that all the kings subsequent to him took on his name. This all came to an end when Quetzalcoatl was tricked by his enemies, led by a man named Tezcatlipoca. Tezcatlipoca showed Quetzalcoatl his own face in a charmed or smoking mirror. What the king saw was a distorted and horrifying face, and as a result of this vision was tempted into drinking a powerful pulque (alcoholic drink) the night of a great ceremony. Tezcatlipoca volunteered to hide the king's "horrific" face and painted it brightly and placed a great feathered headdress upon his head.

Upon becoming drunk, he was manipulated into making love to a goddess-sorceress. Others interpret the story to imply that the woman he made love to was his own sister. Regardless of who the woman was, he was mortified by his own actions when he became sober. When he learned what he had done, he condemned himself to exile. To keep his integrity, he decided to leave his people and go east across Mexico until he reached the Caribbean, where he set sail upon the ocean until he burst into flames and returned to heaven. There he became the morning star of Venus until his return to Earth.

> **Warrior Warnings**
>
> Although he was celibate, pictures often show Quetzalcoatl as sexually potent, possessing a large member that he stored in a specially made loincloth.

Deadly Deception Destroys a Culture

We can see the great influence of the myth of Quetzalcoatl and Teotihuacán all across Mexico. For example, the great pyramid of El Castillo in Chichen Itza is also called the Pyramid of Kukulcan, which is the Mayan name for Quetzalcoatl. Long after the Toltecs were seemingly gone, the worship and legend of the king continued, so much so that the Aztecs, upon discovering Teotihuacán in approximately 1250 C.E., decided to take on the entire Toltec mythology, religious structure, and building style.

This did not fare well for them in the end, though, since they believed that the Spanish conquistador Hernando Cortez was Quetzalcoatl returning to Earth as their messiah. In 1519 this gave Cortez free reign to come into Tenochtitlán, complements of Mocteczuma II, and totally decimate their culture, cities, religious structure, and dignity using their own prophecies to seal their doom.

> **Warrior Warnings**
>
> Perhaps Moctezuma II did ultimately have his revenge on the Spanish. The legend says that before dying, Moctezuma cursed every European that would ever set foot on his land again. If they did, they would suffer from gastroenteritis, or traveler's diarrhea.

Ancient Toltec Life and Times

It is possible that the mythologies are true and that the first sun dawned for the Toltecs over ten thousand years ago. But for now, we will focus on the current anthropological evidence, which indicates that Mexico is the country of their humble beginnings. Although no one knows exactly when the first Toltec city called *Teotihuacán* was originally built, archaeologists say that the earliest structures were created around 200 B.C.E.

The Aztecs gave the city the name that we use today, which in the Nahuatl language means "the place where men become gods."

Teotihuacán is said to have developed in five phases. During the second phase that began around 1 C.E. and extended until 150 C.E., the Toltecs built the Pyramids of the Sun and the Moon and later the Temple of Quetzal-coatl. At that time the city was estimated to have a population of around 30,000. During the third phase of construction, from 150 C.E. to 450 C.E., the residential complexes were expanded and the population was approximately 100,000. The fourth phase, from 450 to 650 C.E., saw the population at its peak of 200,000 people. The last phase ended when the city was mysteriously burnt and abandoned around 750 C.E.

Toltec Topography

Teotihuacán is located in the center of Mexico in the highlands just 45 minutes by car, or 25 miles northeast of the now densely populated Mexico City.

Teotihuacán's Unique Beginnings

Archaeologists believe that the city began as an agricultural community, with peoples who probably descended from the Olmecs, a much older civilization extending back to at least 1700 B.C.E. Most archaeologists agree that the city was always ceremonial in nature and ruled by a class of priests, or Spiritual Warriors, as modern Toltecs like to call them. It was long rumored that a natural cave and tunnel existed that was sacred to the people, which is why the city was created there. Sure enough, a tunnel and cave were identified when the excavation of the Pyramid of the Sun began. I've been in this cave; it's quite lovely to crawl into this deep dark subterranean area and meditate quietly under this massive power object. (Yes, modern Toltecs consider the pyramid a huge power object that can be used to focus your Intent on transcending your physical body.)

Warrior Wisdom _____

Caves have always been held sacred for their connection between the upper world, middle world, and underworld. They are often thought of as wombs and used for ceremonial purposes. The upper world would be representative of the realm of divine life and the underworld the place one passes into upon death. The middle world is the world we live in. The circle of life is the path we take from one world to the next, repeated over and over.

What made this particular cave so special was that it had a four-petaled, flowerlike shape. As you may know, the four cardinal directions are very important in the shamanic traditions of the Americas, and we will be returning to their significance in Toltec mythology in Chapter 3. This long tunnel and cave are in direct alignment with the west-east axis of the city. The Pyramid of the Sun and the Avenue of the Dead were created perpendicular to this axis. The entire city of Teotihuacán was most likely orientated around this sacred cave and tunnel.

Questionable Endings, New Starts

After Teotihuacán was abandoned, there was a short lapse of time until the great city of *Tula* was created in approximately 850 C.E. The name itself is a variant of the Nahuatl word *Tollan*, which means "place of the reeds." Tula was different from Teotihuacán in that it never contained as large a population, nor was it as grand. But it did contain some interesting features that its predecessor did not.

In the city of Tula, a fierce set of Women Warrior statues, called the *Atlanteans*, stands on top of one of the larger pyramidal structures. There are rumors among the locals telling of the sound of thundering footsteps as the Women Warriors march at night. These ladies carry a set of power objects located in each of the four directions. In their left hand they carry arrows, on their chest a butterfly-shaped shield, on their back a solar disc, and in their right hand a weapon that shoots darts.

Toltec Topography _____

Tula is northwest of Mexico City by about 45 miles in the state of Hilalgo.

Toltec Topography _____

Each **Atlantean** stands 15 feet tall on top of a 130-foot-high pyramidal structure.

Another fascinating feature of this city is the ball court. Teotihuacán is the only ancient city *without* a ball court, as all the cities built after it incorporated this particular structure. Because these courts were set up in the central area of the cities, we can conclude that they were important to the people. The game (we don't know its name) was played somewhat like soccer, where the players used their bodies, hips, and heads to advance the ball until it was shot through a circular opening akin to a basketball hoop laid sideways. Based on the huge numbers of skull fragments found in the area of the ball courts, it seems that the losing team was executed. Pretty serious consequences for a game!

There's another gruesome structure in Tula called the *Chac mool*. Legend has it that sacrificed hearts were placed upon these reclining stone-carved figures as part of a ceremony performed every *52 years* to celebrate a new leader's term of service, and also to re-enact the story of the Warrior Quetzalcoatl, who gave his life to bring light to humankind and re-create the world.

Tula also succumbed to an ending around 1170 C.E. that archaeologists find controversial. It seems that the remaining population invaded *Cholula* in the state of Puebla and set up the same religious structure as they had before in Tula. Cholula had been settled before the demise of Teotihuacán around the year 600, and lasted until around 1520 C.E. There are records that indicate evidence of Toltec cultural and religious influence in Oaxaca to the south, Chichen Itza in the Yucatan peninsula, Guatemala, and even El Salvador in Central America. The cultural and religious influence of Teotihuacán and Tula on the surrounding areas was significant.

> **Toltec Topography**
>
> A **Chac mool** is a sacrificial platform that looks like a reclining man holding a platter over his chest. The victim's heart was typically placed upon the platter.
>
> **Fifty-two years** is very important in the Toltec calendar, as it is a cycle of renewal in their cosmology. You will see this same type of calendar system in the Mayan tradition.

> **Toltec Topography**
>
> The name **Cholula** comes from the Nahuatl word "Cholollan," which means the place of flight. You can visit the site today by traveling southeast of Mexico City about 55 miles.

Chichen Itza, a majestic city in the Yucatan peninsula, existed simultaneously to Tula from around 850 C.E. to 1200 C.E. The city has many architectural aspects that are said to be of Toltec influence, including the Temple of Warriors, which has columns of Warriors resembling those of Tula's, a ball court, and the presence of Chac mools. It's important to note that the journey from Teotihuacán or Tula to Chichen Itza was no quick trip in those days as there were no paved roads, just miles of undeveloped jungle and forests. (We can figure the distance between Tula and Chichen Itza to be around 800 miles—a nice hike by foot for sure!)

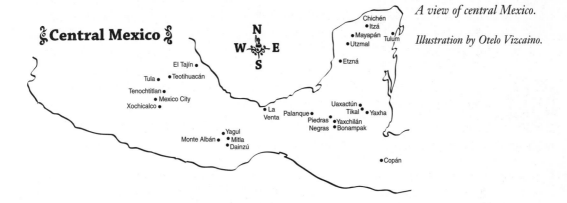

A view of central Mexico.

Illustration by Otelo Vizcaino.

Extraordinary Builders

Did you know that there are pyramids in Mexico that rival those in Egypt? I think we must give credit to these ancient people who built the most amazing pyramids in Central America in a time when they did not even have the wheel or an ox! They fashioned most of their buildings from the surrounding volcanic rock, and thousands upon thousands of tons of stone were used to create these pyramids.

The Pyramids of the Sun and Moon

The Pyramid of the Sun rises 210 feet above the ground, with 242 steps to the top. (Believe me, this is the Mexican Stairmaster!) The base of the pyramid is almost equal to that of the great pyramid in Egypt, except that this pyramid does not go up to a point; instead, it has a flat top perfect for performing ceremonies on. It's estimated that one million cubic feet of dirt and rock was used to assemble this building. There was no metal in those days either, so they used only obsidian knives and stone tools.

Warrior Warnings

Modern Toltecs believe that each stone in every pyramid, plaza, and wall (and that's a lot of stone) was infused with sacred knowledge by the original builders. The ancient Toltecs prophesied that this information would be unlocked in the future by a Toltec who would share their ancient wisdom with the modern world.

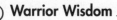

Warrior Wisdom

When Teotihuacán was originally excavated, a huge 22-ton statue of a goddess was found in the Plaza of the Moon in front of the pyramid. This statue now stands in the National Museum of Anthropology in Mexico City.

The Pyramid of the Moon is 147 feet high, and although she is not as tall as the Sun, it appears that she is, due to the slight rise in elevation of the Avenue of the Dead over its 1.2-mile length. There is a mountain to the north of the Pyramid of the Moon called the Cerro Gordo, which the pyramid seems to echo in its appearance in a lovely way. The architects obviously gave great thought to the design of this city.

Painstaking Planning

The layout of the city is fascinating, with the *Avenue of the Dead* extending in a north-south direction, which is off true north by 15.5 degrees bearing northeast. Scientists' best guess is that this directional bearing was determined based on the orientation of the tunnel and cave we talked about earlier. There is also a major east-west avenue

Toltec Topography

The **Avenue of the Dead** is so named because the Warriors who walked down this path had to die to their old way of living before they could continue their spiritual journey toward enlightenment.

that cuts the city into quadrants. The San Juan River was even diverted so that it would cross the Avenue of the Dead exactly perpendicular to it.

Based on the objects that people have found in these quadrants, archaeologists say that each area had certain people living in it: merchants, priests, potters, and so on. The city was never walled off; its influence must have been such that people were not tempted to attack it, or were afraid of it at least until the end of its time.

An Entrance into the Heavenly Cosmos

The Temple of Quetzalcoatl, which is at the southern end of the Avenue of the Dead, can be seen as an opening to the cosmic map that this city represented. Twelve platforms surround the plaza, with the temple residing in the middle along with several other smaller platforms. It's probable that the 12 platforms represented the 12 months of the year. In addition to this, archaeologists estimate that the temple's pyramid contained 365 carved heads of deities, representing the days of the year on its original seven tiers.

This plaza would be the beginning of a Warrior's entrance into sacred space, where the middle world of the human merged with the upper world of the gods. Upon entering the plaza and Temple of Quetzalcoatl, the Warrior officially entered the body of the snake to be slowly digested and transformed as he traveled up the Avenue of the Dead to the Pyramid of the Moon and the Sun. The Avenue of the Dead contains a series of plazas that rise up to meet the Pyramid of the Sun and Moon. Warriors spent years moving forward from one plaza to the next until they were able to reach the Pyramid of the Sun and use its energy to assist them in merging with their personal ray of light, or their Spirit.

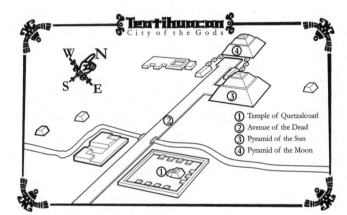

The city of Teotihuacán.

Illustration by Otelo Vizcaino.

Where Did They Go?

Around 750–800 C.E. there seems to have been a mass exodus from the remarkable city of Teotihuacán to Tula, but it, too, reached its ultimate demise around the year 1170 C.E. In Teotihuacán there is evidence of purposeful destruction and fire along the Avenue of the Dead and surrounding buildings, but not around the residential buildings. Archaeologists say that many floors were charred and building stones were thrown off of buildings into the plazas. When Tula was first excavated, many of the Women Warrior columns and other monumental structures were found lying in huge piles of rubble.

A Struggle of Sorcerers and Priests

Many people have proposed all kinds of scenarios regarding why this happened. Some say overpopulation and a shortage of food and water did the people in. Social and civil rebellion has also been cited as a contributing factor. Many people think that Teotihuacán and Tula were sacked, but others feel a huge power struggle took place with the forces of good and evil at play: good priests and Warriors versus bad. It's said that these evil sorcerer priests manipulated the awareness of people so that they would do their bidding, and ultimately destroyed themselves and most everyone else. Some tales say that their abuse of power and sorcery led to the disappearance of many people into thin air and the ultimate destruction of the city.

Impeccable Words

"The Toltec seers were extraordinary men—powerful sorcerers, somber, driven men who unraveled mysteries and possessed secret knowledge that they used to influence and victimize people by fixating the awareness of their victims on whatever they chose."

—Carlos Castaneda, *The Fire from Within*

Some theories suggest that the good Warriors made their final trip to the top of the Pyramid of the Sun and simply merged with their own personal rays of light. I like to imagine that the Warriors who were not corrupted transcended their physical bodies, while some of the others chose to stay here and pass along the knowledge in secret lineages, generation after generation, preventing the corrupted sorcerer priests and Warriors from finding their whereabouts.

The Movement Goes Underground

As a result of whatever happened in this upheaval, the Toltec teachings separated into individual lineages over the subsequent years. Only in the 1960s, as a result of young anthropology student Carlos Castaneda's research (into medicinal plants used by the Native Americans of the Southwest), did the secret teachings end up resurfacing into the public consciousness. In the years between the end of Teotihuacán and Castaneda's books, there were many challenges for the remaining Toltec lineages to face, including the invasion of the Spanish in the 1500s. If any unsavory Toltecs still existed, I imagine they were finished off by the gruesome killing sprees of Hernando Cortez.

Impeccable Words

"European conquest, coupled with rampant misuse of personal power by a few of the apprentices, made it necessary to shield the knowledge from those who were not prepared to use it wisely or who might intentionally misuse it for personal gain."

—don Miguel Ruiz, *The Four Agreements*

In the lineage I am part of, the Intent of our Warriors is to cultivate awareness and live our lives in the most beautiful ways, uplifting humanity and our precious Earth. If ever there was any bad blood around, it seems likely that the long years and intense historical challenges weeded those corrupt folks out of the picture. (And thank goodness for that, because my parents would certainly not appreciate me associating with a bunch of evil sorcerers!)

I think you will enjoy this wonderful philosophy and be able to appreciate it even more in the context of its controversial history.

The Least You Need to Know

- The Toltec were skilled artisans, spiritualists, masterful architects, and powerful Warriors and sorcerers.

- The belief in Quetzalcoatl eventually led to the success of the Spanish conquest.

- Built without the wheel, steel, or the ox, the cities of Teotihuacán and Tula were miracles of human creation and determination.

- Those who abused power were destroyed, and those who sought transcendence passed the Toltec teachings on.

- The modern Toltec consider themselves spiritual Warriors of personal freedom.

Chapter 2

Toltec Traditions and Teachers

In This Chapter

- A philosophy inclusive of all religions and traditions
- Personal freedom, clarity of mind, and loving open hearts
- The three keys to freedom
- The secret teachings become popular

Now that we've covered some background about the fantastic world of the Toltecs, we're ready to explore the more practical aspects of the teachings. Regardless of what happened in their tumultuous past, we have the opportunity to avail ourselves of the best of this exciting philosophy today (evil sorcerers excluded, of course).

In this chapter we'll explore some basics of the Toltec teachings and create a foundation that we will build upon in later chapters. We'll discuss what the Toltec philosophy is today and the purpose of this path as we currently see it. We'll also briefly talk about some of the better-known teachers of Toltec wisdom.

A Way to Personal Freedom

Toltec is not a religion. I was brought up Jewish, and being a Toltec does not preclude me from participating in any of my family's traditional holidays. (Although, on occasion, I must say I wish I could extricate myself from a few of those family events!)

It would be more accurate to say that Toltec is a way of life. The truth is that we are all on a path that starts with birth and ends with death. We can't escape from it, but we have a lot of leeway and choice as to how that journey will turn out: We can live lives filled with peace, or we can accept a life of chaos. The Toltec teachings simply help us to find contentment.

Creating a Magnificent Life

The key to having a beautiful life is to have awareness of all the situations we are creating. Most of us live our lives on auto-pilot, moving from one day to the next feeling like we are the victims of life's circumstances or judging both our lives and others'. Toltec is a philosophy that can be used to create the most magnificent lives we can possibly imagine.

How often do we feel trapped by circumstances, feeling like we can't leave a dead-end job or that we're stuck in a stagnant relationship? Well, a Toltec never feels stuck; he or she always sees choices and options in life.

> **Warrior Wisdom**
>
> In ancient times it was not unusual to refer to a religious path or philosophy as a *way*, meaning that it isn't something to study academically, but instead is a way to live your life.

I found these teachings very exciting and interesting, as I discovered the Toltec path during what I perceived to be a particularly dreadful episode in my life. By using this path for guidance, I was able to extricate myself from a life filled with dramatic relationships, unfulfilling workdays, complaining friends, a lackluster love life, and piles of uninteresting chores.

Are you interested yet?

Expressing Your Spiritual Self

Although Toltec is not a religion, it could be referred to as a spiritual path, as it is concerned with the expression of the creative and spiritual self. As such, it recognizes all spiritual teachers and religious philosophies. The Toltec tradition looks to find commonality among all these traditions, religions, and philosophies; it seeks the truth behind the myths and dogma.

We could say that the origin of all religious teaching comes from humanity's desire to express our feeling or experience that there is something overwhelmingly immense out there, whatever that may be and whatever language we may use to describe that. Modern Toltecs use the term the *Infinite* to describe this phenomenon, but there are literally thousands of words from different traditions and religions that represent the concept of a higher power or consciousness: Spirit, God, cosmic consciousness, divine being, Allah, Krishna, Buddha, Christ, Mohammed, higher self, the light, love, and so on.

The beautiful thing about these teachings is that they survived tens of thousands of years of oral tradition to come to a place where they can be shared in a practical and pragmatic way. By simply looking at what you believe about yourself and the world around you, you can systematically change the way you choose to interact with the world.

Warrior Wisdom

What's most important is to see and acknowledge the sameness of religions and traditions rather than the perceived differences, since difference creates separation between people, and commonality creates oneness.

Toltec Topography

The **Infinite** represents that which is boundless beyond time or space, without beginning or end, absolute, and omnipotent. It is also the part of you that is manifest in this reality, yet is eternal. It is life itself.

Mellow Toltecs

My favorite part of these teachings is that there is nothing to defend, and nothing to fight over or justify. We won't find a true Toltec defending a point of view because he won't want to waste his personal power fighting over anything. Toltecs have absolute respect for others and their traditions; we have no desire to create conflict or disharmony. There is no dogma, nothing to memorize, nothing to recite, and nothing to evangelize. The teachings either resonate with an individual or they don't.

A true Warrior has no conflict with anyone or anything and is at peace with the world. She has no judgment and is working from a place of unconditional love and acceptance of life as it is. An authentic Warrior is a delight to behold and easy to be with.

A Warrior's Path

Toltecs have traditionally called themselves *Warriors*, and although this might lead one to believe this is because they're warlike, this is not the truth. It would be more accurate to say that Toltecs are spiritual Warriors. The battle that a Toltec is engaging in is an internal one.

As Toltecs we want to have wonderful lives, where we are conscious of why we make the choices we do and how these choices create our situations. The war we are engaged in is with our own mind, not with anyone outside of our self. We recognize that the only thing in life we can have any control over is ourselves, the way we act, the way we think, the way we speak to ourselves and others, and our daily decisions.

Toltec Topography

The **Warrior** is a person who is fighting for freedom from his or her own domestication and social conditioning. A Warrior seeks freedom to be able to move through his or her life without having to link self-worth to the beliefs, thoughts, and wishes of one's fellow man. Along with that comes the freedom to be happy no matter what happens in life.

Free at Last!

Chances are, as you're reading this chapter you're having a conversation with yourself about what's being said. Maybe you find yourself agreeing with these theories and teachings, or maybe not, but your brain is giving you some kind of feedback.

Toltec Topography

Just for clarity, you should know that when I use the term **programming** or rational mind I am also talking about what is often called the ego, the small self, or whatever word you use for this purpose.

This thinking is your mind's *programming* letting you know what it believes about everything. Toltecs realize that thinking is only a reflection of one person's point of view and does not necessarily reflect anyone else's point of view. Nor does it represent all possible choices, only those envisioned within one person's mind.

Understanding the mind's programming is important to us as Toltec Warriors because we desire first and foremost to be free. One could say that as citizens of this country, we *are* free—after all, this is a democracy. Well, from a political point of view that might be true, but when we try to behave outside the box of our programmed mind, we realize how imprisoned we really are.

As an example, let's take someone who constantly fights with her parents, siblings, or spouse. Even if she wants to stop this behavior, she always seems to fall into the same patterns. Why? It's simple. Most of us live solely by the rules of our minds' programming, and that programming tells us that we're right, and that anyone who disagrees with us is wrong, and we'll go to great lengths to defend our point of view.

So consider this: If we would rather fight with those we love than detach from defending our point of view, are we *really* free to take action and make choices in our lives? I think not! If we can't stop ourselves from behaving in ways that go against ourselves or others, then we are not free from a Toltec perspective.

Warrior Wisdom

We don't need to argue with others to avoid being taken advantage of. Warriors believe that the same thing can be accomplished with love, respect, and kindness.

Impeccable Words

"Once we have awareness, we have a choice. If we could have that awareness all the time, we could change our routines, change our reactions, and change our entire life. Once we have the awareness, we recover free will. When we recover free will, in any moment we can choose to remember who we are."

—don Miguel Ruiz, *The Mastery of Love*

Fear Is a Terrible Taskmaster

Think about how many things and people we're afraid of. Our choices are too often based on those fears. How many times have we let go of opportunities in our lives because we were too scared to go after them? To be free also means being free from everything we fear most in life. This, my friends, is an incredibly powerful statement! This is true freedom, to create in this world with our hearts and minds open, ready to take chances and opportunities, never fearing anyone or anything.

Warrior Wisdom

We become Warriors once we are able to see our fears as nothing more than smoke. Taking action and having absolute faith in that action is the only way to vanquish fear. Fear never immobilizes a Warrior; we face our fears and move forward.

Victor Frankl once said: "*Everything can be taken away from a man but one thing: the last of human freedoms—to choose one's attitude in any given set of circumstances, to choose one's own way.*" What is so poignant about this quote is that Victor Frankl survived the holocaust and his imprisonment in a concentration camp. He did this by coming to the realization that even though his situation was grim, he was still in charge of the way he chose to see life and how he wanted to feel in any moment. To me these are the words of a true Warrior.

Three Challenging Masteries

Toltec wisdom can be broken down into three masteries. We could say that these masteries are like a college syllabus of life with the first section being the Mastery of Awareness, the second the Mastery of Transformation, and the third the Mastery of Intent. In practice we utilize all three masteries simultaneously, but studying them in a linear fashion helps us to conceptualize them better.

The Mastery of Awareness

Mastery of Awareness is about becoming awake and aware in our daily lives. For the most part we sleepwalk through life, not really paying *attention* to what our mind is telling us or having *awareness* as to why we behave the way we do. The result of this lack of awareness is that our lives may be filled with drama, confusion, and unhappiness.

So how do we master awareness? First we must have a better understanding of what we mean by awareness. For an entity to be aware, it must be capable of perception. As humans, we possess this ability and as a result it is our nature to constantly register information about our surroundings.

Toltec Topography

Attention is an incredible attribute that we possess as sentient beings. Without it we would not be able to focus on what we need to learn. With it we can filter out all the perceptive input we are not interested in receiving and focus solely on what we want to hear or see.

Awareness is the ability to receive information regarding our surroundings. We attribute awareness to being alive in the way that humans or animals are, but the planet earth is aware and perceiving, too; it's just that her awareness does not resemble ours.

An interesting thing happens to us when we are born. Our parents want us to learn to perceive the world just like they do so that we can all be in agreement about what we're looking at. They do this by talking to us from the time we are born and teaching us to focus our attention on certain things. They hook our attention and make us learn language and start naming everything in our universe. Our attention is drawn toward knowledge and information through this process of *domestication* as we are taught words, language, abstract concepts, and behavior. Once this happens we start to feel like we *know* and the rational mind, or ego, begins to form.

Toltecs know that having awareness of what constitutes the entirety of their programming, and that knowledge is the key to understanding themselves. The domestication process is a necessary aspect of our childhood development, but not all of what we were taught was truth or even applicable to us.

The result of this programming? By the time we reach adulthood we have absorbed so much information that's conflicting, untrue, and useless, it's amazing we can function at all! It's interesting that even as adults we end up questioning very little of our programming even if that programming is causing us misery and conflict in our lives.

Toltec Topography

Perception is the act of registering information through our five senses. This information is collected and sent to the brain for processing and to the mind for interpretation. You can also perceive directly with your Spirit, and bypass the interpretation of the rational mind.

Toltec Topography

Through constant questioning we learn how to see and behave exactly like our parents and other humans. This is the process of **domestication** or socialization: being taught how to be a human.

Mastery of Awareness is simply learning to focus our attention on what is propelling us to think and act the way we do. This is empowering because the end result is a change from reacting blindly to life's circumstances to making clear choices. In Part 4 of this book, we cover more about the Mastery of Awareness and learn how to apply this practice to our everyday lives.

The Mastery of Transformation

The Mastery of Transformation is all about taking action and making changes. This is where we get down and dirty and start tearing out all kinds of junk from the storage closets of our minds. And it's amazing what kind of stuff we'll find in there: resentments, anger, grudges, wounds, emotional turmoil, broken hearts, painful incidences, and all manner of things we judge to be best kept locked up someplace dark and inaccessible.

Christ once said *The truth will set you free*. Surely this statement is the best reason for taking any awareness path. Personally, there were many things in my past that were painful for me to look at and other things that I was angry about and didn't want to let go of. But in the end my personal freedom was more important to me than holding on to my judgments, resentments, and painful emotions from long ago.

> **Warrior Wisdom**
>
> We can tell ourselves anything we choose to about the past, and we can justify our point of view to make ourselves right, but if we can't let go and forgive, we will never be absolutely happy and we will certainly not be free.

> **Toltec Topography**
>
> **Intent** is the force that life uses to move and create everything in our universe. Toltecs believe that it directs the very expression of life.
>
> The **void** is where the absolute consciousness of the Infinite resides and originates from. Its location is outside manifest time and space and is connected to the manifest world through one point, which is located both everywhere and nowhere.

A Warrior definitely feels fear and anger, but she doesn't repress her emotions, nor does she allow herself to be immobilized by them. She feels her fear and anger, acknowledges them, and knows that they won't hurt for too long. All she has to do is see what is real, face the truth, forgive, love herself, and move on. This is true transformation.

Fortunately, as Toltecs we have ways of cleaning up the mind. We'll look at these methods in great detail in Part 5.

The Mastery of Intent

There's a lot of confusion about *Intent* in New Thought teachings. People tend to confuse the word *intention* with *Intent*. For Toltecs there is no relationship between the two words.

Intention is something we aim for or plan to do. It involves the thinking process of the rational mind, something we're wanting, wishing, hoping for, or trying to accomplish in the near future. *Intent*, on the other hand, is a force that originates from the *void*, the Infinite. The Infinite, which is life itself, uses this force to create everything that exists in our manifest universe.

There is a huge difference between these two words! Intention reflects the rational thought of a human being; Intent describes a force from the Infinite. All beings in the universe are linked to Intent. As Warriors we spend our lives refining our connection to Intent, learning how to align with it and direct it. Yet there is nothing that the rational mind can come up with that can explain such a statement, as Intent is not in the realm of the rational mind. Only when the mind is absolutely quiet, and we are totally present in the place of *silent knowledge*, can we begin to touch this conscious force. Intent must be felt and experienced, not talked about. Only by living our lives in the most impeccable way can we access this miraculous force.

Toltec Topography

Silent knowledge is all the information and wisdom that exists as universal consciousness that we all are connected to, but have long forgotten how to use or access.

By surrendering to life we are actually aligning with the Intent of the Infinite and following the will of life. To be able to pull this off, we must have absolute faith in life and our Spirit rather than having faith in our mind and what it thinks it wants and should have (desires born of the ego or rational mind). By using the Mastery of Intent our lives become effortless simply because we stop fighting against life. Then, what we want in life becomes exactly what life moving through us wants.

Famous Toltec Teachers

Since Dr. Carlos Castaneda published his first Toltec revelation in 1968, there have been a series of books on the subject from many different authors. Some people claim to have met his elusive teacher, *don Juan Matus* (a Yaqui Indian), and other teachers state that they come from a totally different lineage yet share the same inherent knowledge. I will share with you a little bit about each teacher, the books they have published, and what, if anything, they are currently engaged in. You can refer to their respective works in Appendix B.

Toltec Topography

Don Juan Matus was Carlos Castaneda's teacher, made famous in Castaneda's series of books chronicling his apprenticeship with this enigmatic and mysterious Toltec master.

Carlos Castaneda

Dr. Castaneda certainly deserves the credit for bringing the Toltec teachings to the eyes and minds of millions of people around the world. From the first of his books to the last, there has been controversy regarding whether there was indeed a don Juan, and if there truly is a Toltec tradition. Castaneda was reluctant to answer interviews or lecture in public, and his elusiveness added to this mystery. His apprenticeship with don Juan was the inspiration for 12 books until his death in 1998.

Florinda Donner-Grau, Taisha Abelar, and Carol Tiggs were also trained by don Juan and are part of Carlos's Warriors party (see Chapter 3 for more on Warriors' parties). Florinda and Taisha have both published books, but Carol to date has not. They occasionally lecture publicly and do so through Castaneda's personal website.

> **Impeccable Words**
>
> "Human beings are perceivers, but the world that they perceive is an illusion: an illusion created by the description that was told to them from the moment they were born."
>
> —Carlos Castaneda, *Tales of Power* (as quoted in *The Wheel of Time*)

Don Miguel Ruiz

Don Miguel was born in Mexico to a family of Toltecs and *curanderas* (traditional healers). Don Miguel remembers his grandfather's teachings very well and all the weird and magical stories he shared with him regarding their lineage, the *Eagle Knights*.

Like so many young people, don Miguel had had enough of his family and their stories and decided that he was going to get a real life; he had plans to become a doctor. While he was in medical school, he and a couple of his friends were in a horrible car accident. Strangely, he saw himself in the car asleep, yet he was able to move his friends to safety. This was incredibly bizarre to don Miguel, and he started thinking that maybe all of those family stories were real. That incident started him on the journey of self-knowledge and reclaiming his family roots as the Nagual (spiritual leader) of his lineage.

In the end he realized that it was time to teach, write, and share his tradition openly. As a result, his books have been published around the world, sharing the Toltec teachings with millions of people. Don Miguel and his sons don Mikal and don Jose Luis offer workshops, lectures, and power journeys around the world through his popular website.

Several of his apprentices, including myself, have published books that you will enjoy reading. My fellow Warriors include Heather Ash, David Dibble, Ray Dodd, Susan Gregg, and Bernadette Vigil. All of them teach around the country and overseas, and they have their own websites that you can access for more information.

Theun Mares

Theun Mares shares the Toltec teachings from a different side of the world, hailing from South Africa. He has shared with his readers that he studied with a Nagual he calls J, and feels that he is fulfilling a long-held prophesy that these teachings are to be revealed at this time. Mares has written several books that have been popular and are written quite pragmatically, like Toltec textbooks. Currently living in Cape Town, he has created a foundation to further the Toltec teachings though books, retreats, workshops, and e-groups.

Impeccable Words

"Learning about the inner self is not only frightening, but is also the most consuming of all possible pursuits."

—Theun Mares, *Return of the Warriors*

Victor Sanchez

In 1986, anthropologist Sanchez went to Mexico to study the social customs of the Wirrarika tribe. Sanchez has been a proponent for the indigenous people of Mexico for many years and has done much to support the oral traditions they represent. As a result, he created a program he calls *The Art of Living Purposefully* and sponsors journeys incorporating the experience of nature and spirituality into his teachings.

Ken Eagle Feather

Kenneth Smith writes under the pseudonym of Ken Eagle Feather. Although never proven, he states that he had a 10-year apprenticeship with don Juan at the same time Castaneda did. Ken has been a huge proponent of Toltec teachings over the years, and has worked to make them known to the greater population. Currently Ken is vice-president of Hampton Roads publishing company. He has taught for over 25 years and still travels internationally, sharing his experiences and knowledge with others.

Merilyn Tunneshende

Merilyn Tunneshende has claimed that she also studied with don Juan, although that was not the name she personally knew him by. Regardless of whether she knew don Juan or not, she has been very active in promoting this *shamanistic* tradition and has studied Toltec-Mayan shamanism for more than two decades. Merilyn lectures and presents nationally and internationally, and has led sacred journeys into Mexico.

> **Toltec Topography**
>
> **Shamanism** can be considered a type of religious structure practiced throughout the world. In these traditions a member of the society acts as a medium between the visible world and the Spirit world using magic or sorcery practices for the purpose of healing, divination, or control over natural events.

Will the Real Toltec Teacher Please Stand Up?

Some people may feel that one particular Toltec teacher's writings are correct, and that the others are wrong (or at least less correct). Well, this is nonsense. Being attached to one particular teacher's point of view is like saying that there's only one way to express truth and if we don't follow that way we're doomed!

All Toltec teachers express the path and Spirit moving through them in their own way and according to the times during which those teachings are (or were) being formed. I encourage you to use these teachings and concepts to take you past the mind, past dogma, to a place that is far beyond the known, so that you can touch the true mystery of you.

The Least You Need to Know

- Toltec is a philosophy honed from thousands of years of practical knowledge, leading to personal freedom.

- By learning to master our own awareness, we can change our life so that it aligns and flows with life effortlessly.

- The Warrior's path involves opening the mind to clarity and freedom of choice.

- Intent is the force that life uses to make everything happen; it originates from the Infinite.

- All Toltec publications express their philosophy from the point of view of each teacher; all are equally valid and useful.

Chapter 3

Toltec Philosophy and Perspectives

In This Chapter

- ◆ The Warriors' party
- ◆ The Tonal and the Nagual
- ◆ The luminous egg
- ◆ The assemblage point—where perception takes place

In this chapter I will share some of the more esoteric aspects of the Toltec tradition. Toltecs see everything as energy, and for an ancient philosophy this is fascinating, since this is how science sees much of our universe today!

Since the Toltecs had no advanced scientific techniques to explore their theories with, they explored them through the process of *seeing*. Seeing for a Toltec means bypassing the perceptive abilities of the five senses and viewing the universe with the eyes of their Spirit, or Nagual. Toltecs were able to accomplish this through their ability to shift levels of awareness, which we'll talk more about in Chapter 4.

Ancient Toltecs developed a theory: Humans were not solid mass, but were instead an energetic conglomerate of light they called a luminous egg. As a result of this theory, they created their description of the cosmos and how it relates to them in a way that is quite different from other traditions.

A Warriors' Party

One of the more unusual aspects of the Toltec tradition is the Warriors' party. A Warriors' party is an energetic unit (formed by a gathering of warriors) whose primary purpose is to reach personal freedom and to ultimately transcend their physical bodies and know themselves as light. This party consists of a leader or guide who is called the *Nagual Man* (pronounced nah-'whal) and his energetic human counterpart, the Nagual Woman. The Nagual Man and Woman are then joined by two women in each of the four cardinal directions: north, south, east, and west. One man also stands in each direction, with the Nagual Man representing the south. There may be one or two other people present in each direction whom Toltecs call *the witness* or *assistant*.

Four of the women are *Dreamers*, and four are *Stalkers*. Each group represents two specific energetic configurations of their luminous eggs (which present outwardly like personality traits) that humans can display. We can say that Stalkers are often perceived as friendly, outgoing, talkative, bossy, extroverted, and interested in playing in the world. Dreamers, on the other hand, are often perceived as loners, and a bit spacey, quiet, introverted, and introspective. They are less interested in our daily reality.

Toltec Topography

Nagual means Spirit in the Toltec tradition, but in this case it also means the spiritual leader of the Toltec party of Warriors. This man is the epitome of impeccability, strength, harmony, peace, and sobriety.

A **Stalker** is an expert at functioning in the realm of everyday consciousness. Stalkers can shift their behavior and point of view to become anything or anyone they want to be in order to affect the best outcome in any situation.

A **Dreamer** is an expert at shifting levels of consciousness. Dreamers can shift their state of being to perceive any reality by the use of their attention and control of their own awareness.

The **witness** or **assistant** can be a man or a woman, Dreamer or Stalker, although if the witness is a woman she is usually from the south. The witness or assistant is present to support the members of their direction and to observe without judgment all the doings of their group.

Adding all of these folks up, a full Warriors' party would consist of 21 people, depending on whether there are extra Witnesses present and if the party has been completed. In total, this configuration of Warriors forms a structure that is perfectly balanced energetically to match that of our universe, but on a miniature scale. We can also say that our universe has width, height, depth, and time-space, which is another way of illustrating this energetic configuration represented by the model of the four directions.

Fully formed, a Warriors party would look like this:

> Northern Stalker
> Northern Dreamer
> Witnesses/Assistants
> Man of the North

Western Stalker   Eastern Stalker
Western Dreamer   Eastern Dreamer
Witnesses/Assistants   Witnesses/Assistants
Man of the West   Man of the East

> Southern Stalker
> Southern Dreamer
> Witnesses/Assistants
> Nagual Man
> Nagual Woman

Does this structure remind you of the four-petaled cave back in Chapter 1?

Warrior Wisdom _____

The purpose of this structure is to facilitate the Toltec teachings moving forward, from one generation to the next, through lineages of different Naguals. By passing on the knowledge of our tradition in this way, it survived until modern times in secrecy and in safety until prophesy dictated their public release. Today we do not adhere to the party structure except for use in ceremony, since these teachings are no longer secret.

Now let's take a look at how all this would translate into an actual Warriors' party.

The South

The South is the direction we will start from, as the South is the energetic entrance to the Warriors' party.

Traditionally, in the South we find the Nagual Man and Woman in addition to the three or four Warriors belonging to this direction. The Nagual Man and Woman are called fluid beings because, if they so desire, they may embody qualities of the other directions at any time depending on the situation at hand. They are born with more energy and personal power than average people, which enables them to be natural leaders of their party.

The Dreamer and Stalker Women of the South are warm, delightful, and kind. They remind one of the evening's southerly wind: soft, enveloping, and nurturing. They are a perfect balance to the women of the North, as both groups are strong, but the Southerly women project their strength in a soothing and delightful way, rather than an in-your-face way, which is more typical among the women of the North.

The North

The Women of the North are tough, blunt, and strong. They remind one of the midday northern wind: direct, relentless, and exhausting. Northern Women have no problem getting in your face and telling you what's what. They take action when they need to and are the ones who mix things up between and among people. Then they just sit back, enjoy, and watch all the reactions that result from their actions!

The Man of the North makes things happen, as he is the man of action. He is enjoyable to be with, with a good sense of humor, and plays well in the world. Energetically he is a perfect balance to the strength of the North; his sense of humor eases the directness and severity of these ladies.

The East

The Women of the East are clear-headed, persistent, organized, and serious. They remind one of the morning breeze: lighthearted and delightful. These women come across as lovely people to know; they have a great sense of humor and take any task seriously. These women are great creators and observers. When they take on a task, they complete it from beginning to end in an orderly, logical, and linear fashion without any drama, confusion, or anxiousness.

The Easterly Man is the intellectual, the scholar. As with the women of this direction, he is clear of mind and sober. He can be depended on to initiate projects efficiently and capably and to get the job done. This makes him an excellent assistant to the Easterly ladies.

The West

The Women of the West are emotional, a bit crazy, calculating, and reflective. They remind one of the westerly winds in the late afternoon: uneven and blustery. In general, the Westerly Women have a great ability to connect with their intuitive side and to shift levels of consciousness. The end result of this is that they have an easier time detaching from their rational mind, and, as a result, they come across as a bit nutty or crazy. The Westerly Stalker will be more sober than the Westerly Dreamer and is therefore the more practical of the two.

The Man of the West is quiet, mysterious, unknowable, and is always working behind the scenes. He is the kind of man you will never be able to pin down in any way. Energetically he acts as a balance to the craziness of the Westerly ladies.

The Tonal and the Nagual

The Toltec view of cosmology separates the components of our reality and of ourselves into two aspects: the *Tonal* and the *Nagual*. The Tonal (pronounced toh-nahl) represents the *known*, everything we can experience with our senses, everything we can name, and what we would call matter. Everything we are and everything we think we know is the Tonal; it's the creator of our mental point of view. The Nagual is the *unknowable*, that which we will never know within the confines of the rational mind. It is nothing at all, yet it is in everything. We can also call the Nagual *Spirit* or the *Infinite*, yet when we do so it becomes part of the known because once we create a mental image of it, we think we know, and as a result it becomes part of our Tonal.

Warrior Warnings

Of course this information is a lot of fun and it can certainly be used for guidance, but I would not give my personal power away to it or walk around using it to further define myself in any way. (Having said that, and simply for the fun of it, I will let you all know that I am a classic Easterly Stalker. Some might consider that the reason why this book is so linear and pragmatic!)

Toltec Topography

The **Tonal** is the world of reason, everything we think we know, and the totality of agreements we make about our reality and the order we put to it.

The **Nagual** is the immensity of the unknowable, the Infinite, all possibilities in the universe, and what can never be described. It is who we really are.

A Most Unruly Island

The Toltecs often refer to the Tonal as an island, because this visual makes it easier to understand conceptually. Each of us has our own island of the Tonal floating in an endless sea of Nagual. From our island we can see other people's islands floating all around us. These islands are similar to ours, because the lives we lead are comparable, as are our ideas, concepts, and values. In addition, the things we "own" are on our island, too: our personality, our ego, our body, all of our concepts, and our pet ideals, even our possessions.

> **Warrior Wisdom**
>
> Although the people we share our lives with are not on our island, the ideas and images we hold about everyone we know are there. In addition, we have everything we believe we have experienced in our lives, and the stories we tell about those events, on our island.

The problem with our islands is that they all look like wild forests; some features on our islands are way overgrown, and other aspects can barely get any light or are covered in darkness. Parts of our islands are worn out from overuse (programmed behaviors—discussed throughout Part 2) and other parts appear totally neglected, as if the owners did not even know they existed (our hidden potentials yet to be discovered in our lives).

The overgrown areas might consist of our self-importance, anger, impatience, and our lack of self-respect and love. Areas needing fertilizer could be our self-confidence, faith in our heart and intuition, and our feeling of being good enough for ourselves and others. Aspects that could be hiding in the bramble and underbrush might be our shame about being sexually abused as a child, our drinking or gambling habit, our distain for our bodies, or our jealousy for our brother's good fortune in life.

The challenge here is twofold: We need to get control of our island's unruly nature and learn to break the obsessive focus and attention we have on our own island. When that happens, we can put our attention on the other half of ourselves, the Nagual.

The Totality of Ourselves

When we are born we start to develop our Tonal (what we know). We must be taught and domesticated as to how to form our very own island, but once it is formed, all our attention becomes absorbed and fixated by the Tonal. It forms the rational and linear way that we think and see life.

From the first moment we create our Tonal, we start to develop the feeling that something essential is missing from our lives, something we can't define. This feeling inside is what has each of us searching on a path of self-awareness and personal growth to reach what Toltecs call the totality of ourselves (a body-mind-spirit oneness). To reach that totality on this physical plane, we must incorporate both halves of ourselves, the Tonal and the Nagual, and know them as one. This means that we must come to touch the unknowable within us, which we can only do through experience, not knowledge, and through feeling, not rational understanding.

While the Tonal begins when we are born and ends with our physical death, the Nagual is infinite and continues eternally. It's the source of true creativity, potential, and all our abilities. Learning to take our focus and attention off of the Tonal is a true Warrior's task. When we reach the totality of ourselves, we're living our lives in our integrity, or oneness.

Warrior Wisdom

Our goal is to get the Tonal to give up its absolute control of us willingly, without losing our minds or becoming crazy! At the same time, we strive to give the power back to the true master of our lives, our Nagual or Spirit.

The Known, the Unknown, and the Unknowable

The many things that we believe we know in life constitute the Tonal. On the other hand, most of what is happening in the universe is unknown or unknowable. Take a moment to think about all the things that we think we know in our lives.

- ♦ Do we really have awareness of all the aspects of ourselves, both pleasant and unpleasant?

- ♦ Do we truly understand why our co-workers irritate us?

- ♦ How do we find the guts to do something we never thought we could do?

- ♦ Why are we always arguing with our parents, siblings, or spouse?

- ♦ How well do we really know our beloved?

Impeccable Words

"True knowledge exists in knowing that you know nothing. And in knowing that you know nothing, that makes you the smartest of all."

—Socrates

Although we may think that we know the answers to many of these questions, the fact is that there are many things that are really unknown to us. It's important to understand that the rational mind and Tonal are just doing their job of reflecting an unknown universe to us in a way that makes it appear logical, understandable, and linear. Just remember that Toltecs believe this reflection is not real. It only appears to be that way.

An Island of Safety

Toltecs understand that they don't know anything about anything. They realize that what they know is just an interpretation of what they perceive, and that this interpretation is created using abstract concepts. Concepts represent a description of an experience, and there can be hundreds of them for any issue or situation. In the end, we can see that our concepts can only represent a point of view about our experience, but not the experience itself; therefore, a concept can't be the truth. The whole truth must be inclusive of all points of view.

We can only *know* what is available to us within the context of our times, and in relationship to other known human concepts. The bottom line is that we project our concepts and beliefs out onto our world, making it seem like we *know*. But this is not truth to the Toltec, since our projections are just illusions from our minds.

> **CAUTION**
>
> **Warrior Warnings**
>
> We think we know things, but even if we are an expert on a particular subject, we are only an expert because others have agreed that we are an expert on the subject that we ourselves have created and agreed upon!

This isn't to say that our lives are an illusion—just that what we believe about them is. There's a big difference. Over the years we become reassured by what we *know* about everything, and feel comfortable defending our point of view. It makes us feel safe and secure. But this is a false sense of security. We can see that the only things we really know are the concepts on our islands—and that is not anything substantial. (We'll be learning more about this in Chapters 5 and 6.)

Believing Without Believing

If we understand that we know nothing except agreed-upon concepts, we can go through life in a state of wonderment, rather than boredom. I know my mind contains thousands of interesting concepts and beliefs that are not going to be truth 100 years from now. I don't need to defend these concepts and beliefs against others, nor do I feel that having this knowledge makes me any wiser.

For example, if I were still practicing medicine, I would be using the current agreed-upon beliefs of what is appropriate treatment for any particular condition. As a Toltec, I know that years from now most of this will probably be debunked and found to be false. So rather than labeling everything I know as absolute lies, I simply recognize this is the best of what we have right now as far as concepts and beliefs go, and I believe them without believing and with absolute detachment.

Because of this understanding, I am able to move through my life taking nothing for granted and having my mind and heart open. The best part of this is that I can recognize that I do not even know myself, certainly not the unknowable part of me, the Nagual. Since I do not make any assumptions about myself, I am open to discovering my true potential.

Ponder these questions for a few minutes:

- ◆ Can we ever know the meaning of the universe?
- ◆ Do we really know the purpose of our existence?
- ◆ Can we understand time and space with the rational mind?
- ◆ Can we ever know what is infinite?

Before you jump to answer these questions, see if it's possible to let go of all your concepts, beliefs, and ideas. Ask yourself if you can feel comfortable not having *any* answers, and if you can be okay with that or if your rational mind goes to a place of discomfort and wants to create a story to make you feel safe.

Warrior Wisdom

A Warrior endeavors to learn his or her whole life, knowing that he or she will never really *know* anything.

Warrior Wisdom

A Warrior believes without believing, so that he or she can function within the context of the world of the Tonal. Information constantly changes, but universal wisdom and true knowing always remain the same and are timeless.

Great Balls of Fire!

Like most of us, I was brought up to believe that I am solid matter, but over the course of my Toltec studies I have come to believe that this is not the whole truth.

Toltec theory holds that light is everywhere in the universe and is aware. We are made of light that has crystallized into what we can call matter (our Tonal), and that we also contain light (our Nagual) that exists between our atoms.

Toltecs believe if we could see ourselves as we really are, we would see a huge ball-shaped orb

Impeccable Words

"Human beings are not objects; they have no solidity. They are round, luminous beings; they are boundless. The world of objects and solidity is only a description that was created to help them, to make their passage on earth convenient."

—Carlos Castaneda, *Tales of Power* (as quoted in *The Wheel of Time*)

of light that is much larger than the confines of our physical body. Our luminous (*made of light*) egg, as Toltecs call it, extends slightly farther than the distance our arms would reach if our arms and fingers were extended sideways from our body, all around the body. This is a huge area compared to the amount of space our physical bodies take up. (Just to make things clear, the luminous egg is not an aura and has nothing to do with auras. The luminous egg is you, the real you as a being of light.)

The Assemblage Point

The way that we perceive the world depends on how the energy patterns of light within us align with the energy patterns of light outside of us. These energetic patterns are translated into sensory data, which our brain then processes. This information is interpreted by the mind, which creates our particular view of the world. Depending on what patterns are aligned, we may assemble the world of the Tonal or that of the Nagual.

Warrior Wisdom

What directs us to align certain patterns of energy is Intent, which is the force that the Infinite uses to create and manifest everything in the universe (Chapter 2). Every being in the universe aligns these patterns of light as directed by the Infinite.

Toltec Topography

The **assemblage point** is that area on the luminous egg where the energetic patterns of light that our body is made of intersect with the energetic patterns of light of the greater universe. As a result of this alignment, perception occurs.

The point at which this interaction occurs is on the outside of the luminous egg and is called the *assemblage point*, or the point where our perception is assembled.

Warriors perceive this area to be located on the outside of the luminous egg on the upper part of the back near the right shoulder. Since Toltecs believe the assemblage point is in this area in all humans, we can say that all humans assemble (or see) the world in the same way. The fact that we all have different points of view is just a reflection of the fact that the assemblage point is in a slightly different place from person to person, but always located in the same general area in humans.

According to Toltec tradition, all sentient beings, including the earth itself, are luminous beings just like humans; some just have eggs that are shaped slightly differently from ours and their assemblage points are located in different areas. (Of course, a tree doesn't see the world the same way we do, but it is absolutely aware, just like we are.) Beings that are not organic in nature also have awareness, but their luminous eggs are completely different from ours. This is an important point, as Toltecs believe that the universe itself is one big sentient being and that it, too, is aware.

Fixated or Fluid?

Our assemblage point becomes fixated in one spot by the time we reach adulthood, unlike during childhood when our assemblage point was flexible. In other words, as a child, our point of view about the world was fluid: It could be one thing one day and another thing another day without attachment. This is why children are always in a state of wonderment about their world, and often profess that their imaginary worlds are real.

Our parents spent our entire childhood making sure that we saw the world exactly the same way they did. As a result, they helped fixate our assemblage point where it is today. But just because we interpret the world in a certain way doesn't necessarily make it the truth.

When we become free, not only are we able to shift our assemblage point anyplace within the range of the known (Tonal), but we'll also be able to shift our assemblage point to reach a different level of consciousness that we call *heightened awareness*. From there, *anything* is possible. It is the springboard to the Infinite. To be able to move our assemblage point, we need energy and personal power. When we don't have awareness, we use all of our personal power defending our point of view and beliefs, and we deplete ourselves of the energy needed to move our assemblage point. By letting go of our need to be right and by not believing our own concepts, we start to save up energy, which we can use to shift ourselves into heightened awareness or to create amazing things in our life. (We'll discuss heightened awareness in more detail in Chapter 4.)

> **Toltec Topography**
>
> **Heightened awareness** is the state of consciousness that results from a movement of the assemblage point, enabling you to align different energetic patterns of light outside you, which results in increased clarity and connection with silent knowledge.

I Think Therefore I Am ... Not!

The way humans ensure that we all assemble our world in the same way is by talking to ourselves. The voice in our head constantly talks to us, telling us that the way we see things is the truth. Thinking (our *internal dialogue*) is what keeps our assemblage point exactly where it is as adults; thinking is what keeps us imprisoned in our own minds. It keeps us in a place of self-reflection, which causes us to see the world the way we want to see it rather than the way it is. In this way, life is always proving to us exactly what we already believe about it! Most esoteric traditions encourage students to work at quieting the mind (reaching *inner silence*) to break this trap.

Toltec Topography

Internal dialogue is the conversation that constantly is taking place within our own mind—what we call thinking.

Inner silence is absolute quietude of the mind and is the result of detaching our attention from the internal dialogue. It is the gateway to the second attention (Chapter 4) and the Infinite (the Nagual).

Since our internal dialogue fixates our point of view and our assemblage point, we can never make this shift unless we stop believing what our mind is telling us. The key is to get our mind and its focus on the Tonal to surrender its grip on us so that we can switch our attention to the Nagual. As soon as we stop the dialogue in our head, the world will stop, or at least the world as we *know* it will stop. And once that happens, anything in life is possible.

The Least You Need to Know

◆ Traditionally, the Nagual, or Toltec party leader, assembles a group of Warriors for the specific purpose of gaining personal freedom and total awareness.

◆ A Warriors' party represents a perfect energetic balance of Dreamers and Stalkers, and men and women in the four directions.

◆ According to the Toltecs, the universe consists of the Tonal and the Nagual.

◆ Toltecs believe that we are much more than a physical body and mind; we are all luminous eggs, an energetic conglomeration of light perceiving an energetic universe of light.

Chapter 4

Toltec Mysticism and Magic

In This Chapter

◆ Shifting levels of awareness

◆ Using our attention to choose which reality we perceive and how we perceive it

◆ The one living entity that we are all a part of

◆ The requirements of living impeccably

One of the most interesting aspects of the ancient Toltecs was their knowledge and ability to shift levels of awareness. This empowered them to be in control of how they chose to see life. Depending on where they focused their attention, they were able to assemble different realities. They could choose to see the Tonal world with their eyes, or focus their attention on the Nagual instead.

In Chapter 1, I mentioned that the city of Teotihuacán was laid out as a model for personal ascension. Warriors started in the Plaza of Quetzalcoatl and worked their way up the many plazas until they reached the Pyramid of the Sun. Each of those plazas represented a level of consciousness or a shift of the assemblage point from normal awareness (the first attention or the Tonal), to heightened awareness (the second attention, seeing the Tonal and the Nagual), all the way to the third attention (seeing as light, or pure Nagual). In this chapter we will deepen our understanding of this magical process.

Attention Is the Key

The Toltec saw the ability to shift levels of awareness as an amazing aspect of our magical abilities. What we choose to focus our attention on will determine what kind of world we assemble for ourselves (see Chapter 3 for more on the assemblage point). Whenever we focus our attention with our eyes, we assemble our normal world of the Tonal. When we focus our attention using our Nagual, our assemblage moves and we start to assemble the world of the Nagual. How far we shift from one point of view to the other determines what we *see*. That is why having control over our attention is so important—we use it to determine what reality we choose to perceive.

Let's look for a moment at how we use our attention in our normal world of the Tonal. The ancient Toltecs observed that when a person's attention was focused on something enjoyable, the person was happy, but if his or her attention was focused on something unpleasant, the person would be unhappy. So where do you think our attention would be best focused? I think this is a no-brainer; obviously we would want to train our attention to focus on the beauty of life.

Whenever we find ourselves feeling like things are unfair in life and we're the victim of circumstances, then we'll be unhappy. This is because our attention is on what we *believe* about life instead of on life itself. If we can change our limiting beliefs about life, we will no longer create suffering, disappointment, and heartbreak in our reality. By simply getting control of our attention and choosing to focus it in a different way, our assemblage point shifts and we can change our entire reality and the way we see life. And that, my friends, is real Toltec sorcery and magic in the most practical of ways!

The First and Second Attention

The world we create as a result of focusing our attention for the first time in our lives (through the process of domestication and programming) is this world, the Tonal. Hence, we also call it the reality of the *first attention*.

When we take the time to heal our *wounds*, and let go of our beliefs and concepts, we detach from the fixation we have upon the Tonal. In doing this, we create the world of the *second attention*, so named because we focus our attention for the second time (and move our assemblage point) in a new and totally different way to create another reality we have never perceived before. We become *seers* with the freedom to view the world as it is and without projecting what we think we know upon it. In this way we have the ability to assemble the Nagual's world, where anything and everything is possible.

Toltec Topography

Warriors understand that our use of the **first attention** puts order into a chaotic universe; it creates the world of the Tonal. The key is to realize that this order only represents a point of view and is not necessarily the absolute truth.

The **second attention** is when we focus our attention on what *is*, rather than what we were taught about reality. It involves a shift of our assemblage point and state of consciousness into heightened awareness.

Wounds are those hurts that we have accumulated in our emotional bodies over the years as a result of painful experiences that we took personally.

A **seer** is a person who can perceive the world as *it is*, without his programming or beliefs distorting his perception.

Left- and Right-Sided Awareness

The first attention of our normal world of the Tonal can also be defined as right-sided awareness. This is the level of consciousness that we spend most of our lives in. Many of us, though, at least once in our lives, have experienced levels of heightened awareness. For many, this *left-sided awareness*, or *shift to the left*, as it is also called, occurs during the most challenging or the most intensely awe-inspiring situations. Maybe you were hiking in the Grand Canyon and you were so moved by the utter beauty and perfection of creation that you couldn't speak or even think. Perhaps witnessing the birth of your child put you in bliss, feeling outside of time and mind. Maybe you've suffered an illness that caused you so much pain that you transcended the experience of your physical body. In these circumstances we are so far out of our mind's ability to comprehend our surroundings that we can't hold on to our usual view of the world and the construct of the Tonal falls apart. All of a sudden nothing is the same. Colors are more intense, our minds are quiet, and our focus is more acute. We seem to be suspended in a state of grace where everything is perfection.

Toltec Topography

Right-sided awareness is our everyday state of consciousness, the state of mind that we've been taught to experience and perceive since childhood. This state involves dependence on the rational mind and thinking. When we are in this state we are in the first attention and our assemblage point is in its usual position.

Left-sided awareness or **shift to the left** is when we shift our assemblage point to a place of clarity and absolute knowing. Complete understanding is effortless and immediate, coming from direct knowing. When we are in this state we are in the second attention.

When we shift to the left into heightened awareness, the mind is quiet and stops thinking in its rational and linear manner. That's because we are entering the Nagual's world, where we have direct access to silent knowledge or true knowing. It's a place without words or concepts. Knowing comes as a mass of feelings rather than thoughts. It takes our rational mind time to arrange those feelings in a linear way so that we may express them with language. Sometimes during a drastic shift into heightened awareness, it's difficult to speak or even function normally. This is not harmful; it's just that this state is unfamiliar to us.

Take a few moments to consider the following questions:

◆ Where is your attention focused right now? Is your attention focused outside of you or on the voice in your head?

◆ In general, are you focusing your attention on what is wonderful in your life or on what is "not right"?

◆ Are you choosing to use your attention to see the world from a limited or victimized point of view?

◆ Can you recall a time in your life when you might have shifted into heightened awareness without realizing it?

Warrior Warnings

If your desire to learn to shift levels of awareness is to be someplace other than *this* world, I strongly recommend that you consider otherwise! The key is to learn to be happy in this reality and to treat others with respect, love, and kindness.

Attention is a powerful tool, so asking ourselves these kinds of questions helps us to learn to develop our ability to shift levels of awareness on our own.

Functioning in Heightened Awareness

Once we're comfortable in our heightened awareness, we can navigate perfectly and explore aspects of our reality we've never focused on before. The best way to access heightened awareness with control is through the practice of *Dreaming*. This is a special technique that Toltecs have developed to foster the attention necessary to focus on something other than our everyday awareness of the Tonal, or right-sided awareness. (Dreaming is covered more in Chapters 16 and 22.)

While we're in heightened awareness, we see everything so clearly and we can't imagine why we waste our time focusing on the nonsense we sometimes focus on while we're in normal awareness. But when we're back in normal, right-sided awareness, we can't figure out how to get back to the state of grace of heightened awareness.

We can't make a shift to the left by thinking about it; thinking is strictly an activity that takes place during the right-sided awareness of the Tonal. To make the shift into heightened awareness, you must *Intend* it. From the vantage point of normal awareness, heightened awareness is simply not possible.

For example, during one of the times I shifted my awareness, I was able to see the energetic complex of light everywhere, coming from everything and going everywhere. I actually felt the pressure of the Intent of life upon me, and I knew in that moment when that I died, the Nagual within me would be pulled away by that force and join the larger sea of awareness. As an ex-physician, I can tell you that I didn't see this with my eyes. Yes, my eyes were open so I had the impression that I was physically observing these things, but what was *seeing* in me was my Nagual, *light perceiving light*. From the point of view of my rational mind, what I *saw* was not within the realm of human possibility.

Impeccable Words

"The eyes of man can perform two functions: one is seeing energy at large as it flows in the universe and the other is 'looking at things in this world.' Neither of these functions is better than the other; however to train the eyes only to look is a shameful and unnecessary loss."

—Carlos Castaneda, *A Separate Reality* (as quoted in *The Wheel of Time*)

Warrior Wisdom

During a shift into heightened awareness, we are still in our bodies and on this planet. Our bills and our bosses won't disappear! What's different is that we are able to perceive other aspects of our reality that we have been taught to selectively filter out since childhood.

The Third Attention

There is one more state of consciousness, called the *third attention*. When we focus our attention for the third time, the world we assemble is one of light, or pure Nagual. In this state we have total awareness; in other words, we perceive the universe as light does, outside of time and mind. It's absolute freedom and ecstasy, perceiving the universe at the speed of light, a true somersault into the inconceivable. Every Toltec Warrior desires to reach this state during his or her life by Intending the Nagual within to merge with the Nagual outside of him- or herself (the Infinite). We can also use this state to transcend death (to die with awareness), so to speak. In this case, a person has reached the totality of him- or herself (Tonal and Nagual know each other as one) and has reached a place of absolute awareness. To possess absolute awareness is to have the point of view of light, total knowingness, and consciousness of the Infinite.

Toltec Topography

The **third attention** is total freedom, which comes from the experience of the totality of you as the unknowable or the infinite. It is absolute consciousness and presence, which spans the width and breadth of the universe.

The Mystery of the Infinite

Toltecs know that we live in a universe we can never truly understand, certainly not from our limited point of view as humans on a small planet. We get so caught up in our little everyday world that our focus becomes narrow and finite. It requires a lot of energy to focus on the larger picture. When we do this, it gives us balance and clarity in our lives and also helps us to not take ourselves so seriously. The point is to see ourselves as part of an ever-growing sea of awareness that is constantly moving and expanding.

What we experience in our daily lives, including the results of our individual actions, becomes small compared with the combined actions of all sentient and aware beings in the universe. This keeps us calm when our husband hangs a picture an inch too high on the bedroom wall, for example. (Is that really important in the larger scheme of the universe?) By focusing on the minute, we take the wonderment out of our lives and make our existence boring.

The Infinitesimal and the Infinite

We can say that a person's body and its component systems work exactly like the larger solar systems of our universe. For example, a cell is its own system, and so is the human body, the planet, our solar system, and our universe. This pattern of life is repeated from the infinitesimal to the infinite. Yet all systems, as individual and separate as they may seem, are part of the greater whole.

Toltecs believe there is only light (the Nagual), and it is everywhere and is everything. They know that there is only one living entity (or *one life*) in this universe and that we all are part of it. Just because it looks like we are separate from other people doesn't mean that we actually are disconnected from one another. Our perception of separateness is just an illusion resulting from our constant focus on our Tonal. In other words, there is no this or that, or him or her in the universe. (If I harm you I harm me, just as if you harm one cell within your body you affect the whole of your operational system.) If we can perceive the Infinite, the Nagual, in our own bodies and see the magic of it there, then we can see the infinite as it moves through our universe.

If we accept that we are all part of one universal entity, we won't want to argue or hurt other people (or any other living being, such as plants, animals, or the earth, for that matter) because we'll see them as a part of ourselves. When people murder others in the name of religion or politics, it's because they've never experienced seeing with the eyes of the Infinite. If they did, they would see that they are only inflicting pain upon themselves.

Toltec Topography

The **one life** refers to the knowledge that there is only one living being in the universe, the Infinite, and that we are all parts of this one living being. When we look at creation in this way we realize duality is an illusion both in the concepts of the mind and in the visual illusion that we are separate from each other.

Warrior Warnings

There are many people who are compelled to use their personal power to hurt or manipulate others. Once we see ourselves as one, we realize that every action we take in this direction will result in a reaction that ultimately goes against us. We can call this the Toltec version of Karma.

The human body as the Tonal acts as a mirror for the Nagual, the light that dwells within all conscious beings. The Tonal cannot reflect the totality of the Infinite, but can only afford us a glimpse of its true immensity. Between my cells, in the spaces where matter is not present, the Nagual within me, the captain of operations, is alive. It will remain there until my physical body can no longer maintain operations, and at that time my physical life will cease. I have learned from the Toltec teachings that the aspect of me that is eternal, the small piece of the Infinite that is me, will then return home to the void. And this is a miracle, beautiful in its complexity and grace.

> **Warrior Wisdom**
>
> The part of us that is the Nagual has been around for as long as the universe has existed. It is ancient, patient, and it does not judge. It is impersonal, yet it is unconditional love. On the other hand, the Tonal is only as old as our physical bodies are. It is young and impatient, self-centered and judgmental. It loves nothing but itself and takes everything personally.

If we all treated everyone in our lives as though they were aspects of the Infinite, what sorts of changes might occur—in our homes, in our communities, and in our world?

An Impeccable Life

Living an impeccable life is the keystone of the Toltec philosophy. The definition of *impeccable* is not sinning or going against oneself (hurting oneself in any way). Warriors live their life in the most impeccable way possible, watching the way they speak, and using their energy wisely. An impeccable life begins with impeccable thoughts, which means stopping all that self-deprecating inner dialogue, such as "That was stupid of me!" or "Can't I do anything right?" It also means not blaming things on others by saying, "You're giving me a headache" or "You're making me nuts."

> **Toltec Topography**
>
> In Latin the word **impeccabilis** means not to sin. So in being impeccable Warriors, we are, first and foremost, not sinning against ourselves; we are also careful not to sin against others or the planet.

Warriors are impeccable because they take responsibility for their lives and actions, and don't feel sorry for themselves when they make mistakes. They don't blame others; they simply learn from their experiences and move on. By avoiding this type of behavior they conserve their energy, not having to waste it by getting angry with others or playing with fear-based emotions. They communicate clearly with others, never assuming that others can read their minds or understand their motives. You won't see a Warrior worried about others' judgments; impeccable Warriors don't care what other people may think about them because their self-worth isn't linked to anyone else. Warriors don't get offended, as they have no self-importance, nor do they need to defend themselves against others' beliefs (because they know those beliefs are not ultimately truth). We will be learning all about Warriors' philosophy in Part 3.

Impeccable Words

"The self-confidence of the warrior is not the self-confidence of the average man. The average man seeks certainty in the eyes of the onlooker and calls that self-confidence. The warrior seeks *impeccability* in his own eyes and calls that humbleness. The average man is hooked to his fellow men, while the warrior is hooked only to infinity."

—Carlos Castaneda, *Tales of Power* (as quoted in *The Wheel of Time*)

Wisdom vs. Knowledge

In the Toltec tradition, *Toltec* has been said to mean *man or woman of knowledge*. This doesn't imply that a Toltec is someone with a lot of book knowledge or information. It refers to someone who has access to the silent knowledge I mentioned in Chapter 2. The difference is simple. Information is rational knowledge that we have agreed among each other is truth. It's usually time sensitive and generational, and therefore changes with the era. It's not absolute, and requires the agreement of other humans to make it true.

This is different from wisdom. Wisdom is truth, which comes from the experience of what is. It will be truth regardless of whether any humans see it as such. For example, many years ago humans believed that the earth was the center of the universe. Now we know that the earth is part of our solar system and we rotate around a sun. Fortunately for us, the earth has always happily rotated around the sun, not waiting for humans to come to the correct conclusion.

Impeccable Words

"Being impeccable with your word is the correct use of energy; it means to use your energy in the direction of truth and love for yourself."

—don Miguel Ruiz, *The Four Agreements*

Achieving Action

To become impeccable, we must be willing to change. True change starts with true action, the kind that takes place when one is wide awake. When we live our lives asleep or act in ways that are not impeccable, then we are living from a place of *reaction* and this can only recreate the same results we have always created in our lives.

Warrior Wisdom

A Warrior knows that action is of utmost importance. We will never see a Warrior waiting around for someone else to do his or her dirty work.

As a humble Warrior I can tell you that I am nothing special, no better or worse than anyone else, yet I have managed to change my whole life, including all of my relationships, and I have found true happiness. Most importantly, I have learned how to love and respect myself and never sin against myself. I do my very best to live an impeccable life and I invite you to do the same.

The Least You Need to Know

◆ All of us have the ability to shift our assemblage points from right-sided or normal awareness to left-sided or heightened awareness.

◆ If we learned to use our attention as a child, then we can learn to reuse it as an adult to change our reality.

◆ Knowing that we are matter (Tonal) and Spirit (Nagual) can help us appreciate our part in the greater universe.

◆ By living our lives in an impeccable manner, we develop respect, self-love, and responsibility for our actions.

Part 2

Comprehending the Human Mind

The ancient Toltecs were experts at understanding the human mind; I imagine them to be the psychiatrists of their day. They realized that the function of the mind was to dream all the time, but the problem with humanity was that we were dreaming without awareness. Toltecs saw that as a result of our nonawareness, we humans blamed what happened in our lives on our external circumstances, rather than realizing that we were creating our circumstances based on what our minds were dreaming and projecting. In Part 2, we examine the way the human mind operates, and why it is so important to gain control over it and the way it dreams so that we can become free.

Chapter 5

Your World Is a Virtual Reality

In This Chapter

◆ We are units of perception

◆ The illusory world of the Tonal

◆ Projecting from the virtual reality of our minds

◆ Using our energy in better ways

The most important tool we can have in transforming our minds (and therefore our lives) is having a clear understanding of how our minds work. We've been trained from childhood to believe that we are subject to the whims of the big bad world. But truthfully, it's not what is happening in the world that's at issue, but rather our interpretation of what is happening within our own mind.

Taking a close look at how our minds operate will give us some insight as to how we perceive and create our world. Understanding this fascinating process can make a huge difference in the way we conduct our interpersonal relationships.

Perception Is All in Your Head

Here are a few questions to ponder before we dig into the topic of perception:

- Have you ever considered what exactly constitutes your mind?

- Has the thought occurred to you that your brain may not be the same as your mind?

- Have you ever wondered if your mind is located inside or outside your body?

- Have you ever wondered if your mind has mass and substance?

Scientists have been contemplating these questions for years, and they still have not come to any definite conclusions. What we do know is that when information is received from any of our five senses, it's sent via our nerves to multiple processing centers in our brains. These areas are connected by neural networks, amazingly complex systems that not even the fastest computer processor has been able to beat, to date.

We're Figments of Our Own Minds!

Truly the brain is an astounding organ! But after the input from our senses is processed, what happens next isn't so clear. We know that we assemble our reality within our mind, yet we have no idea where the mind is located. Perhaps the best way to imagine the mind is to see it as a 3-D *virtual reality* filled with information in the same way that the Internet is filled with a universe of information. I know that I have a business website, but where is it exactly? I have a web address, or a URL, but it has no physical location. The same thing can be said for the mind. It also has an address that is your name, so to speak, but where it is actually located is a challenging question.

Toltec Topography

According to the Toltec point of view, the **virtual reality** of the mind is a seemingly real world that is created from light that totally simulates the reality outside of us.

Our five senses are designed to transmit information from the outside world to the processing centers of our brain so that we can then construct a 3-D reproduction of our world. This is because our eyes can't see objects, they can only see light reflecting off of objects (and remember, Toltec theory tells us that we are light perceiving light). It's up to us to create a replica of the outside world within our minds so that we can function in this reality without walking into walls.

So what I'm saying is that we have seen, heard, smelled, tasted, and touched things our whole lives, yet we've never actually seen, heard, smelled, tasted, or touched anything as it actually *is*. We've only experienced an *interpretation* that our minds have created for us, a virtual reality of the outside world. (Wild, isn't it?)

Seeing Is Believing?

The combined input from our five senses contributes to the formation of the virtual reality of the human mind. Let's talk about sight for a moment, as an example of this process. When light bounces off of an object that we're looking at, that light travels inside the pupil of our eye and hits a tiny patch of specialized cells called the retina. The retinal cells record the quality and quantity of light that is being reflected into the eye. The resultant patterns of light are then transmitted via the optic nerve to the visual processing center of the brain, and then are combined with the data collected from your other senses. The input is combined, and the mind's 3-D virtual reality is created.

A human sees things only in the way a human can see things. But what about other living things and their perceptions? Let's take dogs, for example. Their retinas don't have the capability to see in color. Even if we could communicate in dog language, a dog wouldn't understand us if we commanded, "Get the red ball, Fido." Unlike us, Fido sees the world in black, white, and shades of gray.

So who's correct about the color of the ball, us or Fido? Both of us are right, but only from our personal points of view, taking into consideration the tools that we are using to perceive our reality.

> **Warrior Wisdom**
>
> Our virtual reality is a replication of what is outside of us, but a replica that is limited to the capabilities of the organs that are doing the perceiving. According to the Toltecs, just as a dog's perception of the world doesn't include color, our human perception of the world doesn't include all that is out there either, due to the design of our eyes, nerves, and brains.

So What Is Real?

As humans, we make a lot of assumptions about our world and universe because we assume that what we see is absolute, but it's not. Remember, as Warriors, we know that our body has done us the great honor of assembling an entire reality from light for us to function in, and that is truly a miracle! Our great mistake is to assume that what we think we see out there is real. I'm not saying there is nothing out there; what I'm saying is that we have never *seen* what is really out there and we will never know what is out there using our body's perceptive organs.

In Chapter 4, we discussed that when the Toltecs shifted levels of awareness, they *saw* that the entire universe was an energetic complex of light. They were able to see the very concepts that we are discussing here (and without any scientific equipment). When we stop using the perceptive equipment of the body and instead perceive with the part of us that is light, the Nagual, we'll be able to see what *is* instead of the virtual reality. This is possible for every human.

If we have the ability to see one reality with our senses and another reality by shifting levels of awareness, then obviously it's our nature to be able to accomplish these things. Why, then, are we suppressing our magical abilities and talents? Unfortunately, it's not part of the accepted teachings in our society and culture at this time in history, although this is thankfully beginning to change.

A Dream Within a Dream

Edgar Allen Poe once said, "All that we see or seem, is but a dream within a dream," and although he was not a Toltec as far as I know, his quote indicates that he was cognizant of the illusory nature of our reality.

According to the Toltec, the function of the mind is to create what we can call a virtual reality. If we understand this, we can totally change the way we interact with our reality and perceive our world. The ancient Toltecs realized when they shifted levels of awareness that what people see in the first attention is simply a construct, an illusion. But they did not call it a virtual reality, as they did not have computers in ancient times; instead they said that we were dreaming all the time, which is another great way of describing the function of the mind.

Impeccable Words

"Reality is merely an illusion, albeit a very persistent one."
—Albert Einstein

The Dreaming Body

A dream doesn't have physical substance to it and neither does a virtual reality; they are essentially the same. Toltec theory tells us that we are dreaming all the time, both at night and during the day. At night our virtual reality is created from the stored light accumulated during the day, so our sleeping dreams are similar to the way we dream during the day, although they may be a bit more bizarre.

Our memory consists of stored light because all we have ever seen our entire lives is light. While we are sleeping we can use this stored light, or memory, to dream up all kinds of interesting virtual realities. Have you ever experienced flying, traveling, or jumping off cliffs in your dreams? We can do that because, while there's a physical frame (genuine physical constraints) during our daytime dream, there isn't during our nighttime dream.

The ancient Toltecs also learned that we can use the energetic aspect of ourselves that is not the physical body to do this traveling. Through the use of our attention, we can go places with our *energy body* while sleeping. By using our attention in our nighttime dream, we can become better at using our attention in the daytime dream, too. This is a great way to become fluid at shifting the assemblage point during the day away from our normal dream of the first attention. We will discuss this in greater detail in Chapters 16 and 22 when we talk about the Toltec practice of Dreaming.

> **Toltec Topography**
>
> The **energy body,** according to Toltecs, is that part of us that leaves the body at night and travels in our dreams. We can also call this the *dreaming body* or *the double.*

Virtual Limitations

We grow up being taught that things are exactly as they are, even though as Toltecs we can see now that this is not true. If we truly comprehend this, we can understand that we have no limitations in our lives other than the ones that we've imposed upon ourselves.

There are many people who come from meager beginnings who have dreamed big and followed through on those dreams (like Madonna, Oprah, or Jennifer Lopez); they didn't let the beliefs of others stop them from moving forward. If we believe that we are capable, then we will be capable. If we trust our hearts rather than our programming and the desires of our minds, we will dream the most beautiful life. The important thing here is that we take action; otherwise, nothing can change.

We may feel as though we can't accomplish our goals because we have no money, talent, resources, friends, or trustworthy partners (or we may come up with other justifications). I can assure you that even though our limitations seem to be as real as bricks forming a wall, they aren't. They're just statements that our programmed minds are creating for us, and because we believe what our mind tells us, we project that onto the world and make it truth. In Chapter 3 we talked about how concepts are not absolute truth and how challenging them is to disbelieve ourselves. We also said that Toltecs "believe without believing" (more on this in Chapter 17) so that they can experience their world without assuming that they know everything.

Life as a Projectionist

I would like for you to picture the emotional state of the human dream with me for a few moments. Imagine that the six billion humans on Earth are sitting in a big circle together. Each person has a movie projector sticking out of his or her forehead that projects all of the person's fear-based emotions, like anger, frustration, hate, stubbornness, pain, jealousy, anguish, guilt, and righteous indignation into the center of the circle, where a massive hologram containing the combined emotions of all the humans around the world is forming.

An Emotional Hologram

Imagine that every time we've lost our temper, those emotions were projected to the center. Every time we've stubbornly defended our point of view and made someone wrong, those emotions went to the center. The pain of hungry, tortured, and sick people have also gone to the center. Whenever we were hurt, humiliated, or shamed, that was also projected to the center. Every time we have cried or felt pain from what another has done to us, that was also projected to the center. When you imagine this humongous hologram, what does it feel like to you? Does the immensity of the pain and suffering of humans touch your heart?

Changing the Movie

The outside dream or combined virtual reality of humans can be very challenging. We are all responsible for our part in contributing to the immensity of suffering of the human race. Unfortunately, we have not been aware of how we play our part in this human drama. Perhaps now that we understand, we will work harder to be kinder to other people. If we want our world to change, if we want war to end and hate to disappear, let's all do our best to stop projecting these fear-based emotions.

There is war outside of ourselves because we are projecting into the conjoined virtual reality the war that exists within ourselves. When we have an argument going on in our head, this is our personal war. When we are confused and can't make choices in life, this is a battle raging within us. When we argue at home or at work, this is also a war, and all this goes into the combined dream of humanity. Truly the only way to stop war on Earth is to stop war in our minds. Gandhi once said, "Be the change you want in the world." Wise words! He understood that we can make change only by changing ourselves.

Impeccable Words

"It is a man's own mind, not his enemy or foe, that lures him to evil ways."

—Buddha

As a race of beings with the ability to dream, we have taken that great gift and privilege and transformed the majority of our virtual reality into a nightmare. Somehow we fell asleep within our own dream and believed it to be true. Well, the ancient Toltecs realized that it was not true, and we humans could dream any kind of dream once we understood we were dreaming in the first place.

Now that you have this information and understanding, consider how you can change your projections and possibly the world:

- ◆ What actions, however small they may be, could you take to change your personal projection?

- ◆ If you choose to take responsibility for your own creation to date, what effect might that have in your own life and in the lives of others?

- ◆ If you stopped blaming others for all of the difficult things that have happened to you in your life, what changes might occur as a result?

- ◆ There are huge prayer and Intent circles occurring all around the world projecting happiness, peace, and unconditional love. Do you feel you could participate in this kind of activity, and what would that feel like to you? Do you feel you could make a difference in this way?

Impeccable Words

"If humankind would accept and acknowledge this responsibility and become creatively engaged in the process of evolution, consciously as well as unconsciously, a new reality would emerge, and a new age could be born."

—Jonas Salk

Programs, Parasites, and Egos

Here are a few additional ways of looking at the mind, each revealing another important aspect to be aware of.

Malfunctioning Software

In Toltec tradition, we recognize that the mind must be *programmed* to function and that, at least at birth, it resembles a brand-new empty computer in many ways. From the time we're born, our parents start downloading all the programming they feel we need to survive in the world. When we get a little older we add new programming by making friends, going to school, and (yes) by watching TV.

Unfortunately, once information has been added to the hard drive there is no way to get rid of those "files," since our brain does not have a delete button. As a result, we accumulate a lot of information and beliefs that are conflicting in nature. We all have had the experience of downloading new software, only to find that other programs on the hard drive start malfunctioning! Our minds work in the same way.

Let's use an example to see how this works. Let's say that Debbie's mind has a programmed belief (from her mom) that says on a first date a woman should not go back to a man's apartment. She also has a belief (from her peers) that says these are modern times and she can do what she likes. Tonight she goes out on a date and finds she really adores the fellow and feels strongly about going back to his place. Debbie debates back and forth in her mind, because if she goes home with him and he doesn't call her the next day, she will judge herself harshly. (Didn't mom say that would happen?) Yet if she doesn't take him up on his offer, she will feel that she missed out and will berate herself for days. (Why didn't she do what her girlfriends would have done?) Eeek! This is enough to crash any hard drive. So how does our program know which belief to execute? This is a major trouble spot when we depend on our programmed minds to get us through our lives.

> **Warrior Warnings**
>
> Because we drain ourselves of energy in conflict, we rarely have the energy to create new things in our lives or to make major changes. This, in turn, gives us the feeling that we're stuck in our circumstances when we aren't. We're really stuck in our own beliefs and conflicting programming.

Energy-Draining Parasite

We sometimes call the mind a parasite because it's always sucking the energy out of us; take the example of Debbie's date dilemma. Situations arise in life that trigger our beliefs about the way things should be, and as a result we react emotionally, which wastes our energy.

When we argue with another person or even ourselves to defend our beliefs, we expend a lot of energy fighting. So we can see that the mind functions like a parasite, exhausting our energy but giving us nothing in return but a headache.

It's All About Me

Another quality of the mind, or the Tonal, is that it is self-absorbed. We talk to ourselves all day long. Why is it necessary for us to inwardly repeat what we already know? The aspect of the mind that is self-reflective and has a sense of itself is what psychiatrists have been calling the *ego* for many years. When we meet people who talk about themselves endlessly, we say that they're egotistical, but we can see that we are all egotistical because we're constantly talking about ourselves to ourselves!

All of us have that constant inner dialogue going on, telling ourselves either how wonderful or how stupid we are. (We will learn more about the inner dialogue in Chapter 7.) Either way, the bottom line is that the world is all about us: When a friend is late, we are inconvenienced; when cut off in traffic, our life is compromised; when our tire goes flat, our valuable time is being wasted. The focus of our ego is endlessly on itself. We even are under the illusion that we are generous, kind, and loving when in fact we do things because we simply want the approval and appreciation of others. This is very self-centered.

> **Warrior Wisdom**
>
> When we recognize our egotistical tendencies, we can make a choice to be conscious of our motivations and, in turn, be compassionate toward others. True compassion can only occur if we are not in a place of self-reflection.

Ponder these questions about the actions of your mind:

- When did you lose your temper today, even for a moment?

- When did you feel the need to make yourself right and someone else wrong?

- When did you feel the need to defend your point of view to someone?

- When did you judge someone for his or her actions?

- When did you behave like the world revolved around you?

I never realized how self-centered I was until I spent time reviewing my life. I saw that even when I performed acts of kindness for others, I always enjoyed the recognition. (After all, I never engaged in anonymous acts of kindness.) It was the same thing with generosity. I gave but always expected something in return, which is only a way to manipulate others. I never gave my love unconditionally; it was always given with conditions that my beloved treat me in a certain way or behave the way I wanted him to. Our actions as humans do not always come from a pure place, but instead are sometimes filled with ulterior motives. Awareness is the way to see our strategies clearly and to change them without beating ourselves up, which of course would be self-centered again!

The Least You Need to Know

- The mind creates an entire virtual reality for us that is representative of the world we think we know.

- Our daytime and nighttime dreams are the same, except that one has a physical frame and the other does not.

- Our perceived limitations are a result of the fear-based beliefs contained within the virtual reality of our minds.

- We project the 3-D reality of the mind onto our world, and the content of this projection affects what our lives look like.

- The egotistic, self-indulgent mind and the fixation we have on our Tonal keeps us in constant emotional reaction to our world and often drains our energy.

Chapter 6

Beliefs, Concepts, Opinions, and Judgments

In This Chapter

- The cause of the conflict in the human dream
- The judge in our minds
- The programming of the mind
- Humanity's agreement of life's fairness, and why it doesn't work

As humans, we're gifted with the ability to create abstract concepts, ideas, and beliefs. But somewhere along the line we forgot that we were the ones who created those concepts in the first place. We became attached to the very system we created and started to give our power and faith to it. And by forgetting, we have used our very creation to hurt each other.

But we can wake up and become aware of what we're doing. We don't have to be unhappy and use our concepts to hurt ourselves and others. It's not necessary to fight with the folks we love (or even folks we don't know) over concepts. We can simply make a choice in any moment to change our relationship with our concepts. The key is to disempower the judge in our minds and remove the book of law we use to pass out all our judgments with. In this chapter we'll learn how the mind, rather than the life circumstances we find ourselves in, creates our unhappiness. With this information we can make great changes in the way we choose to experience our lives.

Beliefs Aren't Necessarily Truth

The mind is a fabulous tool. Without it we would be unable to communicate verbally with each other. To be able to communicate with our fellow humans we need an agreed-upon code. The first step to accomplishing this is to create words that represent those items and objects that we would like to talk about. Once we have agreed upon the words that comprise our language or code, then we create *abstract concepts* to describe the structures we have created in our society. We spoke a lot about concepts in Chapter 3, so let's explore them now from a different point of view.

Toltec Topography

Abstract concepts are thoughts or ideas that are conceived within the mind but have no physical or concrete existence. We use concepts to describe our personal experience so that we can communicate with one another.

A **belief** is a statement that we accept as true or real. It is also a firmly held opinion or conviction.

An **opinion** is a view or judgment formed about something not necessarily based on fact or knowledge.

A **judgment** is a conclusion one comes to based on one's opinion.

Property, for example, is a human abstract concept that only humans understand. A dog, for example, would have no idea that it traveled from one neighbor's property to another's. Ask yourself this question: Can you really own the earth beneath your feet? No, you can't, but we buy and sell land because we've agreed in our country that this is possible. (The trees that live on our "property" have no idea they "belong" to us!) Other common abstract concepts are money, education, marriage, relationships, family, sports, friendship, good, bad, war, race, and culture.

Transcending Concepts

Once we've created our language and abstract concepts, the next part of the process is for us to make rules about those concepts. Let's continue with our example of property. We can agree that we need to use money to acquire property and that we must sign a contract and have a deed to own the property. Of course, a lawyer is necessary to make this transaction legal.

Can you see that the ideas of a deed, money, contracts, and even a lawyer are just our creation? If we all agreed tomorrow that we can't buy, sell, or own land, the whole structure of real estate would fall apart. Then we would live similar to the Native Americans, who agreed that no one could own land, only live in harmony with it. For them this was truth as much as owning land is truth for us.

According to the Toltecs, we own nothing, not even our own bodies. We only have use of our bodies until they wear out, and then we continue on as life itself, or the Nagual. Objects simply pass through our hands without permanence. Yet we're so attached to the things we believe we own that when they're taken away from us we become upset. When our beloved passes away we get angry at God, as if God took something away from us that was ours. If a hurricane destroys our home we grieve because our possessions are damaged or gone. When a relationship breaks up we get upset and say that we lost our partner. But did we ever *have* that person in the first place?

Take a minute to look at the four definitions in the beginning of this chapter. You will not see the word *truth* mentioned once in regard to concepts, beliefs, opinions and judgments. That's because there can be no *absolute truth* in the realm of concepts. As Warriors know, truth resides in the reality that exists transcendent to concepts and language in a place that can only be experienced by direct perception without the interpretive processes of the mind (remember this from Chapter 3?). Once we put the "truth" into words, it is no longer truth, but instead a conceptual description created by the dreaming mind.

Toltec Topography

The **absolute truth** is simply *what is* without conceptual interpretation. The truth does not require our belief in it to be true.

Concepts as Weapons

Concepts are practical in our daily lives and it's important to see our creations with clarity and to have respect for them. But to wage war on other humans over the concepts of property is using the concepts we've created to kill each other with. Can one country's concepts wage war against another country's concepts? If the United States attacks a communist country, is the concept of democracy fighting with the concept of communism? No, concepts cannot fight, only humans can wage war, and they are the ones who will be sacrificed in the name of those concepts.

Let's take a moment to reflect on how often we wage war against the people we love over concepts and beliefs. Consider the following questions:

Impeccable Words

"Our ideals, like the gods of old, are constantly demanding human sacrifices."

—George Bernard Shaw

◆ Today, what concepts or beliefs have you used to create conflict in your life?

◆ What would it feel like if you could spend one day not defending any of your concepts or beliefs?

◆ How have you used concepts to create anger and other fear-based emotions inside you?

These are challenging questions to answer. But our freedom lies in our ability to see what *is* in order to rise above the reality of concepts.

Here Comes the Judge

Once we have taken the time to create all of our concepts and beliefs, we then must have a way to make sure that they are implemented. Our minds, being the creative entities they are, have figured out the perfect solution: the judge. Every mind has a judge present and ready to make sure that all of our concepts and beliefs are perfectly executed.

The Book of Law

The totality of information that is contained in our programs, from the day we were born until now, constitutes our book of law (all part of the island of the Tonal—see Chapter 3). We use it to operate in daily life at all times. We refer to it when we need to make decisions in our life, and we use it to make the other people in our life wrong. Worse yet, we often use it to make ourselves feel wrong.

I'm not saying that all concepts are bad. Take friendship, for example, which is a lovely ideal. But if we believe that a friend is someone we can whine and complain to, or whom we can expect to be at our beck and call, we're not going to have many friends! Using a friendship in this way may cause our friends to back away, leaving us hurt and angry. Can you see how the judge can take a beautiful concept and twist it to hurt ourselves and others just because of our personal interpretation of that concept? Because of the programming of our mind, we are always manipulating our concepts to help us get what we think we want and need.

> **Warrior Wisdom**
>
> One way of looking at the totality of beliefs and concepts in our minds is to perceive them as a book of law containing everything that we believe is right and true in our virtual reality.

Let's look at a fairly serious example of how this might be applicable in real life. Let's say we know someone who has just found out that her partner has been cheating on her. Her book of law states that this is a crime worthy of great punishment. She feels anger, and then all the other fear-based emotions start to follow: humiliation, revenge, sorrow, betrayal, jealousy, righteous indignation, guilt, anguish, panic, self-pity, insecurity, rejection, pain, depression, inadequacy, and frustration.

Fear-Based Emotions Rule

If this person feels humiliated, it may be because she believes that everyone knew about the affair except her. She may believe that everyone is talking about her and judging her. But she should ask herself these questions:

- Does her partner's having an affair *really* have anything to do with her?

- Does it really matter what others think about her?

- Does it matter if other people are talking about her or judging her in any way?

The point is that her partner is not making her feel humiliated or angry—*she is doing it to herself*. She has taken the concepts and beliefs she holds about cheating to hurt herself. Of course, she's involved in the consequences of her partner's actions, but still, those actions are not about her. Perhaps this woman feels betrayed because she believes her partner broke the marriage vows they both promised to keep. Here's another point to consider. Since the breaking of marriage vows is not an uncommon event, perhaps it's time to look at the concept of marriage and ask ourselves if it needs to change.

All of us have broken commitments to people at some time in our life, sometimes by mistake, sometimes due to overcommitment of our time, sometimes by forgetting, and other times because at the last minute we just didn't want to do what we thought we would when we made the promise. If we know this, why would it surprise us that a partner broke a promise? Why would we choose to get upset over something that is not an unusual occurrence in our society? The feelings of betrayal and pain come from our concepts not being upheld.

I realize I've picked a touchy subject to use as an example, but I also know that this is a common-enough situation. Wouldn't it be great if we could go through life not losing our happiness to the judge and the book of law in our mind? To be truly happy in life, we need to be free of all the judgments our mind puts out against ourselves and others. These concepts and beliefs are the very things that have overtaken our island of the Tonal, and need serious pruning and weeding out.

Impeccable Words

"There is no need to blame your parents or anyone who abused you in your life, including yourself. But it is time to stop the abuse. It is time to free yourself of the tyranny of the Judge by changing the foundation of your own agreements. It is time to be free from the role of the Victim."

—don Miguel Ruiz, *The Four Agreements*

Warrior Wisdom

Toltecs say that fear-based beliefs and concepts create fear-based emotions. Concepts and beliefs that are created from love make us happy and benefit humanity as a whole.

Victims of Our Own Minds

I think we can clearly see how the mind can victimize us and make us sick and unhappy. Every time the judge uses the book of law against someone else, someone is going to suffer, and guess who that is? Ourselves! Even though it looks like we are judging someone else, what is really happening is that we are judging ourselves. Toltecs understand that the Nagual will not judge us, but we certainly will take every opportunity to berate ourselves.

We can spend our lives feeling offended, victimized, and insulted by situations and people. We might perceive certain information, pit it against what we believe we

know, and use it to irritate ourselves. There's
something about this system that's just not
working for us! Of course we often perceive
our reality and the result is joy, but the key is to
increase the amount of joy and happiness in our
lives, and to decrease the amount of irritation.

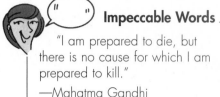

Impeccable Words

"I am prepared to die, but
there is no cause for which I am
prepared to kill."

—Mahatma Gandhi

Disengage the Autopilot!

When we live our lives at the mercy of the judge, we are functioning on autopilot,
allowing our programmed mind to handle the challenges in life. The rational mind
compares every situation we're in right now with something that has happened in
the past. It tells us that we already know what this situation is. Based on that, it does
what it did in the past, not fully accessing the current challenge at hand. What a poor
strategy, since every situation is unique! No wonder we're constantly surprised when
things don't turn out the way we thought they should.

To stop functioning this way, we need to be aware of what our mind is telling us in
every moment, and take control of the process. This requires that we stop the judge
in its tracks and recognize that what our mind says about what is happening is not
necessarily truth.

A Warrior never underestimates her challenges because she knows that she really
doesn't know anything about anything. (Yup, that again!) Yes, she recognizes that
her mind is evaluating whatever is going on from her mind's point of view and all the
data contained within it. But she also recognizes that her mind is just like a computer,
which is only as good as the information contained within it.

Stop Thinking and Start Feeling

The mind is like a computer, great for adding
numbers and doing calculations, but it can't
give us a gut feeling based on the silent
knowledge we constantly have access to. A
Toltec uses his silent knowledge in addition to
the information he has available to him. He
acknowledges what he is feeling and pays attention to that rather than *just* his rational mind.
He trusts himself and his heart 100 percent
over his programming.

Impeccable Words

"A warrior lives by acting, not
by thinking about acting, nor by
thinking about what he will think
when he has finished acting."

—Carlos Castaneda, *A Separate
Reality* (as quoted in *The Wheel
of Time*)

Since we grew up learning to think before we act, this type of advice goes directly against everything we were taught as children. Consider this Toltec advice: Listen to your inner wisdom and let that direct you. How many times have we deliberated for days over some decision and ended up doing what our intuition told us to do in the first place? So why did we waste all that time *thinking*? Because we didn't want to make a mistake. We didn't want to go against the judge in our own mind. After all, we know how badly our mind would punish us if we dared to make a mistake!

> **Warrior Wisdom** _____
>
> Stop for a minute and picture your favorite heroes from the movies. Can you imagine them sitting for hours mentally contemplating what they should do? No way! A Warrior trusts the feelings that propel him to take an action. Then he makes any adjustments in his plans based on what he observes as a result of those actions. A Warrior can do this because he has cleaned his mind of all its conflicting beliefs and it is easy for him to make choices in life without wasting time in deliberation and circular thinking.

The Judge Is Corrupt

With that judge hanging over our heads, it's challenging to take chances in life. The consequences are just too great! We worry about what other people will think about us and how they will judge us for our errors. We all make errors in life; this is how we grow and learn. But once we deal with the consequences of our actions, that is enough. Of course, our inner judge is a hundred times worse than outside criticism since it's in our head and we can't escape it. Every time we tell it to be quiet, it starts berating us all over again, keeping us awake at night and preventing us from having peace in our life. But we do not have to be in fear of our mind or the minds of others punishing us repetitively for things that are long over-with. If we aren't happy in our lives, we need to look at the power we've abdicated to our personal judge and the judges of others. True justice is taking responsibility for our errors and then forgiving ourselves and moving on. It is a kindness to extend this same courtesy to others.

Ask yourself the following questions:

♦ How do you judge your family members?

♦ What things do you judge harshly about yourself?

♦ What have you done in your life that you have a lot of self-loathing about?

♦ What things have happened in your life that you feel are unforgivable?

If we can recognize that our judge is not our friend, we can work at bouncing it right off the bench. Imagine how peaceful it would be if we didn't have to hear that judge saying horrible things about us and other people all the time. Or if the judge would stop telling us how to run our lives.

Warrior Wisdom

The judge has had un-opposed power for way too long and is a dictator. Now is the time to stage a *coup* and get control over it and its book of law!

Pain, Suffering, and Injustice

There's a belief floating around that says we can't enjoy life and appreciate pure joy unless we also experience pain and suffering. No pain, no gain.

I don't subscribe to that belief. I feel that it encourages our need to hurt each other with our concepts and justifies our own suffering. Consider children for a moment, before they are old enough to have concepts. They're happy unless they are physically uncomfortable or hungry. They don't accept that pain is an insurmountable part of life.

Choosing Happiness, Not Suffering

Pain is a fact of life as far as the physical body is concerned. Kids can't reach the age of five without falling down and scraping a knee. But whatever they're feeling physically, children are usually able to find happiness. Somehow, without being told, they realize that the body can feel pain but that they don't necessarily have to suffer.

While in medical practice, I treated many children and noticed that it was often the parents who created drama based on their judgment of what was happening. Meanwhile, the child was doing fine and even being brave, as long as I told the truth about what she was going to experience. Even the sickest child will do his best to play if he can find the energy to do so. Kids are truly Warriors. (If you have

Warrior Wisdom

Children will cry one minute and forget why the next. Warriors strive to live in the moment this way. We can fully experience sadness or pain in one moment, and then return to our natural joy-ful state in the next.

Warrior Wisdom

As a whole our society has made the choice to believe that pain and suffering are necessary, but if we are awake and aware, we can make a conscious choice to change that belief if it is not serv-ing us.

72 **Part 2:** Comprehending the Human Mind

never had the opportunity to witness this, consider volunteering some time at any cancer hospital's children's wing, and you will see this miracle for yourself.) So what am I saying? We have it within ourselves to be happy, and it really is our nature to find that happiness, no matter what the circumstances are.

It's Just Not Fair!

A question I started asking myself years ago was "Why do I want to have concepts and beliefs that cause me to get upset and make me sick?" The truth is I had never realized it was my beliefs that were making me ill; I always thought it was everything outside of me. As a Warrior I learned to take responsibility for everything I was creating in my life, and that included my emotional state of being. I started watching my mind carefully, and what I saw was that my internal dialogue got me all riled up about whatever I perceived in the moment. In other words, the constant analysis and judgment by my programming was hooking my attention and getting me emotionally involved.

I used to see everything as unfair or unjust. Either life was not going the way I wanted it to go, or I wasn't getting what I thought I needed. People weren't doing what I wanted or needed them to do. Others were not keeping their promises or doing what they were supposed to. My time was not flowing smoothly and my computer did not behave properly. Salespeople were taking too long to talk to me and unruly drivers were speeding dangerously close to me in traffic. The line in the bank and the grocery was too long and even the drive-through line was too slow.

Then one day I realized that I had a belief that said life should be fair. I realized it wasn't really any of these things that were making me unhappy, but the fact that I had expectations about the way life *should* be.

Impeccable Words

"Almost all of us long for peace and freedom; but very few of us have much enthusiasm for the thoughts, feelings, and actions that make for peace and freedom."

—Aldous Huxley

Truth be told, life is what it is. My beliefs and concepts aren't going to change that one iota. I realized that my happiness depended on making some serious choices about what I wanted to believe about my reality. I didn't have to suffer and I didn't have to go from one unhappy emotion to another. I could live my life feeling good, having lots of energy, and not feeling victimized by everything. This change didn't happen in one day, of course; actually, it happened over the course of several years, as it took me that long to inventory all the nonsense that I had in my book of law. Giving up my addiction to doling out judgment was a challenge, but in the end I learned that it's possible to live life being happy all the time. I don't miss suffering one bit, and I don't think you will either!

Now that you have a better understanding of the power of concepts and beliefs and how we use them against ourselves, ask yourself this:

◆ Can you think of some beliefs you would find beneficial to change?

◆ What would you have to do to make those changes?

The Least You Need to Know

◆ It's our responsibility to evaluate our attachment to our beliefs and concepts and whether they are causing us unhappiness.

◆ Our belief system is held in effect by the judge in our mind, whose sole job is to enforce our concepts.

◆ It isn't life's circumstances that we are victimized by, but by the very concepts and beliefs that we put our faith in.

◆ Life may present us with challenging situations, but we can make the choice to be happy in the face of adversity and avoid the need to suffer.

Chapter 7

An Insane Species

In This Chapter

- The repetitive blind behaviors of circular thinking
- How internal dialogue traps our attention and enslaves us
- Learning to silence our internal dialogue
- Engaging in not-doings to "stop the world"

By now we have a good understanding about the way our beliefs, judgments, and opinions can affect our lives. But do we really understand how we are at the mercy of the voice in our head that expresses those sentiments to us all day long, day after day? We often kid around that people who hear voices are crazy. Well, we listen to the voice in our head—but we call it thinking, yet feel that we are sane. The problem is that this voice keeps us locked into doing things the same way we've always done them, and that can be very limiting.

In this chapter we will look at how our internal dialogue corners our attention and has us do things that are not always in our best interest. By observing this internal dialogue and our programmed behaviors, we can stop our mind from making choices for us that would be better addressed by our intuition and heart. This in turn opens us up to a multitude of different possibilities and opportunities in life.

Madness Is Epidemic

Albert Einstein defined insanity as "doing the same thing over and over again and expecting different results." This is a simple but stunningly accurate observation. Let's consider how this might apply to our own lives:

◆ Do you have personal relationships that look like repeat performances?

◆ Do you seem to always attract partners from hell?

◆ Have you gone from one unfulfilling job to another?

◆ Do you always choose a job that ends up requiring more than 40 hours of your time each week?

◆ Do you seem to attract whining, complaining, unhappy friends?

◆ Does your life consist of one dramatic episode after another?

If anything about our lives is a repeat performance, this is a sign that we are creating life on autopilot. Yes, it seems like we're taking different actions, but actually we're doing the same things over and over. The universe works on the physics principle of action-reaction. If we always take the same actions, we'll invariably receive the same reactions.

A Tricky Trap

We only have certain information available within our programmed minds, because we each have a specific education and set of life experiences. If we use our minds to make choices in life, then we limit ourselves to only the possibilities contained within our program.

I'll give you an example. I went from college and medical school to private practice. As a result of my programming, I believed that I was logical, intelligent, and reasonable. My education taught me that this was the correct path to follow in life. I judged other people who didn't seem to follow logical actions as flighty and ignorant. I had to think about everything and would only take actions that fit my program's requirements of what was appropriate to do.

But blindly following my program had serious consequences in my life. I turned away many wonderful opportunities because they weren't logical and didn't fit my mind's profile for proper actions. I didn't date certain men because they weren't the right ones, according to my programming; conversely, over and over I picked men who were supportive of my unhealthiest beliefs.

My decisions were based on the contents of a program rather than on my heart's desires. My program did whatever it could to execute itself, even if the results created pain and suffering in my life. How insane is that? Our minds constantly tell us what we're capable of doing and not doing, based on what we believe about ourselves and about our world. This is the trap. We believe that we *are* our mind and that our beliefs and points of views about life are truth. But they aren't. (Remember this from Chapters 3 and 6?)

If we believe the mind, then we'll take the advice of our program and be severely limited in our life's expression. For example, if we're always thinking of ourselves as shy, are we going to apply for a job that requires us to speak in front of people? Probably not, but that job could be an opening to a whole new world of possibilities and opportunities. Instead, we'll be tempted to keep doing the same thing over and over, even if it's making us unhappy, because this is all we've ever known and done.

If we become aware of this trap, we'll realize we don't have to take the advice of a program anymore. We have choices. If we don't have the information contained in our own program to do something different in life, all we have to do is obtain the information needed to proceed in that direction.

> **Impeccable Words**
>
> "The voice of knowledge is telling you what you are and what you are not. It's always trying to make sense out of everything. I call it *the voice of knowledge* because it's telling you everything you know. It's telling you your point of view in a conversation that never ends."
>
> —don Miguel Ruiz, *The Voice of Knowledge*

Repetitive Relationships

Let's go a little deeper. If we keep attracting partners who aren't right for us or we can't sustain healthy relationships with, who's responsible for that? We are, of course. Let's consider the following set of questions:

◆ If you have beliefs in your program that say you're never going to have a wonderful mate, or if you believe you're not good-looking enough or smart enough to find a decent partner, what choices will you make in a partner?

◆ If you believe that the people you love hurt you or that the people you love abandon you, what kind of person will you choose?

- If you have been taught that you need to yell to be heard, what type of person will you attract?

- If you believe that you are poor and will never have financial abundance in life, who will you marry?

- If you believe you need to fix people and solve everyone's problems to be worthy of love, what type of person will you attract?

- If you feel that you need to control everything and everyone in your life, what type of partner will you meet?

- If you feel that you are worthless or deserve to be punished, what type of relationship will you end up in?

Can we nail down a pattern in our own lives and see the beliefs in our own programs that have prompted our choices? If we believe that we're never going to have a successful relationship with a worthy mate, for whatever reasons our programming throws at us, we'll never find a worthy mate; it's that simple. Not only that, we also may fall into the same destructive patterns in relationship after relationship, all because of a self-sabotaging program.

Humanity Insanity

On an even larger scale, let's take a look at the world for a moment. We have experienced war for at least as long as we have written history to record it. Never has there been a time of absolute peace in humankind. We've engaged in war many times, destroying families and causing horrific suffering, yet we keep doing it over and over.

Here are some questions we must ask ourselves:

- Do you believe that war can create resolution and peace?

- Does war create more resentments, grudges, feelings of revenge, and ultimately more war?

- After thousands of years of war, why are we still fighting?

- Is it necessary for humans to exterminate themselves to finally realize that war is futile?

The Toltecs speculated that the human race is very ill to want to perpetuate these repetitive cycles of war. They saw that humans were trapped in a prison of their own minds, only able to exercise the possibilities contained within. They saw that the limitations they placed upon themselves were enormous. It was obvious to the Toltecs that people were taught to place limitations upon themselves from the programming of their parents and society. They realized that humans were unaware of what they were doing and creating in their lives. Watching humans suffer in this way was a great impetus to spur the Toltecs to become free of their own minds, to be able to enjoy life and create new things all the time.

Internal Dialogue of the Mind

In Chapter 3 we talked about how the mind's dialogue keeps us fixed in our point of view about our world. As Warriors we spend our lives getting our inner dialogue under control so that we can be free of the mesmerizing effects of the Tonal. Most of us hardly notice the voice in our head that chatters all day. We are so used to it that we can't imagine how lovely it would be if we could turn that sound off. Ahh, absolute silence, quietude, and peace!

Silencing the Judge

It's critical that we begin to listen to what that voice is saying so that we can make choices as to what we want to focus our attention on. Much of the time the voice is like a personal organizer, constantly telling us what we need to do and at what time, what appointments we have and when to pick up the dry cleaning. But the rest of the time it's a dictator, telling us what to believe about everyone and everything, judging others and ourselves. This is where it becomes torture to be trapped in the presence of this manipulative judge. Not only can it be painful to listen to its insults and opinions all day, but it also tries its best to control our life by making all of our choices for us, often taking us down the road to ruin.

So what can we do to get control of our mind again? The first step is to understand that if we willed ourselves to have this internal dialogue in the first place (since we weren't born with it), then we can will ourselves to ignore it. It's imperative that we believe we have the power within us to change this and anything else in our virtual reality. Let's take a few minutes to look at the voice in our head:

- ◆ What things did your mind say to you today that were insulting or limiting?

- ◆ What unkind things did the voice tell you about others in your life today?

◆ Did your program judge anyone to be rude, inconsiderate, annoying, frustrating, or irritating today?

◆ Has your mind told you that you should not take an action because you will fail or because that action scares you?

The best way to get a handle on what our programming is telling us is to keep a running record of all the judgments it makes over the course of one day. We'll find that we're mean and vicious to ourselves and to others, even though not one word has been uttered from our mouths. In watching my own mind, I was able to see the assault starting from the moment I looked in the mirror in the morning. I "heard" statements like "Gosh, your thighs are getting gross, you'd better do something about that," or "You're going to need a lot of makeup today to look halfway decent," or "You're looking so old, maybe you should consider plastic surgery."

Alright, so anyone's programming might be a bit harsh in the morning; how about what it says as the day progresses? It might say "Don't bother flirting with that man, you can never have him," or "Why apply for that job? It's way above your credentials," or "Don't bother asking for what you need here; that's selfish and you need to make everyone else happy first."

How many of these kinds of statements sound familiar to you?

Once we can clearly see the strategies of our own mind, we can start to make changes to it. We uphold our view of the world with this kind of internal discussion; it keeps our island looking exactly as it always has. Things are the way they are in our lives simply because we say so. If we tell ourselves it's *this* way, then it is. The best thing about looking at the contents of our mind is that the end result will be letting go of our egotistical nature and the self-absorption that results from putting all of our attention internally in our virtual reality.

If we all expressed what we were thinking out loud, we would all be walking around talking to ourselves, looking quite insane. The Toltecs realized that it doesn't matter if we talk to ourselves out loud or in our heads; it's insane either way!

Impeccable Words

"Whenever the internal dialogue stops, the world collapses and extraordinary facets of ourselves surface, as though they had been heavily guarded by our words."

—Carlos Castaneda, *Tales of Power* (as quoted in *The Wheel of Time*)

Warrior Wisdom

A Warrior knows that it's a challenge to stop our internal voice, so until we can totally silence it, at least we can have it tell us nicer things, less limiting thoughts, and less vicious commentary about everyone else in our lives.

A Mesmerizing Story

By taking an inventory of everything on our island of the Tonal, and everything in our belief system, we can start to get a good idea of exactly what we're dealing with. Many events have happened to us over the years, and we've made many agreements based on how we've interpreted what we've experienced. Looking at the whole story of our lives clearly and without judgment enables us to see the repetitive patterns in our lives and the reasons for those choices. We can start this process by keeping a special journal just for writing the story of our life.

In this journal, we'll put everything we can remember about everything that has happened to us, year by year. Remember to write without censoring the story and without determining whether or not the writings are okay from the judge's point of view. Reread the story at a later date, separating what is not absolute truth from the emotional fiction, and take special note if the story sounds in any way like you were a victim. If you've felt like a victim at any time in your life, this is something to be addressed.

The purpose of this journal is to detach, forgive, heal, and let go of all of the stories we believe about ourselves and our life. When this happens, the mind has little to say to us anymore. If we come to a place of total forgiveness and absolute gratitude about life, what kinds of judgments can we possibly believe? For example, if we can't forgive our parents for certain things dating back to our childhood, this may be because we felt, and perhaps still feel, victimized by them. The truth is that our parents' actions, in many cases, didn't have anything to do with us, even though we may have suffered the consequences of those actions.

As children we internalize everything and make it all about us. We become hurt and wounded. Our less-than-perfect parents couldn't help themselves; they had their own issues, problems, and wounds. This doesn't make their actions right; it just makes them not about us. When we can rewrite our story from the

> **Warrior Wisdom**
>
> For a Warrior there are no victims, only participants in life, so retelling our life stories in a journal can be a powerful exercise. We'll discuss this exercise in depth in Chapter 19 when we talk about the process of recapitulation.

> **Warrior Wisdom**
>
> The Toltecs recognized that we can advise people not to believe what their minds are saying and to work toward inner silence, but if people believe in their virtual reality and the voice in their heads, that advice will be useless.

point of view of the truth above the concepts, we'll be able to let go of what we believe, and then we'll never feel hurt by our parents (or anyone else) again. This is freedom from the mind, since it's not our parents who are hurting us now that we're adults; we're inflicting our own pain by what we tell ourselves about the past.

This is powerful stuff. I think it's obvious that as long as we still believe ourselves and our stories, it's unlikely that we'll be able to silence our mind. We have to rise above the stories to find the truth and let the rest go.

What Are We *Doing?!*

The Toltecs realized that we must take drastic action to break the fixation we have on our internal dialogue and Tonal. To be able to shift our attention at will and focus on the Nagual within us and outside of us, they knew that we needed systems to purposely break that attention. It was a challenge to find ways to end our focus on our mind's linear processing, and our stubborn belief that we know everything. By observing humans, the Toltecs saw that everything we do and everything we think in our daily lives constitutes our *doings.* If we could disrupt the chain of doings, it would, in turn, break our view of the world. Toltecs call this process *stopping the world.*

Toltec Topography

Doings are activities that we engage in that are directed by our mind's programming. They cause us to create our world exactly as we want to see it according to our domestication and socialization, rather than the way it is.

Stopping the world is when we finally silence the mind, and the world of the Tonal stops. Then we can assemble any reality we desire.

Doings Are Your Undoing

So what constitutes a doing? Anything you do in a consistent way, without thinking, that reflects you as the personality or program, is a doing. A doing might be the way you interrupt people when they speak, not allowing them to finish what they are saying. Or perhaps the way that you are cutting with your sense of humor, or the way you talk down to people to make yourself look better. When you feel threatened, a doing might be how you use your intelligence to keep people away from you. Even your internal dialogue is a doing. Anything you do that another person can identify as *your* particular behavior pattern is a doing.

Some of you might be thinking, "What about my positive doings?" If some of your doings are causing happiness and joy in your life, there is no reason to address them right now. But if your doings are sabotaging your life in subtle and not-so-subtle ways, this definitely deserves immediate attention. In the end, a Warrior will eliminate even his "positive" doings as they are still programmed activities and his ultimate goal is freedom.

Our doings are simply a result of putting ourselves on autopilot and letting our program live our lives for us. For us to discover the remarkable beings that we are, it's necessary for us to stop our doings and the internal dialogue that prompts them. Our thinking is the main support for our seeing the world as we do and for our particular way of interpreting everything that happens to us. The challenge is to force ourselves to see the world differently so that we can experience it differently, and, as a result, create our lives differently. Every time we do something that purposely goes against what we believe or is different from what we normally would do, we expand ourselves and our possibilities exponentially.

Not-Doings Will Set You Free

Engaging in *not-doings* can be a painful affair. In other words, it is not easy to go against the prescribed behaviors we have been participating in our entire lives. It almost feels like we are going against ourselves. The truth is that we are absolutely going against ourselves, but who is the self we are talking about? The programmed self, of course—the ego or the parasite (see Chapter 5), not the Nagual. Since we believe that we *are* the program, this is a challenging activity for "*us.*" The Nagual within, pure life or Spirit, wants to express itself freely through us in our manifest form. It is these aspects of our personality and the clinging to what we believe about ourselves that prevents us from being all we can be in our lives. It is a Warrior's task to take new and different actions even though they are not comfortable for us, knowing that the reward will be considerable.

I myself have engaged in hundreds of not-doings and we will be talking a lot about them in Chapter 17. It is so exciting to see aspects of the real you revealed in the most amazing ways. Even though this process is tough, it is well worth it, and it actually becomes entertaining to design things to do that challenge who you

> **Toltec Topography**
>
> **Not-doings** are specific activities that we design to break our addiction to our doings. They enable us to break free of the limiting ideas and beliefs we have about ourselves and expand our possibilities in life.

believe you are. The result of doing this is experiencing the real you, maybe for the first time in your life.

Here are two simple not-doings you can try. Feel free to design more complex and challenging activities for your "self":

♦ Try eating your lunch at a different time than you normally do and don't eat your normal choices. If you only eat two meals a day, perhaps you can eat five small ones. Don't believe the story your mind tells you, just make note of what it is saying and look for the nontruth in your internal dialog.

♦ If you dress in a particular way that people identify as "your style," take one week and dress in an entirely different manner. Pay attention to the story and judgments your mind is telling you, but again, don't believe yourself.

Impeccable Words

"The internal dialogue is what grounds people in the daily world. The world is such and such or so and so, only because we talk to ourselves about its being such and such and so and so. The passageway into the world of shamans opens up after the warrior has learned to shut off his internal dialogue."

—Carlos Castaneda, *Tales of Power* (as quoted in *The Wheel of Time*)

The Least You Need to Know

♦ By taking inventory of our mind and our thinking, we can have awareness regarding the choices we make in life, rather than functioning on autopilot.

♦ Addressing our internal dialogue will keep us cognizant of the judge in our mind and the constant barrage of insulting commentary.

♦ By keeping track of our doings, we can create actions that are different from our normal behaviors, leading to alternative outcomes in our life.

♦ Experimenting with not-doings will bring our habitual behaviors to the forefront and enable us to clearly hear the limiting commentary in our mind.

Chapter 8

Checking Out of the Asylum

In This Chapter

◆ The human addiction to drama, suffering, and stress

◆ Being brutally honest with ourselves to break free from stressful habits and situations

◆ The distorted concept of perfection

◆ Being aware of the origins of our behavior patterns

We invest a lot of money and time in the pursuit of happiness. We buy pretty things to decorate our homes, spend time with friends and family, and go on vacations to relax, but something is still missing. We have hectic, stressful lives that we don't know how to change, as we have no role models for a different kind of life. It's like one big insane asylum with billions of people searching for something that seems to remain elusive no matter how hard we try.

The problem is that we're looking outside of us for the solution. We keep trying to change everything out there, to make it better and better. But it isn't what's out there that needs to be addressed; it's the agreements we have with ourselves that drive the choices we make. All of our answers lie deep within the programming of our minds. By having clarity, we can see the beliefs that are contributing to the creation of drama, stress, and suffering in our lives and in society. This is the prison that can keep us trapped in unfulfilling, treadmill-type lives. Just because everyone else is living this way doesn't mean that we have to.

Breaking the Addiction to Drama

I love to go to the movies and see a great drama, one that has all the elements of a good story: a little infidelity, family feuding, double-crossings, and emotional crescendos. Movies and TV shows hook our attention and get us involved in either questioning or supporting our morals, values, and beliefs. It would be nice if we could confine drama to the big screen and keep it out of our lives.

There are a few of us whose lives are as peaceful as a Buddhist monk's; however, those people are in the minority!

When I started studying the Toltec path, I spent time looking at the amount of craziness in my life and realized that I was so used to constant drama that I didn't even see how stressful my life was or what was causing that stress (like my 60-hour workweek or difficult relationships). I suffered the effects of that stress, experiencing heart palpitations, rashes, and stomachaches. After observing myself and my life with deeper scrutiny, I saw that most of my stress, suffering, and drama was self-created, and totally supported by the other people in my life. With awareness I saw that although I said I wanted change, I really enjoyed my stress, just like an adrenaline junkie.

It wasn't easy admitting to myself that I was responsible for all the drama in my life. I spent a good portion of my time blaming my unhappiness and suffering on everyone and everything that I possibly could, like my ex-husbands, my mother, my profession, the government, and the weather. It was never about me, until I realized it *was* all about me. Even though I was the one who decided to be a doctor and have a busy practice, I used to complain that my profession was too hectic and nerve-racking.

> **Warrior Warnings**
>
> Warriors know that stress, anxiety, and drama cause the heart rate to increase, blood pressure to rise, hormones to be released, gastric juices to flow, and blood vessels to constrict. This can result in migraines, heart palpitations, rashes, strokes, ulcers, and all sorts of diseases.

> **Impeccable Words**
>
> "Tension is who you think you should be. Relaxation is who you are."
>
> —Chinese proverb

A Sick Strategy

Upon observing myself carefully, I found that I was perpetually late in the morning, arriving at my office 10 to 15 minutes *after* hours officially began. As a result, I had to rush to catch up, patients had to wait, and of course they were cranky before I even saw them. Since I was behind schedule all morning, it meant that I would be late for lunch and my consults, setting me up for a belated start for afternoon patients. As you might guess, if we had to squeeze in one emergency patient during the day, all hell broke loose! To make matters worse, I was also director of a surgical residency program at my hospital, loaded down with all the responsibilities inherent to that job.

 **Warrior Wisdom**

Warriors know that drama and stress drain us of our personal power and energy, and that is just not acceptable.

I realized that if I *chose* to arrive at work 15 minutes before hours began, to have my coffee and start my day on time, I wouldn't be running behind all day. Also, if I *chose* to book my appointments more efficiently, I wouldn't feel so rushed and pressured. And who made the decision to be residency director on top of everything else? Me! I was totally responsible for my stress and my drama, as I created the way my day looked. I created life exactly the way it needed to look to be hectic and frustrating.

We rarely take the opportunity to look at our lives with this kind of objectivity and honesty. In the beginning I didn't want to admit that I was driving myself crazy and hurting myself. I was in total denial with all kinds of good excuses and justifications, like "Who else could run the residency program as well as me? No one is as qualified," and "I have to see that many patients or I can't pay my office staff and bills," and even "I need to sleep as much as possible in the morning because my schedule is so tiring." See my rationalizations, justifications, and total denial of the truth?

The unfortunate thing was that I believed my excuses and stories 100 percent, which in retrospect seemed logical, but were clearly not the truth. Now when I hear people share tales of woe, I don't believe them any more than I believe my old stories. We love to argue for our limitations, which are never worth supporting from a Warrior's point of view.

Here are a few questions we can ask ourselves about the level of drama in our lives:

♦ What things do you do to create a hectic daily schedule?

♦ Are you putting too many things into your day because you're convinced that they have to get done, or that no one else can do them but you?

◆ Are you sure that your life must absolutely, positively look the way it does, or are you trapping yourself in your own asylum or prison?

Saying NO to Drama

If we can't get our tasks done by the end of the day and have some time for rest, we have too many things scheduled. The question we need to ask ourselves is *why* do we want to be addicted to something that is making us sick and stressed? This inquiry applies to anything we are addicted to, whether it's drugs, alcohol, sex, work, food, or shopping. The Toltecs saw that we are always creating situations that go against ourselves, hurt us, stress us out, or create some level of drama and suffering in our lives. But then again, as kids we were trained to harm and reject ourselves.

Beliefs that we were programmed to have in childhood, like "I can never be good enough," "I will never have what I need in life," and "I will never have someone who really loves me" act as viruses in our programming that cause us to take actions that sabotage us rather than empower us. That's why it's important for us to have a clear understanding of what we believe about ourselves and our life. Then we can address what the true issues are. As you can see, once I was able to identify exactly what I was doing, I was able to take action to change it. When I went a little deeper, I was able to unearth the beliefs that were causing me to create that dramatic life in the first place. As a result, my life became strikingly different.

Self-Rejection Is Insanity

It wasn't just my work that contained drama, but so did every aspect of my life, including my personal relationships. So it was a great exercise to look back into my childhood and figure out why I set things up the way I did. When we're kids, we're unaware of how the greater world-dream works. We need to be domesticated by our parents so that we know what kind of behavior is appropriate for humans. We become domesticated through a method of rewards and punishments. If we behave against our parents' wishes, we're punished, and if we obey, we're praised and loved. Unfortunately, there's a problem with this method, even though it's effective for controlling little humans and pets.

Mommy, Please Love Me

Children in general aren't able to distinguish between their parents not loving the *act* they have just engaged in, and not loving *them*. They don't have the intellectual and conceptual abilities at that age to understand the difference. As a result, if parents yell at a child for something they have done, or punish them, they perceive it as a personal affront. They feel that they aren't loved or lovable. It's confusing from a child's point of view to have their parents love them one minute and not love them the next based on something they did or didn't do.

Children want to do their best to please their parents without really understanding what their parents want from them. This starts the pattern in our lives of wanting to please other people for love and approval. We want to be perfect for our parents but we realize at an early age that this is not possible. As a result we begin to believe that we're bad, not worthy of our parents' love. None of this happens consciously; instead it becomes an unwritten agreement that we make on an emotional level within our belief system and programming. You could say it's one of the first viruses that enters into our little program.

So while we're doing our best to please others for the reward, we're also denying ourselves and our *integrity* because we believe we're bad. This is how the pattern of self-rejection gets started, as we give away pieces of our self just to be loved by others. Self-rejection takes all kinds of forms as we get older and gain more experience in the world. We become better and more efficient at hurting ourselves and giving our integrity away. It becomes second nature and unnoticeable to us because our behavior is further supported by all the other people around us.

> **Impeccable Words**
>
> "In that system of reward and punishment there is a sense of justice and injustice, what is fair and what is not fair. The sense of injustice is like a knife that opens an emotional wound in the mind."
>
> —don Miguel Ruiz, *The Mastery of Love*

> **Toltec Topography**
>
> **Integrity** is the state of being whole and complete, experiencing the totality of ourselves as Tonal and Nagual. It involves living and expressing our lives honestly from our heart and Spirit, rather than from the lies of our programming.

A Self-Fulfilling Prophecy

In the example I gave you from my own life, most of the other physicians in my hospital suffered from the same dramatic lifestyle as mine. We would gather at lunch to complain about how dreadful life was and how we were victims of the horrible health-care system. Of course we all agreed with each other, so obviously we were all correct! In turn, I was empowered to continue creating my life just the way it was because everyone else agreed that what I was experiencing was truth. Since everyone else had the same unhealthy beliefs, they were creating their lives in the same way. It was a self-fulfilling trap that none of us could see and that all of us supported.

I was angry with myself for buying into that story and using it to hurt myself for so many years. But I realized that I needed to forgive myself, because I had simply been doing the best I could with what I knew. The key was to make changes with my new realization, and to not use it to further support my behavior of punishing myself.

> **Warrior Warnings**
>
> Just because everyone is behaving a certain way doesn't mean it's a healthy way to behave. We don't have to be like mice following the Pied Piper into insanity. We have free will and can choose to live in a different way.

Looking from this point of view at the way we create our lives gives us a different perspective on our behavior. When you get down to it, most of us are acting insanely. Is there another way to describe a society that encourages us to fabricate a reality to hurt ourselves—through draining our energy, manufacturing fear-based emotions, or taking a toll on our physical bodies? Let's ask a few questions about how we allow ourselves and others to define our reality:

- Can you see, within your own life, situations that resemble the personal example I gave? What is one adjustment you're willing to make tomorrow to reduce the stress, worry, or drama in your life?

- Is there anything you do to please other people in your life just to get the reward of love or approval? How can you begin to shift to rewarding and pleasing yourself instead of others?

- Do you create situations that hurt yourself and are supported by your friends and family? How could you stop this cycle?

Once we can see what we're doing to hurt ourselves and why we're doing it, it's insanity to keep doing it. Exiting the insane asylum involves taking action to change our behavior and coming to the place of knowing deep within our own heart that we are perfect just the way we are.

This is a process of self-realization; we aren't children anymore and we don't need anyone's approval or love to be good. We are and have always been good people. It's our actions that haven't always been the wisest. As Toltecs, we know we are not our actions, even though we are responsible for them. This information helps us to forgive ourselves for not having faith and love in ourselves and for always wanting to please and love others before we please and love ourselves. Of course, we can never truly love anyone else unless we totally love ourselves first. After all, it's not possible to give away what we do not possess for ourselves.

Perfection Is Unattainable

As children, part of the silent agreement we make is about our lack of perfection. We feel like no matter how hard we try we can never be what our parents and teachers want us to be. Perhaps we aren't good enough in sports or school, or our siblings are always getting more praise than we are. There's a strong desire to be perfect and to meet everyone's ideal of how we should be. As adults most of us are still trying to meet our parents' opinion of how we should be living, the type of job we should have, or the kind of mate we should marry. In the eyes of our parents, we're still little kids no matter how old we get! This is often what's at the root of our adult conflict(s) with our parents.

Getting That Carrot!

What does it mean to be a perfect little boy or girl? Our parents' ideas about what's perfect are always in a state of flux, so how could we as children live up to something that was constantly changing? Worse yet, as soon as we lived up to a certain degree of "perfection," our parents may have set the bar even higher. Some children under that type of pressure succumb and agree that they'll never be anything, and become under-achievers. Others go into rebellion and make a silent agreement to fight everyone and everything, to try to keep their integrity. They become the black sheep in the family. The rest of us keep trying to please the ever-growing demands of perfection by being the "good girl" or the "good boy."

The problem is that this type of perfection can never be attained. We can *never* live up to an idea of perfection that's constantly shifting and ever-increasing. The only thing we can do for ourselves is to be happy and to do everything we can to please ourselves. As adults, we take on that drive for perfection from our parents, even when they're gone. If we're still being driven by some obscure idea of perfection, we need to ask ourselves when we'll be happy, and under what circumstances. Will a better job or a nicer house fill us with inner love and peace, or do these material things translate into a temporary high that fades as a new goal comes into view?

The type of happiness I'm talking about is the kind that constantly exudes out of your skin and lights up your whole countenance, not the kind of happiness that's dependent on temporary external circumstances. How many times have we had the experience of working *so* hard for something we wanted, only to realize that attaining it left us feeling so-so? Has running the race for the proverbial carrot made us happy yet? I doubt it!

For those of us who have been the rebel or black sheep our whole lives, we need to ask ourselves when we're going to stop fighting something that no longer exists except in our minds. As an adult, the reason for our initial rebellion no longer exists, so why are we still holding on to our rebellion as a position to defend in life? If we've made the agreement that we'll never live up to our parents' dreams, we need to stop living that sad story and take the chance to live up to our own wonderful potential, whatever that may be. (Or is it easier to blame our lack of success on our parents rather than take responsibility for our creation?)

Warrior Wisdom

Perfection is the ultimate moving target. The more you strive to reach it, the further away from you the goal becomes.

True Perfection Is Intrinsic

This is the bottom line: The Nagual or Spirit within us is perfect and always has been perfect, as there are no mistakes in the universe. There's nothing external in life that we must live up to. If we detach from the false concept of perfection, trying to measure up to some idea of perfection outside of us, our lives will look totally different. We could find peace and contentment in our lives and be happy creating every moment. We wouldn't be worried about how others will judge our creation. If we disbar the judge in our minds, we could even stop being worried about how we judge our own lives and creation. And even better, we would stop demanding that *other* people live up to *our* personal idea of perfection. How nice would that be?

The most important thing to recognize is how we have taken the concept of perfection and used it as a weapon to hurt ourselves. We've distorted the idea of the perfection of the universe to make ourselves suffer. We are part of the universe and Spirit; we are perfect. It is insane trying to live up to some false idea of perfection that society has set up for us and that we have agreed to.

Having a six-figure job is pleasant, but if you have it, will you be perfect? If you drive a Jaguar rather than a Buick, will you be perfect? Those things are nice to have from a certain point of view, but they can't make us a better or worse person. Maybe others will envy our professions or possessions, but that's only their lack of self-worth speaking.

Self-worth and self-love come from the knowledge that we're perfect the way we are, with whatever we have in life. We're perfect even with all of the mistakes we've made in life, the people we've hurt, and the things we've done against others. This isn't about judgment, but about understanding that the process of life looks like this and it's okay. As humans who've been gifted with free will and choice, we can decide to use our expanding consciousness to move to a place of integrity, self-acceptance, and forgiveness for ourselves and for others. When we choose these acts, we're expressing the Spirit that we really are, and that is *true perfection*.

It's Your Prison—Love It or Leave It

So now that we have awareness of our apparent insanity, what are we going to do about it? We don't have to be stuck in a trap of our own making. Nor do we have to be mad at ourselves once we have awareness of our behavior. If we're unhappy with our creation, let's start taking action right now to change what we have. If we don't take action, then let's make an agreement with ourselves to love where we are in life and to stop complaining to anyone willing to hear us.

The first action to take is to look at your life with complete objectivity. Take some time to identify all the aspects of life that go against your integrity:

♦ List the situations that are causing you stress, anxiety, and drama.

♦ Which situations and doings in your life are being supported by the beliefs of others around you?

♦ Have you been justifying situations in your life that are going against you or creating stress in your life? If so, what are your justifications?

Remember that we can't ask people in our same situation for help, because they may be as blind to the problems and the solutions as we are. If I had asked any of my medical colleagues for advice, they would only have been able to support what I already believed. Their point of view was fixed just like mine. If they believed that another way of seeing the situation was possible, they probably wouldn't have been in that position in the first place! It helps to have someone who isn't invested in your story or someone who has a completely different point of view to be your sounding board. This creates objectivity and room for you to consider other possibilities.

Impeccable Words

"To see your drama clearly is to be liberated from it."
—Ken Keyes

Old Agreements Must Go

The next step would be for us to look back into our childhoods and determine those agreements we adopted when we were small. If we had parents who were always setting the goals higher and higher, is it possible for us to make an agreement with ourselves to stop chasing the carrot? If we were the black sheep or rebel in the family, is it possible to end our need to fight against everyone and everything? If we see ourselves as a failure in life, never being able to meet anyone's expectations, is it possible to let that go and take a chance at enjoying life for ourselves rather than for others?

It's important to answer these questions, because unless we *want* to change, no change will occur. Unless we admit what we're *doing*, there will be nothing to change. The most significant question of all is whether or not we're ready to stop blaming our state of affairs on everyone and everything else in our lives. I had to want to stop blaming everyone else for my stressful situation. The truth is that many people don't want to do that because this shifts the burden of responsibility directly onto them.

The way out of that trap is to anticipate the judge's strategy and to be prepared for its assault. If the judge is coming, then we can disempower it simply by refusing to accept any kind of judgment and verdict. The judge is just reflecting our own book of law; since it's our book, we can change the rules at any time. Refusing the judge is an act of self-love and respect; it means that we know we have done our best. Resisting the habit of self-rejection is honoring the perfection that we are and the divinity we embody.

The Least You Need to Know

- Many of us are addicted to creating suffering, drama, pain, and stress in our lives.

- Humans have been domesticated to believe that we aren't really worthy of love.

- Our false concept of perfection has us racing for the proverbial carrot, never to be obtained.

- By having awareness, we can make a choice to change what we believe about ourselves and what we deserve in life, and live in peace and contentment.

Part 3

Living a Toltec Warrior's Life

As Toltecs, we consider ourselves Warriors on the path to freedom. The war we are engaged in is personal; it is one where we are working to gain control over our minds so that we can express our real selves without limitations of any kind. Like most Warrior traditions, we have a code of conduct, so to speak—one that we respect and use on our path when times become challenging. In Part 3, I introduce you to what it means to be a Warrior and the principles we live by. In the end, these tenets are practical ways to be happy and to live in love, and we all can put them into use in our lives, even if we don't consider ourselves Warriors. No matter how esoteric-sounding these teachings can be, they are always based in plain old common sense.

Chapter 9

Becoming a Warrior

In This Chapter

- The characteristics of a Warrior
- Going into battle
- Knowing your opponent and being focused on the task at hand
- Weapons that can make life effortless
- The practice of acceptance and surrender to life

Back in Chapter 2 we introduced the Toltec teachings as a Warrior's path. In this chapter we will explore what that means in a much deeper way, and will ask ourselves if it's possible to incorporate some of these aspects into our own lives. When I first started this path, I thought that the idea of becoming a Warrior was a little much. After all, I desired more love in my life, which seemed incongruous with becoming a soldier at war! But since then I have come to understand that it's actually a practical way to look at life.

In fact, I feel more at peace with my family, society, and the planet now that I recognize that I was fighting the wrong war in life. I thought that I needed to fight everything and everyone outside of me to get what I wanted. Now I know that the only war is within my own mind and its self-limiting beliefs and concepts. How's that for a drastic change?

The Characteristics of a Warrior

Many esoteric traditions contain the concept of the Spiritual Warrior. You may be familiar with the high code of ethics of the Japanese Samurai Warriors, as we have been exposed to a great number of these kinds of movies in the past few years. Of course, as Toltec Warriors we don't brandish sharp, pointy weapons! Instead we have other weapons to create a life of integrity.

Dedication to the Path

One of the most important characteristics of a Warrior is his dedication to his path and to himself. Being dedicated to the path means that your spiritual growth is first and foremost in your life. A Warrior recognizes that he lives in the *dream of the planet* and has normal life activities that he must take care of. But even with his responsibilities, like having a job and taking care of family, he knows that his personal freedom is his number-one priority.

For many of us, spiritual and personal growth is something that happens on the weekends when we go to church or to a workshop we're interested in. Then during the week the commitment dissipates as we are pulled into the daily conflicts and challenges of our lives. This isn't unusual for us since the dream of the planet is set up to hook our attention and keep us from paying attention to our mind. It's one of the strategies the mind uses to keep us imprisoned (which we'll discuss more in Chapter 13).

Toltec Topography

The dream of the planet refers to the combined beliefs, rules, and concepts that all the humans on our planet project onto our shared reality.

Warrior Wisdom

A Warrior is dedicated to experiencing the totality of himself in his lifetime. This task is first and foremost in his life, as there is no other way to touch the Infinite within himself.

Radical Respect

This brings us to the next characteristic of the Warrior: respect. A Warrior has absolute respect for herself and will never put herself in a situation that goes against herself or is harmful to herself. An example of this is that a Warrior will never enter into a relationship with someone who yells at her or is abusive to her. A Warrior won't allow herself to be put into a situation that goes against her feelings toward other humans, like engaging in dishonest practices at work. A Warrior doesn't end up drunk at a party and in bed with someone she doesn't know or doesn't like "by mistake." Nor is she tempted to do things that she knows are not healthy for her. She will not insult herself to herself, or insult herself in front of others.

A Warrior has respect for other people, too. He may not agree with what other people are doing, but he understands that people do things because their belief system and programming has compelled them to behave that way, even if he doesn't agree with a particular person or action. A Warrior doesn't judge, he just watches carefully. It's not about making the other person right or wrong. A Warrior respects others by not forcing his path or beliefs on to the other person. This respect is a reflection of his belief that everyone is part of the one life, and even if someone has a belligerent personality, there is still a divine presence behind his or her programming.

> **Warrior Wisdom**
>
> A Warrior's self-respect is never at the expense of others. In other words, she always recognizes that her actions have consequences; it's necessary to make a choice that respects as many beings as possible, yet is absolutely true to herself.

Patience Is a Virtue

A Warrior has patience, a quality that we often run short of in modern society. A Warrior knows that she's always moving toward her death so she has no place to be except right here, right now. She doesn't need to be in a rush, yet she doesn't slack off either, as she respects time. She doesn't demand that people move at her pace, nor does she force her time schedule onto others. A Warrior makes her choices carefully and has patience to sit and observe her circumstances until she has a gut feeling about what she should do. She never sits spinning the wheels of her mind trying to make a decision. A Warrior never demands what she wants *right now*, because she knows that life works in a certain way and that she'll get what she needs when life is ready to give it to her. That doesn't stop her from taking action, though. A Warrior has the patience to let relationships and situations develop to their full potential and doesn't push or rush things because of her own insecurities about life.

> **Impeccable Words**
>
> "Nature does not hurry, yet everything is accomplished."
> —Lao Tzu

A Warrior has patience for herself most of all. She knows her path is a challenging one filled with uneasy times, rocky roads, and uncertain turns. She doesn't rush her personal and spiritual growth, nor does she feel that she has time to waste. She has patience for the mistakes she has made in life because she knows that this is the way to learn and grow. She has patience for her impatience and the weaknesses in her self-restraint. A Warrior knows that she'll learn no matter how long it takes, even if that process takes longer than this one lifetime.

Take a few minutes to ponder these questions:

◆ Could you be more dedicated to your personal development and spiritual growth? What would it take and what would that effort look like?

◆ Do you let others walk over you? What could you do to respect yourself more?

◆ Do you show disrespect to yourself by insulting yourself in your mind or by making fun of yourself in front of friends?

◆ Have you been in any situations that went against yourself? What were they like and how did you allow them to happen?

◆ When are you the most impatient with yourself? Could you work at changing that?

◆ How do you impose yourself on others and show disrespect to them and their boundaries?

These may be challenging questions but they will help illuminate some of the ways we hurt and disrespect ourselves, often without us knowing it.

The Preparation of a Warrior

A Warrior looks at life as if he is going to battle. (And sometimes life feels like a battle, doesn't it?) This is because he recognizes that he is always projecting the internal battle in his own mind out into his life. In addition he knows he is creating issues in his life because of his rigid beliefs, agreements, and internal dialog, which keeps him from seeing with clarity what is going on around him. As a result, he drains his personal power and energy in conflicts that exist only in his own mind rather than outside of him. Once the battle for control of our mind is finished, then life becomes effortless, but never free from challenges! We just are prepared for them and face them with respect and due consideration. In other words, until our internal battle is complete, a Warrior understands his battle will be played out within the circumstances of his life.

For example, a Warrior is always ready. He knows that life is happening around him all the time, and he's not sitting around waiting for a cosmic two-by-four to hit him upside the head. How often do things happen in life that we didn't anticipate, but that our friends or family could see coming as clear as day? If it wasn't a surprise for them, why was it a surprise for us? (Our mind was too busy believing some story we had about our circumstances rather than seeing the truth.) A Warrior who has control of his own mind has eyes that are always open and ready to see what is, not what they want to see. That's why they're able to anticipate possible impending issues with ease rather than shock.

Discipline and Focus

A Warrior is also focused and present. You'll never see a Warrior spending time worrying about the future or bemoaning her past. She lives in the here and now. This is an important quality because most of us spend very little time in the now, focusing instead on comparing the present to the past and future. Worry is just the practice of indulging in our feelings of anxiety, and Warriors don't indulge in this practice.

A Warrior focuses on the task at hand. She doesn't let her mind wander all over the place, especially when faced with a challenge. How often do we find ourselves thinking about something else when we need to be addressing the issue at hand? This happens because we don't want to be facing the challenge in front of us, and our mind wants to escape to someplace else. The ability to focus our attention is one of the most important weapons we have.

Warrior Wisdom

A Warrior knows that if he worries or engages in clinging to people, things, or concepts, he'll lose personal power and drain himself of the energy needed to face his challenges.

This brings us to another great aspect of the Warrior: discipline. It takes great discipline to be focused and ready when the dream of the planet is always conspiring to divert our attention elsewhere. It takes discipline to spend time on our personal growth when we're tired at the end of the day and would rather just turn on the TV.

Most people have plenty of discipline when it comes to executing their unhealthy habits and behavior patterns, but not when it comes to breaking those habits and patterns. It took a lot of my own personal power and energy to stop engaging in what I had been doing for 40 years of my life. We're all familiar with how important discipline is, since most of us have started an exercise program or have chosen to break an unhealthy habit, such as smoking, at some time in our lives.

Knowing Thy Enemy

When going into battle, the most important things we need to know are the habits and behaviors of not only our own programming but the programming of others. No use taking an action in life only to find out that we're outwitted, cornered, and out-manned. Watching other programs' actions is the key to our success. If we were going into business with someone, for example, it would behoove us to learn as much as we could about our potential partner's past behavior and current activities. In our relationships, do we see what we want to see about the person we're dating, or do we watch them carefully and observe all of their actions with clarity and without judgment? If we have all the information there is to have about a situation, we'll have a better idea about what our options are and the possible outcomes. The chances of our situation and choices working out well increase significantly when we don't make choices out of haste, blindness, or listening to our mind telling us things that are not truth.

> **Warrior Wisdom**
>
> Warriors live life in a state of war, but the war is with our own mind, beliefs, self-importance, and self-centeredness. Our greatest opponents in life are the self-sabotaging strategies of our programming, not the people in our lives.

If we have patience and aren't rushing to get what we believe we want so quickly, we'll observe a situation until we're satisfied we understand the behavior of the other person. Then we can do what we need to do, feeling confident about our actions. This doesn't guarantee that everything will work out well, but it will increase the chances of success considerably.

Here are a few important questions you can ask yourself:

◆ When you're nervous about a challenge in your life, do you allow your attention to be hooked by other challenges so that you can get out of having to address the issue at hand? What happens when you procrastinate in that way?

◆ Which unhealthy behaviors are you supporting with your discipline and how could you use that discipline in a better way?

◆ What decisions have you made quickly out of fear, rather than taking your time to watch the situation more carefully? What were the results of those choices?

The Weapons of a Warrior

The most effective weapon that a Warrior can draw on is his detachment. In Western cultures detachment implies that someone is uncaring, aloof, or cold. This isn't the way a Warrior looks at detachment. To a Warrior, detachment means to move through life with an absence of prejudice or bias, and with a degree of separation from the things he's involved in.

Detachment gives us clarity, something most of us don't have. This lack of clarity is what makes it so difficult for us to make decisions in our lives. You know the saying that we can't see the forest for the trees? When we're too close to what we're looking at, we have no perspective. When this happens, we make choices that are not based on what is, but instead are based on a distorted perspective of things.

Attachment and Detachment

It's especially challenging for us to make clear decisions on issues surrounding family because we have an emotional attachment to these people. We also have opinions, points of view, and beliefs about them that color the way we see them. These prevent us from backing up and seeing the bigger picture. We're so attached to our beliefs about our family and the way we want to see them that we have no perspective. Everything we believe about them is based on what our mind is telling us, which is not necessarily the truth. When dealing with a nagging mother, for example, it helps to be able to detach and see the truth, which is that she loves us and cares about us and that her behavior is the only way she knows how to express her love.

Impeccable Words

"Detachment does not automatically mean wisdom, but it is, nonetheless, an advantage because it allows the warrior to pause momentarily to reassess situations, to reconsider positions. In order to use that extra moment correctly, however, a warrior has to struggle unyieldingly for the duration of his life."

—Carlos Castaneda, *The Eagle's Gift* (as quoted in *The Wheel of Time*)

Warrior Warnings

A Warrior never uses detachment to stop herself from experiencing her emotions or from being present in her life. That is escapism, and a Warrior always faces her challenges with respect and appreciation.

Being attached to doing things a certain way can also steal our clarity. If we're working on a project and insist that that job must be done our way, we could be missing out on a more enlightened way to do it. The mind may be telling us that we have a lot of experience and knowledge, but we really only have the experience that *we have*. There are other people out there with other experiences. Not being attached having things go the way our programming dictates can open a whole new world to us. With this type of weapon in our arsenal, we can become extremely open and creative at work and find solutions to our challenges in more effective and inclusive ways. Detachment from our way of doing things will also make us a more pleasant person to work for or with, and will enable others to be creative in their work process, too. This in turn leads to happier and more interested co-workers.

When we're attached to our concepts, we also limit our life possibilities, something a Warrior would never do. Maybe we believe that we must have a traditional marriage rather than entertaining the possibility of a spiritual union. As a result, we may end a relationship that could have been incredible if it didn't conform to the structure our mind defined as right. Detaching from all our beliefs and points of view that aren't absolute truth will give us the opportunity to explore relationships in new and exciting ways, and will give us the clarity to see how we've been cramping our own lifestyle. This kind of clarity is what a Warrior counts on to assist him in making the best possible choices for himself with the best chances of a positive outcome.

The Desire of Spirit

Another critical weapon that a Warrior has is his desire and *will*. Normally we humans are constantly exercising the desires of our rational mind and programming. These desires come from cravings that arise based on the fear that we don't have what we need to survive, or that what we have will never be enough. The truth is, most of the things we want have nothing to do with what we truly need. They're simply a reflection of the desire we have to fill the emptiness in our hearts. Of course we can't fill that kind of emptiness with physical things, and that's why we are always wanting more.

> **Toltec Topography**
>
> **Will,** for the Warrior, is a force that he cultivates. It is a purposefulness, determination, or deliberate desire that transcends thought or rational mind. It comes through him from the Infinite and can also be seen as the personalized force of Intent.

Creation is happening around us all of the time. Birth and death are normal processes that keep a constant balance in the universe. As a result, we are creative beings in the process of producing and ending things all the time. The problem is that our programming is forever clamping down on the expression of our Spirit by deciding what's appropriate or not according to the judge and its rules. A Warrior creates in his life with joy and abandon, without concern of what others think about his creation. He knows that he has the choice of creating hell in his life or creating great beauty and loveliness. A Warrior's desire to be the medium that Spirit uses for creation is forged into being with his will, which he uses to implement his heart's desire; yet he never imposes his will onto others. Just to be clear, we are not talking about exercising the will of the mind in our life, but instead the will of Spirit, life, and creation moving through us. Can you see the difference between the desire of a Warrior and that of a person who is not aware of his motivations and programming? Certainly the weapons of detachment, clarity, and desire are things that all of us can use to create our lives in better ways, once we make the choice to incorporate them into our own reserve.

◆ Can you see your attachment to your beliefs as a limiting factor in your life?

◆ Have you actually lost an opportunity or destroyed a relationship as a result of the demand of your belief system on others? How could you have done things differently?

◆ Is there something you are willing to detach from now that could make your life lovelier?

◆ Has your desire for things to be the way you want them, according to *your* fear-based beliefs, created conflict in your life? If so, how?

◆ Is there a situation happening in your life right now that you could use more clarity in? If so, what opposing pieces of information is your mind telling you that are causing you confusion?

 **Warrior Wisdom**

A Warrior has no desires of his own; he wants and needs nothing but to be happy and to lead an impeccable and free life. He trusts that Spirit will direct him through life as the Intent of the universe becomes his Intent.

A Warrior in Action

A Warrior in action is a sight to behold. What makes a Warrior's life so amazing is the ease with which he or she glides through it. We've all seen people who seem to have gifted lives; everything, even their challenges, go effortlessly. What makes those people different from most of us, who seem to struggle and suffer through life?

Surrender and Acceptance

First and foremost, a Warrior accepts life on life's terms, not on the terms of her programmed mind. She recognizes that fighting life is insanity (as discussed in Chapters 7 and 8), when the true war is within her own mind. When situations arise that aren't in accordance with her plan, she just assesses what is and makes choices based on intuition, feeling, and consideration of what the possible outcomes may be. We have many grand expectations about the way things *should* be, but the truth is that life has other plans for us. There are no guarantees that anything will work out the way we want it to.

Trying to fight life and everyone and everything in it is exhausting, and it drains us of our personal power and energy. If you take some time to look at your life, you'll probably find that all your fighting was probably not worth it. Mine certainly wasn't! But it took a lot of detached self-observation to be able to admit that to myself. In reviewing my life, very little of it went the way I thought it would go. In fact, if it had gone the way I originally thought it would, I would be living a very predictable and boring life. Life has always brought me bigger and better opportunities than my mind would have dreamed for itself. Life may be uncertain, but at least it's interesting.

This is the process of surrender and acceptance. In general, most of us are terrible at surrendering to life. In battle, though, a Warrior must be fluid enough to change strategies at any moment since life changes constantly. That keeps a Warrior on her toes and ready for action. We, on the other hand, rarely change our strategies quickly enough. How many times in life have we complained about something we didn't like, but felt as though we had no choice or say about what was going on? While we're busy being angry, life is constantly flowing and moving along.

> **Impeccable Words**
>
> "You are alive, so take your life and enjoy it. Don't resist life passing through you, because that is God passing through you."
> —don Miguel Ruiz, *The Four Agreements*

Let Go and Let Life

To move through life with the grace of a great Warrior we must learn to let go over and over again. Whether it's letting go of the way we think things should be, or letting go of our resentments and judgments against others, letting go is the way to be happy. (We'll talk more about detaching from our resentments, grudges, and judgments in Chapters 18 and 19.) Even if a Warrior is facing a challenge in life, he does it with a gracefulness that's intentional, as every act the Warrior performs is with great purpose. No move is wasted, no act is purposeless. He never does things just for the heck of it. This is because he never knows when his act will be the last one he takes.

Most importantly, a Warrior in action never abdicates his power. He may have to concede his strategic position, he may lose a challenge now and then, but he never gives up his power willingly. This is an important concept; we'll focus on personal power in Chapter 15.

Warrior Wisdom

A Warrior is 100 percent clear about the reasons for her actions. She acts without any doubt, remorse, or concern about the thoughts or judgments of others. If she has made an error, she takes full responsibility for it, remedies what she can, forgives herself, and she never looks back.

Anyone can be a Warrior. All it takes is the desire to change our mind-set and the way we perceive our life. The bottom line is that a Warrior knows that in the end, whenever that is, he's going to die. So compared to that, all challenges appear small. I'm not making light of people who undergo severe challenges in life. Take Christopher Reeve, for example. Here was a true warrior. In spite of facing the overwhelming physical and emotional challenges of a spinal-cord injury, he lived a full life, without blame or regret, taking responsibility for his life. Do we need any further examples of what a Warrior's path might look like? The Dalai Lama is one of my favorite Warriors, yet he has no sword other than his word, the most powerful of weapons. Despite living in exile from his own country, he has dedicated his life to slaying ignorance, suffering, and nonawareness for all sentient beings, and this is truly beautiful.

These types of people inspire us to be the best humans we can be in this lifetime. Warriors are not myths from the past; they're all around us making changes in the world and uplifting us simply because they are who they are.

You are capable of introducing everything I talked about in this chapter into your life. Take some time to go over the following list of Warrior traits, realizing that nothing on the list is impossible to put into action. I can tell you that if you put even *one* thing on this list into practice, your life will change considerably for the better.

So to summarize …

 ◆ A Warrior's acts are imbued with purpose.

 ◆ He moves with grace and alacrity.

- Her mind and her body are ready for action.

- He is detached, so he can see life with clarity.

- She is always in the process of surrendering to life.

- He is dedicated to his path and himself.

- She has respect for herself and for others.

- He is patient and waits and watches his opponent.

- She never gives away her power.

- He lives in the moment.

- She is focused, present, and in charge of her attention.

- He takes the time to know the habits of other programmed minds without judgment.

- Her desire comes from Spirit and life moving through her.

- Warriors live with joy and abandon, without worrying about the judgment of others!

Are you ready to be a Warrior?

The Least You Need to Know

- Respecting oneself and others and being dedicated to oneself and one's path are common-sense suggestions for living a happier and more fulfilling life.

- Being in the here and now, focused and ready, enables us to enjoy life fully in every moment.

- Patience, detachment, and the practice of letting go foster clarity and awareness.

- When we allow ourself to be a channel to Spirit moving through us, creativity and joy become second nature.

Developing the Eyes of a Warrior

In This Chapter

- The Warrior's choices

- The Warrior's path to happiness

- The ruthless Warrior

- The practice of compassion without judgment

In Chapter 9 we talked about the many wonderful characteristics of the Warrior. In this chapter we'll explore the Warrior's view of the world and the qualities he possesses that enable him to see it that way. Most people believe that the way they see life is exactly the way it is. But by now you know this is not true. Since we are always viewing life though the lens of our beliefs and past experiences, we must *learn* to see the world differently.

A Warrior loves life to the maximum with all his heart and soul. But that kind of love doesn't come easily. We must practice this way of being and stop engaging in our petty dramas and emotional behaviors. During our domestication we were taught to give our love only to people we know, rather than to all sentient beings. But a Warrior gives his love and opens his heart just because he wants to—and because it feels good. You'll have a lot to ponder and practice in this chapter. See if you can keep an open mind and have fun with the concepts presented here. They will all help you retrain yourself to get to a place of peace and unconditional love.

Seeing the World as a Warrior

A Warrior sees the world as a magical and mysterious place in the most unfathomable of universes. She knows that this universe is beyond the capabilities of her rational mind to comprehend, and she feels humble in comparison to that immensity. Only the perfection of creation is in her field of vision, and its beauty is far beyond the ability of words to capture it. In the morning when a warrior wakes up, she is stunned by the glory of the day and the abundance of opportunities she is presented with. Nothing is beyond her reach, yet she wants for nothing. Her heart is open and her unconditional love for life is boundless.

Training Your Eyes

A Warrior sees the world as an enchanted and exquisite place. She sees the world with the eyes of a child, but one who has a lifetime of experience. Children are constantly surprised and amused by life. You can play peek-a-boo with a child over and over again, and that child will squeal with delight. That's because they're engaged in being, loving, enjoying, and not judging what they're doing. Once they get older and realize that they're playing a baby's game, and understand what that concept means, they lose interest. It's our judgment and beliefs about what we're perceiving that limit our enjoyment. We start to understand that some activities are stupid, childish, and not cool. But is this really true? What makes something interesting or not interesting? Can we enjoy every activity without letting our beliefs and opinions about it interfere?

Impeccable Words

"A warrior knows that he is waiting, and he knows what he is waiting for, and while he waits, he feasts his eyes upon the world. A warrior's ultimate accomplishment is to enjoy the joy of infinity."

Carlos Castaneda, *The Eagle's Gift* (as quoted in *The Wheel of Time*)

We think that we don't enjoy something because we judge that the activity is not what we should be doing, instead of engaging in the activity and seeing how we feel about it *in that moment*. This is the difference between thinking and feeling. Before children learn judgment, they make their choices based on fun, not on thought. We can have that as adults, too. We can fully enjoy life each day as if we never saw a day before. Can you remember how old you were when the world became mundane?

A Warrior uses her eyes in a different way than the average human. She trains her eyes to see each day anew, so that the wonder of life is always present. Practice looking at each and every day as if you've never experienced it before. Once we start doing this on a consistent basis, we find that we've been missing a lot of pleasure in life.

A Warrior Lives for the Challenge

A Warrior knows life is giving him challenges in every moment. Now, for most people, as soon as you say "challenge," they fear that their lives are going to become difficult. Not so for a Warrior. They live for the challenge. Think about it: If we see every moment of life as a challenge, how can we possibly become bored or unhappy? In addition, without challenges how can we grow and learn?

Let's say that today I must make some changes on my business website. I turn my computer on, and for whatever reason, it starts behaving totally crazed. I suspect a virus has invaded my computer and start to take action to do whatever is needed to remedy the situation. Five hours transpire before I can complete a task that was supposed to take me one hour.

Situations like this pop up all the time and affect all of us. Our reaction to the challenge is the important thing. Ask yourself this:

♦ Has something like this happened to you recently, and how did you handle the situation?

♦ What underlying beliefs were causing your emotional reaction? For example, were you angry and frustrated because your time is limited and you have too much to do as it is?

♦ How could you shift your point of view to one of a Warrior, to have a more positive experience in the future?

If we lose our temper and become impatient and irritated by these types of situations, it's because we see them as an obstacle to our day. Well, guess what? We're the ones making our

Warrior Wisdom

Challenges are neither good nor bad, neither a curse nor a blessing. They are only what we make of them depending on the *meaning* we assign to them.

day bad by making the *choice* to let these events upset us. We're the ones making our day bad by deciding to believe that life is out to get us. We're the ones making our day bad by thinking the world revolves around us and that life should be without challenges.

The Gratitude of a Warrior

Our enjoyment level in life is based upon how much gratitude and appreciation we have for our lives. Most of us begrudge all of the "bad" and "painful" experiences we've had, and only have appreciation for the supposed "good" things. A Warrior doesn't see his experiences in terms of good or bad, but instead as learning experiences. He knows that without the many challenges in his life, he certainly wouldn't be where he is today. A Warrior gets excited by challenges because they give him a glimpse of the magical being that he is and the hidden resources within him.

Gratitude is a reflection of how much peace and resolution you've made in your life. If we haven't made peace with the many people and events that have transpired in our life, we will carry our resentments on our shoulders. These resentments will prevent us from seeing as a Warrior sees, with absolute love and appreciation for life. It's impossible to be absolutely happy if we haven't reconciled the difficult and painful parts of our life. If we can come to a place of acceptance, we can shift the way we perceive our existence to one of *grace*. That means we must *choose* to see life that way.

I've said before that a Warrior always sees choices in his life. For example, if you do not want to forgive your mother for something she has done, then you do not want to see your other choices. One great choice is to have gratitude for whatever happened between the two of you, and to know that you learned something from the conflict. If you came out of that event a stronger and more self-aware person, then why not choose to have gratitude?

Here are some things you can do to develop your Warrior's eyes:

Toltec Topography

I'm using the word **grace** in the theological sense here. When we are given divine approval, favor, and mercy, divine acceptance is bestowed upon us. What better gift is there than to give *ourselves* divine ac-ceptance for our lives?

- ◆ When you're about to get upset about something that is happening to you, take a deep breath and pause. Make a choice in that moment to shift your point of view and see your situation differently.

- What activity do you enjoy that you haven't engaged in for a while? Why haven't you? Make a choice to do something fun that you enjoy that feels good, just because.

- When you're about to judge something that is happening in life as bad, take a moment to imagine the good that could possibly come out of that event, even if you have to use your imagination quite a bit.

Warrior Warnings

Resentments and grudges are like a malignant cancer that grows slowly within us, aging us prematurely over the years and turning us into sour old people.

Essential Qualities

One of the most important qualities a Warrior possesses is her ability to not take the things that happen in life personally. As we can see from our discussion so far, our lives are filled with daily challenges. It's how we approach those challenges that makes one a Warrior or not. Most of us spend our days on an emotional roller coaster, happy when things are going our way and angry when they aren't. If we understand that things happen in life that are outside of our control, like viruses in our computers, car accidents, and delayed flights, we can choose not to be upset about them.

Don't Take It to Heart

In our daily lives we communicate our beliefs and feelings to each other without much thought, and often we feel hurt or angry about the things others say to us, especially if family is involved. A Warrior understands that people have their own point of view and beliefs that are being generated from their programming. So when other people say things to us that we feel are hurtful, or when they promise something to us that they don't follow through with, we don't have to get upset. We simply recognize that what they're thinking is different from what we're thinking.

Impeccable Words

"When you take things personally, then you feel offended and your reaction is to defend your beliefs and create conflicts. You make something big out of something so little, because you have the need to be right and make everyone else wrong."

—don Miguel Ruiz, *The Four Agreements*

For example, when your mom invites you for dinner on Friday night and you can't come, she might get angry with you and say that you're a bad son. This is her point of view based on how she believes a good child should behave, and you aren't playing by her rules. Her judge has no choice but to sentence you as a bad son. If you can see what is happening clearly, you don't have to argue your position with your mom. After all, you can't win here, and indeed there is nothing to win. You don't have to take her belief system personally, yell at her, or explain to her how busy you are. If you do, you will be trying to make her wrong and yourself right, by justifying your point of view. Then she will want to make you wrong and herself right. There can be no understanding or resolution when people are defending their points of view. A Warrior would simply say, "Mom, I love you so much and would never want to hurt you. I'm sorry I can't make it this Friday. How about we compromise and schedule dinner at another time?" A Warrior knows you can't clap with one hand. In other words, if you don't argue, there can be no argument.

Accepting No Assumptions

Another powerful quality a Warrior possesses is her ability to ask questions and get more information without feeling embarrassed. A Warrior has no desire to make assumptions about things that are happening in life. She knows that people have all kinds of ideas, and that it's better to ask what they mean and get more clarification instead of guessing. We make lots of assumptions about situations because we believe we know what others mean or what they're thinking. In reality, we can never know what another person has in mind, not even the people we're closest to. How many times have we been sure we understood what someone said to us only to have that person later swear they never said such a thing?

These misunderstandings are the cause of *so* many arguments between people. A great example of this is something that happened to a friend of mine at work recently.

> **Warrior Wisdom**
>
> We can only take what someone else says and run it through what we believe in our programmed mind. Now it becomes what we believe they said, instead of what they actually said.

She was chatting with her boss and she shared something personal that was happening in her life. After telling the boss this story, she saw the boss's face change and her attitude shift. Immediately, my friend assumed that her boss was upset about what she had said and had made judgments about her. She assumed that her boss thought she was a terrible person and avoided talking to her boss for weeks! Turns out that her boss was touched by the story because something similar happened to her a while back, but she was too embarrassed to share her experience with her employee! So my friend took her boss's reaction personally and assumed the worst, which propelled her to take the action of avoiding her boss, all for nothing.

How many times do we imagine all kinds of things because we make assumptions about our circumstances? If we don't ask, how will we know?

Doing Your Best

Another wonderful quality a Warrior holds is his ability to do his best without the burden of self-judgment. This is a very important quality to possess if we're interested in living an exciting and full life. If we're always judging and being critical of our actions, we'll never want to take chances in life. Our fear of being victimized by our own mind will keep us locked into a life of mediocrity and boredom. The people who have the most interesting lives are the ones who don't care what anyone thinks about them. And most importantly, they don't care what their own mind thinks of them! In other words, they don't take *themselves* personally. How often do we beat ourselves up because of something that we did or said? Most people will forgive us our transgressions; we're hardest on ourselves.

> **CAUTION**
>
> **Warrior Warnings**
>
> Doing our best is not an excuse to be a control freak or to do 110 percent to try to impress others or our own judge. A Warrior acts to please herself and her Spirit; she does her best simply because it makes her happy to do so.

It's an act of self-love to be kind to and have compassion for ourselves. One of the ways to do this is to know that no matter what we're engaged in, we're doing our best. If we truly acknowledge this, how can we beat ourselves up afterward? It's important, though, to keep in mind that a person's best changes daily, depending on all sorts of factors, including whether they're physically well or not.

A Warrior always does his best, at whatever level he's capable of, and when he's done, he detaches from the situation. What's done is done. This isn't to say that a Warrior does not assess his performance and learn from his actions. But there's a huge difference between an honest evaluation and a mind-lashing filled with insults and degrading self-commentary. If we know we've done our best, we can let the judge in our mind take a vacation, *permanently*.

Here are some ways we can cultivate these Warrior's qualities:

- Next time your judge wants to tear you apart, tell it "Thank you for sharing your opinion, but your comments are no longer welcome here!" Keep telling your mind this every time it starts up with you.

- When you're about to take something personally, count to 10 and create some detachment between you and what's happening. Use that moment to remind yourself that you have a choice as to whether you're going to make what's happening all about you or not.

- Appreciate that you have no idea what anyone else is thinking. Ask for clarification about anything that is not 100 percent clear to you by repeating back to people what they just said. For example, at work you might ask your boss, "I just heard you say that you want me to type this letter in this way on this stationery. Am I understanding you correctly"?

Warriors Are Ruthless

One of the best qualities of a Toltec Warrior is her ruthlessness. We tend to think that this word implies coldness and meanness. I used to think that being ruthless was a nasty way to be, but then I actually looked the word up in the dictionary. Turns out that it simply means *no pity*. But why would a Warrior want to incorporate this quality of having no pity? Of what benefit is that?

Toltec Topography

To **co-create** means that we are conscious partners with life and that partnership is 50-50. As Warriors we know we are totally responsible for our 50 percent. In an equal relationship there can be no victims, only partnership.

No Pity, Please

The average person has been taught to feel bad for him- or herself and for others. We've been domesticated to feel victimized by the things that happen in our life. This isn't the truth, though—at least not for a Warrior. A Warrior understands that we are *co-creating* with life all the time. Because of this, there can be no victims in life. Since this can be a challenging point of view, I would ask you to suspend your opinion for a while and read on.

We're constantly making choices in how we participate in and perceive life. Because of this, we're responsible for the outcomes we experience. Even though we can't know the outcomes ahead of time, and they're not always what we expected, we're still responsible. We can have an outcome that we don't like, a challenge lost, so to speak, or we can have an outcome that we're pleased with. But it isn't whether we win or lose that's important, but the way we choose to experience that situation. If we perceive every challenge as a learning experience, we can still be happy even if we don't like the outcome. But if we don't detach from our expectations, then we give our power away in our anger and feelings of injustice.

The person in charge of that choice is us, so when we get upset about the things that happen in life, we're the ones victimizing ourselves. Look at Lance Armstrong, the cyclist who overcame cancer and went on to race again. He didn't feel victimized by his disease; instead he felt empowered *because he chose to see it that way*. Taking this one step deeper, we can say there is only one life and all of us are part of that one life (discussed in Chapter 4). From that point of view, can life victimize life? Only if we choose to see it that way. Life is expressing all around us and through us and it is not personal. We will spend more time considering this concept in Chapter 19.

> **Impeccable Words**
>
> "Cancer is my secret because none of my rivals has been that close to death and it makes you look at the world in a different light, and that is a huge advantage."
>
> —Lance Armstrong

Injustice or Gratitude?

When I was in medical school I had to go through the process of applying for residency programs. It was a very nerve-wracking experience, as I had a lot of fear and self-judgment in those days. I spent one month on externship at the hospital where I wanted to do my residency. My plan was to impress them so that I would be a top choice at interview time. At the end of my month rotation, all the residents agreed I was a shoo-in for one of the two available positions. I had a good interview, and yet I didn't get into the program. I felt victimized when I found out that the person who got "my" spot was the son of a doctor who donated a huge sum of money to the hospital. How unfair!

I was accepted at another program, but I never truly appreciated that situation because I felt I *should* have gotten the other program. The truth is, I was not a victim. In looking back at my externship with ruthlessness, I saw so many things that could have led to my not being considered, things I didn't want to admit to myself at the time. (After all, there were two spots and only one was taken by the doctor's son—who was a strong candidate.) Once I acknowledged the truth of the situation, I was able to take total responsibility for my actions, and I forgave myself for any behavior that led to me not receiving the program. As a result, I could appreciate and have gratitude for the program that I did participate in. Accepting the fact that what happened was actually perfect for me is what helped me to create the gratitude.

Warrior Wisdom

You know the saying about seeing the glass half full or half empty? We're talking about the same thing here. Our point of view determines everything in life. We can see any incident from the point of view of injustice or gratitude. Changing our point of view doesn't change the incident. What changes is our emotional reaction to that incident.

I have had many things happen in my life that could be judged to be terribly unjust, but I've forgiven myself (and others involved, as well) for co-creating those situations. This is why I can tell you that I have absolute gratitude for my life and that I live my life in joy.

This is ruthless thinking. I have no pity for myself for any of the things that I have co-created. As a result, I know that I can transcend anything that has happened to me and will happen to me, and so can you. I can see the greater purpose in life and forgive the ignorance of myself and my fellow humans. (And by ignorance I mean nonawareness, not stupidity as a judgment.)

Now we can see why on a much deeper level we call this a Warrior's path. It asks us to find the Warrior that lives inside us and to live our life with faith and strength in the face of the most challenging circumstances and situations.

Here are some questions we can ask ourselves about ruthless thinking in our own lives:

♦ What situations have occurred in your life that you feel shame or great anger about?

♦ How could you take responsibility for your part in those situations so that you can move to a place of forgiveness and resolution?

♦ If you can't do that at this point in your life, what would it take so that you might be able to do this in the future, knowing that your happiness depends on it?

♦ If you're unable to take responsibility for your part in past events at this time, might it be because you feel your own anger and pain is more important than your happiness? Why?

Compassion Is Not Pity

Although a Warrior is ruthless, that doesn't mean he's also not compassionate. As you know, a Warrior has great respect for others and an immense love for humanity, the earth, and our universe. This love is expressed in a Warrior's *compassion* for other humans and our world. First and foremost, a Warrior knows he must heal his own suffering before he can address the suffering of others effectively. This means he must look within his own experiences and let go of anything that he's attached to that's continuing to hurt him. It's challenging for a suffering person to help another suffering person be happy!

Toltec Topography

Compassion simply means a deep awareness of the suffering of humanity and our planet and the desire to heal it.

Curtail Criticism, Cultivate Compassion

A Warrior will make sure that he's not causing suffering in the lives of his family, friends, or colleagues. He'll be cognizant of the way he talks to others, making sure that he's using his word impeccably, with kindness and respect, and is also doing his best to be thoughtful of others. This entails being as aware as possible of the effect his actions are having on others. (Of course, he's not responsible for the way people interpret his acts, nor is he responsible if people take what he says personally. He can still be considerate of what comes out of his mouth and the way he does things.)

For a Warrior to have compassion for others, he must also have compassion for himself. We spoke about having respect, love, and patience for ourselves. It's not possible to have any of these things for another person unless we demonstrate them to ourselves first. Recognizing that we have suffered and granting ourselves forgiveness enables us to show compassion to others without judgment.

Warrior Wisdom

There is *no* element of judgment in compassion; it's recognition of a shared human experience. We can do that without feeling bad for others, pitying them, or losing our happiness because of their pain.

When a Warrior has compassion, he's willing to lend a hand in support of ending another's suffering. But that doesn't mean that he interferes with what that person is doing. It's important that people move to end their own suffering. We can help others help themselves, but doing things for them that they could be doing for themselves is self-importance, not compassion. There's a huge difference. When we make the judgment that someone can't do something, and that we can do it for them, then we're putting them below us, as if we're somehow better qualified than they are. We're all equal, and the humility of a Warrior reflects that understanding.

Being Like the Buddha

A Warrior expresses her love and appreciation for her life in every moment just because she wants to. When you walk through life with an open heart, it's possible to be compassionate. On the other hand, judgment prevents us from feeling compassion, and we end up having pity for people instead. There's a lot of human pain and suffering in our world-dream. But projecting the emotional energy of pity won't change that hologram of emotions we talked about in Chapter 5. Conversely, by projecting the energy of love and compassion, we can make immense changes in our world.

Many religions and philosophies ask us to do kind deeds and to help our fellow humans because they also have the awareness that we are only one life. If each of us made an effort to perform a kind act every day, the world would be a better place. When we have the choice to smile at someone or to glare, let's choose the smile. When we have the choice to be critical or understanding, let's choose understanding. Let's make the effort to be as compassionate as possible, having the awareness to see the effects that our behavior has on others. It's wonderful to treat people the way we would love to be treated, and to do so without expecting *anything* in return.

Here are some activities that you can do to assist you in developing compassion in your own life and mind:

- Watch how many times you say things like "I feel so bad for her" or "What he's experiencing is so dreadful." Instead, try changing those judgment-heavy statements to "I've had an experience like that before; it was challenging, but I have faith that she will get through it just like I did" or "That is a challenging situation, and I feel for him."

- If someone is having a difficult time, ask the person if you can be a listening ear for him or her. Often by talking about your challenge out loud, you can get clarity about it. This does not mean telling someone what to do, but simply listening without judgment.

- Do a kind deed for a neighbor, a friend, or a family member. Open a door for someone, give someone your parking space, or let someone ahead of you on the grocery line.

♦ Observe how often you smile during the day, and increase your smile quota. Your smile is a message of love and a great gift to others.

The Least You Need to Know

♦ It is up to us to change the way we use our eyes to perceive life.

♦ Not taking anything personally gives us emotional immunity from the acts and words of others.

♦ We should always ask for clarification and never assume that we know what anyone is thinking or feeling.

♦ If we do the best we can in life, we'll avoid having to beat ourselves up for our actions.

♦ Being ruthless means not having pity for ourselves or for others.

♦ Compassion is the understanding of human suffering and the desire to overcome it.

Chapter 11

Enemies of the Warrior

In This Chapter

- Self-importance: the number-one enemy to a Warrior's personal freedom

- Self-pity as the twin sister of self-importance

- Letting go of self-importance and self-pity

Congratulations—you're well on your way to seeing, thinking, and living like a Warrior! In this chapter we'll look at three of the major obstacles on the Warrior's path to freedom. Of all the challenges we face, self-importance, self-pity, and fear are the most significant. As humans we all suffer from these afflictions. It's up to each of us to look deep within ourselves and at our behaviors with honesty. I'm not going to tell you this is a pleasant task; it's not. But it's an extremely effective task in finding our happiness.

In this chapter I'll use real-life situations to illustrate these obstacles. By using real scenarios rather than theories, my intent is that you will be better able to apply these teachings in your own life. If you're able to change just one situation in your life after reading this chapter, I believe you'll see a big difference in your overall happiness.

Self-Importance Is the Root of All Evil

One of the most challenging and significant fights of a Warrior is to overcome his or her self-importance. And what a fight it is! It's truly a battle to stop believing that everything is about us, to stop taking everything personally, to end our selfishness and self-centered behavior, our manipulative and controlling conduct, our defensive actions, our need to be right, our need to have things done our way, and our obsessive pride. Wow, that is a pretty significant list. But we can sum it up by saying that this task is one that takes our focus off of our Tonal and places it on our Nagual, thereby enabling us to move our assemblage point. The result of this battle is claiming our freedom from the ego or the mind, which is normally the driving force in our lives. (All of these issues were discussed back in Chapter 3.) So let's talk a bit about how these aspects manifest themselves in our lives and what we can do to change them.

> ### Impeccable Words
>
> "Any movement of the assemblage point means a movement away from an excessive concern with the individual self. Shamans believe it is the position of the assemblage point which makes modern man a homicidal egotist, a being totally involved with his self-image. Having lost all hope of ever returning to the source of everything, the average man seeks solace in his selfishness."
>
> —Carlos Castaneda, *The Power of Silence* (as quoted in *The Wheel of Time*)

In Chapter 10 we spoke about not taking things personally in our lives. We can weed out so much self-importance from our lives just by being cognizant of when we're behaving in this way. Instead of just talking about the concepts of self-importance, let's illustrate these ideas with real situations so that we can be clear about them, and relate to them in a personal way.

A Growing Grudge

Timothy grew up with a father who was a well-known physician in town. He loved and respected his mother, a hard-working lady with a good temperament and an open heart. On the other hand, his relationship with his father was strained for as long as he could remember. His dad had a strong personality and demanded perfection from his son. Tim always felt like his father never loved him; he felt as though he was expected to produce good grades so that his father could boast about him to others. Tim fought with his dad over anything and everything. Although his mom told him that his dad loved him, he didn't believe her, choosing to see his father as a horrible and abusive man, thus making himself a victim of his father's stern ways.

As an adult with kids of his own, Tim faced off with his father yet again. His dad had finally retired and was excited to have the time to enjoy his grandchildren in a way that he was never able to with his son. Tim was angry with his dad for being so good and loving to his kids (although he would vehemently deny taking that position). He thought his dad was a mean old hypocrite and he didn't want that type of person around his kids.

Tim would say, "Can't you get that we need to spend time with our own kids? You can't just come over whenever you want! You're so selfish and always want things your way. Can't you have consideration for our lives?" His father felt guilty because he believed he was at fault for the poor relationship he had with his son, but he had too much pride to apologize for hurting his son in any way. So they were both at an impasse, angry and hurt and unable to see each other's point of view.

This is a great example of how our self-importance prevents us from being in a place of unconditional love, happiness, and gratitude. Tim made a choice as a child as to how he was going to see his father. He made that choice because he wasn't old enough to understand the dynamics of his father's life. In other words, he didn't know the pressure his father felt to provide for the family, and he couldn't understand that his dad even thought that by working so hard, he was actually doing his son a favor (financially, anyway), even if that meant missing out on Tim's childhood. Tim didn't understand that his father wanted him to have all doors open to him in the future, which was the real reason for encouraging those good grades.

Because Tim chose to be victimized by the lack of his father's presence in his life and by his father's choices, he felt justified in punishing his father for the crimes he felt his dad was responsible for. Can you see how Tim's point of view and beliefs have determined the tone of his present-day relationship with his father?

Warrior Wisdom

A Warrior's greatest enemy is self-importance. Constantly feeling offended by the acts and words of his fellow human drains his personal power and makes him weak. Holding on to his self-importance forces him to spend his life insulted and angry.

Resolution Required

As an adult, Tim is behaving like a child who is unable to see what is and to forgive and appreciate his childhood. He has no gratitude for his father and the sacrifice he made for his son's comfort. I'm not saying that his dad's choices were right or wrong. I'm simply stating what is, and being happy in life requires us to accept what is regardless of whether or not we would have done the same thing in a similar situation.

Tim is manipulating and controlling his father by denying him visitation to his grandchildren. He's also defending his point of view against his father by insisting on being right. Things have to be his way or the highway at the expense of his kids enjoying their grandpa. This is true selfishness and self-centered behavior. He's taking his dad's actions personally, since from his dad's point of view, he did what he did so that his son could have a good life!

Tim's dad understands that his son is angry with him and he feels bad about their relationship. But his own guilt, fear, and self-importance are preventing him from communicating what he feels with his son. If he forgave himself for not being present in his son's life, he would no longer have the emotion of guilt to deal with and he would be able to talk about the past with his son.

Having said all of this, ask yourself these questions:

- Do you have a situation in your life similar to this one? Knowing what you know now about letting go of self-importance, what could you do to change the situation?

- Does your need to be right show itself in your life? Do you find yourself consistently defending your point of view to others?

- Can you list three ways you behave selfishly or from a self-centered point of view?

- Are you manipulative and controlling of others? How do others feel about it when you behave this way?

- If you feel that others in your life are manipulative or controlling, can you look at their behavior from their point of view and see any underlying factor(s)? If their behavior has affected you, can you forgive them?

- Do you catch yourself insisting that things have to be done your way? When you behave like that, how do people react?

♦ When has your pride prevented you from saying you were sorry? When has your pride prevented you from forgiving someone?

We can clearly see how self-importance is the root of the unhealthy relationships we have with the people in our lives. Letting go of our need to be right and our one-sided points of view enables us to enjoy the people we love and, in turn, enjoy our lives.

Self-Pity and Whining Warriors

In Chapter 10 we spoke about how Warriors are ruthless and they don't participate in pity, not for themselves or for others. Picture a coin for a moment, with self-importance on one side and self-pity on the other. Self-importance and self-pity are the same thing, two sides of the same coin. You might be wondering how that can be possible. Simple. In Tim's situation he felt victimized (self-pity) by his dad's treatment of him during his childhood. It's all about him and his painful childhood filled with suffering and maltreatment. He wants people to feel bad for him, and he wants to be right (self-importance) at his father's expense. This is selfishness no matter what point of view you take, the side of self-pity or self-importance.

If Tim were a Warrior, he would recognize that his dad did the best he could under the circumstances, and would see that he did have a good childhood and that his father loved him the only way he knew how. It might not have been the way Tim wanted it, but it was the way it was. As a Warrior, Tim would be able to forgive himself for treating his father with disrespect and then forgive his father for not knowing the effect he had on his son. Leaving his self-pity and self-importance behind would change his life and his relationship with his dad completely. And perhaps for the first time in his life, he would be able to accept his father's love and return it with pleasure.

> **CAUTION**
>
> **Warrior Warnings**
>
> Watch out for your fear-based emotions. They are like an alarm letting you know that something is not right. Pay attention to them, for they are a gift that will lead you to your fear-based beliefs.

A Seething Situation

Marla always had the tendency to be a bit of a martyr, telling her kids that she got pregnant when she was young and never finished school because she was too busy raising them. She always let the kids know that she had given something up for their welfare (for example, the kids were well aware of the fact that their mom couldn't join the neighborhood bridge club, because she was too busy carting them to and from band practice or some other activity).

When Marla's husband passed away, her daughter was in college and her son was living in a nearby city, busy with his promising career. All of the self-pity that Marla had seething within her for so many years came to bear at that time. Once her husband was gone and she had to fend for herself, she felt that everyone owed her big-time. She was so lonely that she wanted her daughter to quit school and come home to be with her and help out. (There was no reason for her to be at school, Marla reasoned, when she could get a job back home and take care of her mother.) She told her son that it was necessary for him to move back to their hometown so he could take over his father's responsibilities.

Marla felt it was terrible that she was all alone, and blamed this on the fact that she had such ungrateful children with no sense of responsibility. Although she loved her children, it was obvious that she had never done anything in her life out of true generosity, but instead figured that she would get something in return at some point. This situation put a huge strain on her relationship with her children since her son was not about to move home and her daughter had no intentions of leaving school and living her mother's life.

> **Impeccable Words**
>
> "To be self-centered means that we do not uphold the interrelationship of life, for this is the very meaning of the term. To be self-centered quite literally implies that you see yourself as being the center around which the rest of the world pivots, an idea which expresses a gross sense of self-importance."
>
> —Theun Mares, *The Mists of Dragon Lore*

No More Martyrs

In the end, Marla had to come to terms with the fact that she had never enjoyed her life and had always felt resentful that she had never finished school like her friends did. She admitted to herself that she was the one who got pregnant; it was no one else's fault. Marla also saw that she could have earned her high school and college degrees at any time; her husband offered to support her in that venture repeatedly over the years. But her fear of failure stopped her and it was easier for her to be a victim and to martyr herself than to take the chance of going back to school. She realized that she was being selfish to ask her children to give up their lives for her.

Marla took responsibility for the way she chose to see her life and for the actions she took as a result. In doing that, she was able to forgive herself for her behavior over the years and for her fear of taking a chance and failing. She also realized that she always felt a bit resentful toward her kids for "stealing" her life. But once she was able to admit that the only thing that stole her life was her own fear-based beliefs, she let that lie go, too. In the end, her relationship with her kids blossomed, since all her resentments, deep-seated anger, and fear were gone. She felt as though a weight had been pulled off her shoulders and she became excited to go back to school and get involved with new endeavors. Marla decided that there would be no whining Warriors in her home ever again.

In this story you can see how Marla made her husband's death all about her, and how she took her children having their own lives personally. Her selfishness and self-centeredness was huge. She did her best to manipulate and control her children into getting what she wanted without any concern for how her requests would affect their lives. She felt she was right and set out to make her children wrong.

We can see how self-pity and self-importance go hand-in-hand in these stories. As a Warrior, it's so important to have clarity about our own behavior and motivations. It's the only way we can move toward our freedom. It does take admitting the truth and getting over our fear, but there is no other way to go about it.

Having heard Marla's story, ask yourself these questions:

◆ Have you ever martyred yourself in your life in any way? Think carefully about your personal and work relationships. Does martyring yourself really make you feel satisfied?

◆ Have you ever tried to make someone feel bad for you by embellishing a story to make it sound worse than it was? Did you feel empowered by doing that?

◆ When you've felt victimized in your life, did you try to blame your circumstances on the other person(s) involved? What was your responsibility in the creation of those circumstances?

This is a great opportunity to journal incidences that you can remember of any times you have played the victim and indulged in self-pity. If you can take responsibility for your part and forgive all parties involved, you can increase your freedom quota immensely.

These Are a Few of My Favorite Fears

It's certainly challenging to move through the maze of the human mind. But even more than that, I believe it can be frightening. There are so many things we're afraid of in life: Fear of changing jobs, of ending relationships, of moving to where we have no friends or family, or even of changing something simple, like the style of our hair. Our fear extends to looking into the closet of our mind (or the overgrown bushes on our island of the Tonal) to see the pain and wounds we have buried there. We're afraid to admit to ourselves that we have sabotaged our lives, as Marla did. The biggest fear of all is our fear of being judged by our own mind or by the minds of others.

When we look at this a bit more closely, is it logical to be afraid of the judge that lives in our minds? Our minds contain our own beliefs, which are creating our fear. Concepts and beliefs can't hurt us, and we don't have to be afraid of them. We created them and we can disempower them, too (remember Chapter 6?).

We create all kinds of things in our minds that are not truth. We turn small situations into huge issues with our assumptions. We worry and create fear about stuff that never even happens. Of course, none of this is going on outside of us; all of it is occurring in our minds. As President Roosevelt once said, "The only thing we have to fear is fear itself."

Fear of Judgment

When we say we're shy, what are we afraid of? I'd be willing to bet it's the judgment from others and our own self-judgment. We're worried about what other people are thinking about us and we're self-conscious. In this way we're linking our self-worth to what others think. Who cares what anyone thinks about us? Most of the time people are too busy thinking about themselves to be paying attention to us. What's happening is that we are thinking that others are going to judge us the way we have *already* judged ourselves. And that's what creates our shyness. When we're shy our mind is victimizing us, and this is yet another example of self-pity and self-importance.

Fear of Loneliness

When we stay in a relationship that we're not happy in, what are we afraid of? Are we afraid we won't find someone else to love us or that we aren't worthy of love? Do we feel that we aren't pretty or handsome enough to find someone else? Or do we believe that having someone, even someone who's clearly wrong for us, is better than having no one at all? Do we believe the judge in our mind when it insults us in this way and says we don't deserve a good life?

Are we afraid to hurt the person we're in a relationship with by leaving? Because if we are, that is our fear of being judged by them, and that is selfishness. We're saying that we'd rather stay in a relationship we don't enjoy just because *we* do not want to deal with someone's possible anger or hurt. Is it kind to be with someone whom we don't want to be with, preventing them from finding someone who might really enjoy being with them? Is that not self-importance and selfishness?

Fear of Self-Expression

When we dress the same way or keep the same hairstyle for years, what are we afraid of? For how many years has our "look" remained the same? Life is constantly changing as it is moving through us, and it's not possible to remain the same person unless we are in resistance to life. Perhaps we feel uncomfortable with change, and this is our way of trying to control life and feel safe. Maybe we are afraid to change because of the way our own mind or others might judge us. By looking different, we might attract new and exciting people and we could be afraid of that. Do we always do things the same way, listen to the same music, and tell people that this is just the way we are (more doings [see Chapter 7])? This is not truth, as people are the reflection of the Infinite, which is *no-thing* and is always in motion, evolving. Therefore, it is not possible that "this is the way we are." Nope, "this is the way we *think* we are" is more accurate. What we believe about ourselves is not necessarily the truth, but it does reflect our level of fear.

Toltec Topography

No-thing in Toltec terms refers to the understanding that life, the Infinite, God, the Nagual, or any term we choose to use for Spirit is not and cannot be defined or limited by any concept or idea. That would immediately make it Tonal or some-thing.

Fear to Dream

When we stay in jobs or careers that aren't going anywhere, what are we afraid of? Are we afraid of not making the "right" choice? Is it truth that we can make a mistake in life? Isn't that just our judgment about something life is teaching us? If a job move doesn't work out, are we afraid of the endless beating our own mind will give us?

What about the fear of being judged by our colleagues and family? Have we already judged ourselves incapable of finding a new job that we might be interested in? Life is waiting for us to explore, expand, and experiment. If our own fears are the limiting factors in our lives, then as Warriors, let's put them aside and dream daringly and bravely.

Fear to Ask

When we can't ask for what we want in life, what are we afraid of? Do we believe we are so lowly that we don't even deserve to ask? By not asking, we are martyring ourselves into a position of "poor me." Why be worried about what other people will think of our requests? It doesn't matter if they think we are asking for something that *they* might judge as unreasonable. Are they living our life or are we? When we do not ask that man or woman out, we are setting the limitations in our life. If we do not ask our boss for a raise, how will he or she know we want one? If we do not communicate to our partner what we want for our anniversary, how will he or she know?

When we are unable to forgive someone or to ask for forgiveness, what we afraid of? Perhaps we will feel uncomfortable giving up our resentments. Or maybe we are addicted to holding onto our grudges. Is it better to feel victimized our whole life rather than to take a chance on letting go? Does our judge feel that we deserve to suffer in life rather than be happy? It is important for us to practice asking for what we want without fear, because if we don't ask, how can we receive?

> ### Impeccable Words
>
> "I must not fear. Fear is the mind-killer. Fear is the little-death that brings total obliteration. I will face my fear. I will permit it to pass over me and through me. And when it has gone past I will turn the inner eye to see its path. Where the fear has gone there will be nothing. Only I will remain."
>
> —Frank Herbert, *Dune* (from Bene Gesserit, *Litany Against Fear*)

Fear Is as Real as Smoke

Fear is like smoke. It has no solidity to it. It lives solely in the mind and is not real. I know that it *feels* mighty real, but once we move through one fear, it becomes easier and easier to conquer each subsequent fear. No matter how many fears we work through, we'll still feel discomfort, but the exciting end result propels us forward and helps us get through our illusory pain. Once we walk through the smoke and look back, we realize there was nothing there in the first place.

Having said this, try the following:

- Make a list of what you feel are your greatest limiting fears right now. Can you make a commitment to work on moving through just one of them? What will it take to do so?

- For the fears on your list, write down what could be the worst possible result of each situation. Will you die from moving through any of those scenarios? Are you more afraid of moving through your fears than dying?

- When have you taken the chance and moved through one of your fears before? Since you obviously survived that challenge and things worked out for you, what's stopping you from doing something like that again?

A Warrior has absolute respect for fear and understands that it's part of life. But a Warrior will never allow fear to stop him or her from moving forward, enjoying life, or becoming free. I know you can do it because I have, and I have faith that you are as capable as I am.

The Least You Need to Know

- Self-importance prevents us from being in a place of unconditional love and happiness.

- Self-pity is the flip-side of self-importance.

- We are responsible for evaluating our own issues of self-importance and self-pity and changing them.

- Fear lives only in our own minds, and it only takes a choice to make it disappear.

Part 4

Mastery of Awareness

As we know, the Toltec tradition consists of three masteries, the first one being the Mastery of Awareness. The Toltecs realized that we can't change what we don't know needs fixing, and they set out to develop ways to achieve clarity about the way we dream our lives. In Part 4, we look at the different strategies that our minds use to keep us trapped into seeing the world and creating our lives the way we do. By watching the way we use our word, the justifications and rationalizations our minds propose, and our tendency to go into denial, we can literally change our entire lives. Last, we'll discuss personal power and how we can prevent ourselves from losing it or giving it away. We'll also learn how to gain personal power.

Chapter 12

In the Beginning There Was the Word

In This Chapter

- The impeccable word of the Warrior
- Using our word to create a better life
- Learning to communicate clearly
- Changing our behavior so that we don't harm others

In Chapter 5 we discussed the virtual reality in our mind and how we're dreaming all the time. Then in Chapter 6 we spoke about how we use concepts and beliefs to define the structure of the virtual reality. We learned how our concepts are entirely our creation and are supported by the agreement of other humans, but aren't necessarily truth. In this chapter we're going to put all of that together and discuss how we create what we call our reality with our word.

The way we use our word in life is critical. It's the way we create everything in our lives. By having a deeper understanding of the ways we use our word, we'll be empowered to make changes that will shift the way people react to us. This in turn will shift the outcomes of many of our situations, making our lives easier and more pleasant. If we can have absolute faith that we can create in this way, we can make it so.

Use Your Word Wisely

We mentioned that being impeccable for a Warrior means living a life in which we aren't sinning against ourselves or others (Chapter 4). We accomplish this by not using our beliefs and concepts (or our words) as weapons. Impeccability is also refraining from projecting meaning from one's belief system (which is not absolute truth) onto situations or other people.

We use our word to create our entire reality. Our spoken word is a reflection of the words contained in our belief system. That's why it's so important for us to have a clean belief system and nondistorted concepts. So how can we use our word to create a wonderful life and avoid hurting ourselves and others?

Vacuous Verbiage

One of the first ways we can do this is by asking ourselves about the intent behind what we're saying. Most dialogue consists of people talking just to hear themselves talk. Do we ever stop and wonder why we say the things we say to people? Are we talking to fill up space and time or because we're uncomfortable with silence? A Warrior doesn't need to fill up anything. If there's nothing to be said in the moment, a Warrior will just enjoy the presence of another person rather than talk about nonsense. There's a lot we can communicate without saying a word, just with a smile or by holding someone's hand.

When we talk just for the heck of it, what are we creating with those words? When we speak about Intent in Chapter 21, it will become clearer why we as Warriors want to be so careful about the message we put out there. But until then, think about this: If we put out thousands of words per day, and our words create our reality, how many of those words are spoken with true purpose?

> **Impeccable Words**
>
> "The word is not just a sound or a written symbol. The word is a force: it is the power you have to express and communicate, to think, and thereby to create the events in your life."
>
> —don Miguel Ruiz, *The Four Agreements*

Many of us are extremely wordy. We talk and talk when we could have said something in half the time. How many times have we found ourselves getting impatient with someone because we felt they were taking forever to get to the point? Certainly others feel this way about us at times.

It's great practice to only say what we need to say and in as few words as possible to get our point across. This way the message we send out to the universe will be explicit and precise. Our reality will, in turn, respond more specifically to what we're saying.

Oppressive Opinions

On one of my first Toltec spiritual journeys to Peru, my teacher asked me not to speak for three days. He saw that all I was trying to do was impress others with all the wonderful stuff I thought I knew. While in silence, I could hardly contain myself, I wanted to talk so badly. I felt what I had to say was important and pertinent.

Well, I was wrong. After a couple of days in silence, I realized that everything I wanted to say was just "stuff" and really didn't matter. I observed how much I loved to give my personal opinion and point of view about everything. My opinion was usually not being solicited; I was the one wanting to give it because of my self-importance. I saw that people occasionally asked me what I thought, but most of the time I gave my opinion without even being asked! This was simply a reflection of my programming wanting to justify its existence and make itself right, which was *not* an impeccable use of my word.

What *was* really important was my presence, my smile, and my love for others, all of which were being obliterated by my motor-mouth. I learned a powerful lesson that trip, one that I have never forgotten.

> **Warrior Wisdom**
>
> An interesting thing starts to happen when we put ourselves into silence. The mind becomes quiet, the voices in our head stop speaking, and the sounds of nature become more compelling. Even better, we start to feel the presence of our Spirit, which is bliss.

Boring Stories

Do you often rush to tell people about yourself and your story? When someone tells you about something that happened to him or her, does it trigger a similar experience in you that you have to share? After my experience, I realized that people really don't want to hear someone else's story; for the most part, they just don't care. What they want is to use us to listen to *their* story! This is obviously not the way to have true heart-to-heart sharing. For example, how many times have we asked someone, "How are you?" only to regret asking? We just gave someone the opportunity to start telling a story we may not be interested in. Or look at how many times we aren't finished sharing what we have to say, and the other person is already talking. We may even find ourselves doing this at times.

When we're anxious to tell our story to someone, we have to ask ourselves why. Do we want to tell it because we think the other person really wants to know? Maybe we want to tell it because we think our story is scintillating or important. Or perhaps we're telling it to get an emotional reaction out of others.

Unpleasant Voices

Another aspect of our speech that we need to be aware of is the type of emotion that's being sent along with our words. Often people are more affected by the tone of the message than the message itself. Other times it seems that the tone is not in alignment with the words being spoken. Whenever we speak there's an emotional component that's transmitted along with our words. It's very important when speaking impeccably to make sure that the two transmissions match and are appropriate. For example, we could thank someone but say it in the most sarcastic of tones. When we speak like that, people usually go into defense mode against us.

Often we don't realize how we sound. It's a great exercise to record ourselves during the day. I once did this for several weeks and it was *very* enlightening and surprising. Friends often told me I sounded very cutting but I had no idea what they meant. I kept blaming it on the fact that I was from New York and folks living in Florida aren't used to people who speak like me. Of course that was nonsense, but I couldn't admit that until I was able to hear myself. I actually sounded very self-important and I could tell that my tone made other people feel stupid. Amazing that I never heard that before! I listened to the way I sounded and realized that I was doing it to make myself feel better. Yuck!

Once I paid attention to the emotion behind my words, I found that my whole reality started to change. People who didn't know me reacted kindly to me, and people who did know me were happy to be in my company because I was pleasant. My whole life shifted just from putting my attention on that one aspect of making my speech impeccable. You can

Warrior Warnings

The result of a discrepancy between the words that are spoken and the emotional quality being sent is that the person we're talking to will often feel an instant distrust of us.

try this, too. Just get one of those small recorders and record yourself at work, speaking to your family (that's always fun!), and during an argument. I promise this will be a *very* revealing exercise.

Here are some things you can practice to become more impeccable with your word:

◆ Try putting yourself in silence for a day. See what it feels like to not have to be talking all the time. If this isn't possible at work, practice responding only when absolutely necessary.

◆ For one day, promise yourself you won't give an opinion unless it's asked for. I bet this will be extremely challenging to do!

◆ Tape yourself and listen objectively to how you sound. Don't judge yourself, or you'll get defensive and the exercise will be worthless. Just listen and change what isn't creating happiness in your life.

Using Our Word for Mal-Intent

Most of the time we're doing our best to use our word kindly and to create a lovely reality. But other times we use our word for *mal-intent* and to hurt others. Often this happens without our awareness because we aren't paying attention to the effect our words are having on others. One example is if we use our words to put someone down or to insult them. In an argument, we often take the other person's point of view personally and our self-importance gets the better of us. We may end up saying things to justify our position and our need to be right, and, in turn, regret those words later. As Warriors it's important to put our self-importance shields down and put our awareness radars up so that we don't make these kinds of mistakes.

> **Toltec Topography**
>
> **Mal-intent** simply means with bad intent, or with the specific purpose of harming or hurting another.

Gossip Is Gross

One of the ways we use our word for mal-intent is through gossip. It never results in a reality that is nice, and more often than not it ends up hurting someone. We've all experienced being both the gossiper and the target of gossip, and neither position feels good. An important question to ask is whether we're gossiping about ourselves when we're sharing a story with others.

Consider how other people know what they know about you. Ninety-nine percent of what they know is based on what you've told them. Many times we disclose something to a friend, only to find out later that others are aware of what we said. The best strategy is to keep our personal information private, because when we trust others with our thoughts and feelings, we're actually trusting them to do exactly what *they* are going to do with it, not necessarily what *we* had in mind.

Warrior Warnings

The only way that someone can try to hurt us is if the person knows something that we have done or said that was not impeccable. Therefore, a Warrior never gives another person information that can be used to manipulate or control him, and he never engages in acts that are not impeccable.

Another way to use our word wisely is to not gossip about others. Many times we feel compelled to share a piece of information that we know about a friend or neighbor. The question to ask ourselves is if that person wanted another person to know what happened, wouldn't they have shared that information themselves?

We need to ask ourselves what kind of reality we're creating when we gossip. We often feel empowered to tell people things that aren't our business. If we feel compelled to gossip, we need to ask ourselves about the purpose or intent of our communication. People have actually told me that if they didn't talk about other people, they would have nothing to talk about. If that's so, then it's important to read the paper, listen to music, see a movie, read a book, or take up a hobby, because there are plenty of other things to talk about besides other people's business.

Malicious Malapropisms

Why would we want to hurt someone purposely and use our word for mal-intent? Revenge is one example, and is the ultimate in self-importance and self-pity. Feeling like we've been hurt by someone else really means that we've victimized ourselves. Feeling that we must get back at someone is a reflection of our self-centeredness and taking the incident personally.

When we use our word for mal-intent, we're turning it into a sword that can cause harm in the lives of others. It doesn't matter if someone says something mean to us. We must try to understand that that person is in his own world and feels justified by his own beliefs. We don't have to agree with what the other person says, nor do we have to take it personally. Let it go and walk away. If we use our word with mal-intent, what kind of life will we have? Again, using our word for mal-intent will eventually come back to us, because we are all part of just one life.

Using our word as a persuasive force to control or manipulate others is another way we engage in mal-intent. Many of us are adept at using language, and we give in to the temptation to try to get what we want by manipulating weaker or less-aware people with our wily words. There have been many powerful speakers over the years who have convinced millions of people to do harm to others. They used their words to play upon the fear-based beliefs of others and their emotions. On a lesser scale, there are those of us who know just how to manipulate and control our loved ones by purposely upsetting them or pushing their buttons.

I encourage you to watch yourself carefully for any signs of this type of behavior. If we're manipulating for personal gain at the expense of others, then we're harming life, and in the end we'll suffer from the suffering we have caused. There are kind ways to get people to assist us or to get what we believe we need, mostly by simply asking. If we simply treat people well and with respect, life will reflect our kindness back to us.

Warrior Wisdom

People are gullible and easy to manipulate because they have so many fears. A Warrior cannot be manipulated because she isn't afraid of other people, different ideas and beliefs, or things that people say or do.

Lastly, it's important to look at the way we use cursing in our daily language. The words that we use as curses were originally created to send mal-intent and unhealthy energy to others. Even if we use these words just for the purpose of "coloring our speech," so to speak, we are engaging words that are not uplifting.

Coming from New York, I used to use curse words a lot, both as adjectives and also when I was angry. My teacher suggested that I stop using my word in this way, just to see how it felt. I was surprised at what a difference it made in my life. After a while I became sensitive to the cursing in other people's speech, and it sounded awful. My environment had become nicer without the curse words, and I saw that these words acted like toxins.

Here are some strategies that you can use to remove the mal-intent from your words:

♦ If people are gossiping around you at work, or if a friend is gossiping to you, see if you can steer the conversation elsewhere. If you can't change the conversation, get up and leave if you can. This isn't about judging others for gossiping, but simply respecting your own new way of conducting your life.

◆ Make an agreement with yourself to end using your word for mal-intent. Don't speak to people when you're mad. Wait until you get a grip on what your mind is telling you and speak when you have clarity and presence of mind.

◆ We live very toxic lives in many ways. Try to decrease the "bad vibes" by removing all cursing from your life. That may also include changing some of the music, radio, or TV shows you might currently be listening to.

Wordy Advice to Live By

In the last two sections we talked about the way we use our word both for good and harm in our everyday lives. I mentioned several times that my life changed when I started to use my word in a different way. By realizing how we're speaking, the words we're using, the emotion we're sending, and the intent of our communication, we can literally change our life.

As I shared with you earlier in this book, I used to believe 100 percent that the problems in my life were all outside of me. I thought that the only way my relationship with my mom would improve was if *she* went into therapy. But when I stopped talking to her the way I always had, my whole relationship with her changed. I changed the way I used my word in my life, and the results were amazing. My teacher had told me this time and time again, but I didn't believe it until I experienced it for myself.

> **Warrior Warnings**
>
> Once we say something out loud, we can't change the chain of actions and reactions that follows the energies we have set into motion. Speak wisely.

I encourage you to take a chance and put these ideas and suggestions into practice. In this section, we'll take a look at four things we can do to change our life and reality using our word.

Quash Conflicts

First and foremost, stop arguing with people. There's no reason on earth to argue, and I mean that. If we understand that all we're doing is defending concepts that aren't even absolute truth, why even go there? Arguing makes our physical bodies sick, drains our energy, and weakens us. We won't ever find a true Warrior who argues. There's no reason to defend any opinion, point of view, or belief. We can share our beliefs or point of view, but defending them is an act of war. If we're going to engage in a war, let's engage in the right one, the war with our own mind to be free of our self-importance and our need to be right.

Liberate Your Love

Second, let's change the emotional message in our communications. If we come across as whiny, angry, bitter, frustrated, or disgruntled, how can we expect people to react to us? There's only one emotion that needs to be present no matter what words you are using, and that's the feeling of love. As my dear friend Angelo from the Bronx would say, "That's it and that's all." If we aren't sending all the love that we *are* in every communication, why are we speaking?

We can't share concepts with another person, really. We can only share ourselves, *using* the concepts. Can you see the difference? We're all the embodiment of love, and communication gives us an opportunity to send that aspect of ourselves to another human. We aren't our anger or our jealousy, but we can feel those emotions. So if we care for another person, why would we want to send them our fear-based emotions? It's like taking our garbage and putting it on our loved one's front lawn. If we are going to send emotions to others, let us send ourselves and our love instead.

End Malevolent Messages

Third, let's pay attention to the intent behind our words. If we're sending a message that we know could or will hurt someone, we have to stop and put our verbal sword back into its sheath. There's absolutely no reason to purposely want to harm another human. In an emotional moment we may say something we know we shouldn't have said, but there are no excuses. We are responsible for our emotions and behavior; no one can get us upset or angry. We must choose to have those emotions and say those words. It's never necessary to get our message across in a hurtful or rude way.

Cultivate Clear Communication

Fourth, let's be succinct with our words. It's important to do our best to get our message across as clearly as possible. We can pretend that we only have a certain number of words that we're allowed to use in our lifetime. Certainly we would want to make sure that we have enough words to last that long, so we wouldn't waste them on conversation that's going nowhere.

We can't assume that others know what we're saying. We need to be as clear as possible so that they have the greatest chance of comprehending us. If we feel embarrassed, ashamed, or uncomfortable about what we want to say, this is going to cause us to beat around the bush. If we do that, be ready for that person to misinterpret what we say.

We're 100 percent responsible for the words we use and how we use them. We aren't responsible for the way people hear them or interpret them, however. So, on our side, it behooves us to take responsibility for our messages and make them as unmistakable as possible.

 Warrior Wisdom _____

A good many of us were taught the golden rule. How many of us really live that rule?

"All things whatsoever ye would that men should do to you, do ye so to them; for this is the law and the prophets."
Christianity: *The New Testament*, Matthew 7:12

"What is hateful to you, do not do to your neighbor. This is the whole Torah; all the rest is commentary."
Judaism: Rabbi Hillel, *Talmud*, Shabbat 31d

"Treat not others in ways that you yourself would find hurtful."
Buddhism: *Udana-Varga* 5.1

"This is the sum of duty: do not onto others what would cause pain if done to you."
Hinduism: *Mahabharata* 5:1517

"No one of you truly believes until he desires for his brother that which he desires for himself."
Islam: The Prophet Muhammad, *13th of the 40 Hadiths of Nawawi*

"Lay not on any soul a load that you would not wish to be laid upon you, and desire not for anyone the things you would not desire for yourself."
Baha'i: Baha'u'llah, *Gleanings*

"Regard your neighbor's gain as your own gain and your neighbor's loss as your own loss."
Taoism: Lao Tzu, *T'ai Shang Kan Ying P'ien*, 213–218

A Succinct Summary

Now we have four specific tools that can make a huge difference in the way our reality looks if we put them into action. At first the people in our lives may be confused because we're acting differently. Have patience; people need to see that we really have changed and that this isn't a temporary glitch in our behavior. Once they feel confident that we really are different, they will feel comfortable in reacting differently to us.

The Least You Need to Know

- We create our reality with our word, and it behooves us to use our word as impeccably as possible.

- When we're communicating, let's be succinct, loving, clear, and only say what we need to say to transmit our message.

- Engaging in communication for the purpose of gossip, cursing, manipulation, control, or the harm of others is using our word with mal-intent.

- By practicing using our word wisely, we can change our reality and the way people react to us.

13

The Strategy of Sabotage

In This Chapter

- ◆ The most subversive being in our life
- ◆ Finding and revealing the unhealthy patterns in our lives
- ◆ Seeing the strategies that our minds use to keep us functioning in denial
- ◆ Being undermined by the mind

As we already know, we are Warriors at war. The war is with our own fear-based beliefs and concepts. What's at stake is our absolute freedom to live our lives without fear, with open hearts, and in happiness and joy. We spent time talking about how our mind is our greatest enemy (at least until we get control of it) in Chapters 7 and 8, and I mentioned then that our minds have excellent strategies for keeping us locked into behavior patterns that create unhappiness, drama, and pain in our lives.

In this chapter, we'll examine how those strategies work and how we can transcend them to lead more pleasant lives. Since we can't—and wouldn't want to—"kill" this enemy (after all, you do need your mind), the best we can do is convert it into a lifetime assistant or ally. I'll use real situations to illustrate these concepts, and I encourage you to look for any similarities to yourself in each one.

We Are Our Worst Enemy

The Toltecs observed that the most effective way to investigate the mind is by becoming a nonjudgmental witness. That means we can use our mind to watch our mind and ultimately to re-program it. This is the technique that we as Warriors use to see our behavioral patterns and deep-seated beliefs. (We'll learn more about this in Part 5.)

I want to make it clear that this process is not about hating our mind. After all, we would not be able to communicate without it, and it did get us to where we are today, drama or no drama. Our mind may often be our worst enemy, but we still have gratitude for it. Instead, we focus on transforming a serious saboteur into a useful assistant. The day that our programmed or parasitic mind is no longer in charge of our life, we can say we have created an ally. We accomplish that by reprogramming our fear-based beliefs to ones based in love, and then finally by detaching from our mind and putting all our faith and personal power into our Spirit. Then the real us is running the show instead of our programmed mind.

Let's look at some situations that illustrate how our mind can be our biggest downfall and how we can change that role.

People Never Hear Me

Samuel grew up in a home with a father who was a stern, serious disciplinarian. Many times Samuel would get in trouble for things that his sisters did or for things that he wasn't responsible for. His father would punish him severely for these perceived wrongdoings. Samuel would try to explain to his dad that he didn't do anything, but his father, a hardworking and impatient man, had no time to listen to a little boy's explanation of the supposed truth. In fact, his father would often get even angrier if Sam tried to defend his point of view to him.

> **Warrior Wisdom**
>
> Always remember that people can only function at the level of awareness that they are in that moment. Our parents did the best they could, operating from what they believed at the time.

As a result, Samuel developed a habit of repeating himself over and over to people who he thought didn't understand him. At work, for example, he could see that people were not interested in the ideas he had to share and so he would repeat himself in a different way, hoping people would comprehend him. Co-workers would get impatient with him because they understood what he was saying; they just weren't interested in what he was proposing. Sam thought he just was unable to communicate what he wanted; he felt unheard.

At home, he would ask his kids to do something and then ask them again 15 minutes later in a different way. They would complain, "Dad, you *already* told us to do that." When he would discuss something with his wife that perhaps she didn't agree with, he would repeat the whole thing all over again hoping she would "hear him" the following day. He was never able to see this irritating behavior pattern within himself. He was totally blinded to his ways.

Children Should Be Seen but Not Heard

One day he had a huge argument with his wife about this behavior. She told him that she loved him very much and always respected what he had to say, but just because he said something didn't mean that she had to agree with it. Somehow he heard his wife in a way he had never heard her before. He thought very carefully about what she had said. He sat with it for quite a while until it hit him: Samuel realized that people were hearing him just fine, but they didn't always care for or agree with what he was saying! He saw that he had *chosen* to believe he was not heard, which empowered him to keep behaving in this repetitive way.

> **Impeccable Words**
>
> "There is a condition worse than blindness, and that is seeing something that isn't there."
>
> —L. Ron Hubbard

Sam saw that as a child he thought if he could explain to his dad just once what *really* happened, he wouldn't be punished anymore and everything would be okay. The truth was, his father believed children should be seen, not heard, and had no interest in hearing Sam's point of view. Once Sam saw this, he was able to release the anger he had toward his dad that he had been carrying around for so long and forgive himself for all those years of irritating behavior. In this way he was able to change the way people perceived him at work and in all aspects of his life. He could not believe how he was sabotaging himself and all his relationships with just this one behavior pattern!

Can you name one unhealthy behavior pattern that you have been using, after reading this? If so, ask yourself the following questions:

- Are you able to look back through your life and see how that pattern came to fruition?

- Who was the one who helped you create that pattern and cement it into place?

- What was your responsibility in creating that pattern?

- Are you able to forgive yourself and the person who helped you create that pattern?

- Do you see how your life presented you with situations that always proved your fear-based beliefs to be true?

We all have our own behavior patterns that we use to hurt ourselves without even realizing what we're doing. The key is to wake up and see that it's not about those folks out there but, instead, is all about us. Can you see how Samuel was creating this entire situation with his word and how he was creating his reality to look just the way his programming needed it to look to support his fear-based beliefs?

Repetition and Revelation

The trick to locating these unhealthy patterns and strategies is to look for the repetition of certain happenings throughout our life. Once we see the repetition, we can experience the *revelation* that comes from seeing the truth. In our example of Samuel, that's exactly what happened. He saw the repetition and then he had the revelation. The more we keep on searching for these patterns in our own lives, the easier it becomes to find them.

Toltec Topography

Revelation is an important concept in many religions. For us, we see it as the uncovering of what is truth, an enlightening or astonishing disclosure. It can also be a dramatic disclosure of something not previously known or realized.

Three Dastardly Divorces

A number of years ago I was in a workshop where we had break-out groups for the purpose of doing a specific exercise. Everyone was divided into groups of three. The assignment that day was to tell the other group members the story of a particularly difficult time in your life. The three people in the group that I was leading ended up sharing the story of their divorces and the circumstances surrounding them. When each of them had completed their stories, they were going to discuss what they observed about their experiences. But right before they were about to speak, they all just stopped and looked at one another. They all had the same revelation at the exact same time! What was shocking was that, although they had all experienced divorce as adults, they each saw it from a perspective developed from childhood. Childhood experiences had caused them to make certain agreements with themselves. As a result, they tended to interpret adult experiences in the context of that agreement.

Frank felt that his ex pulled the wool over his eyes when she first met him. In other words, she presented herself to him one way, but was really a very different person inside. She always told him how great he was and how much she loved him, and then she cheated on him. What this confirmed for him was that people always lie, they present themselves in ways that aren't true, and they can't be trusted.

Sharon, on the other hand, was hurt from her experience because her husband had abandoned her for another woman. She spent years feeling terrible about the whole event, and it confirmed to her that the people she loves always leave her. In fact, she felt that it wasn't worth loving people and opening her heart because she would always be left abandoned.

Lastly, Anna shared that her husband also left her for another woman, and she felt that was unfair. She complained that if one person loves another, then he or she shouldn't hurt the other person and should have respect and consideration for the other's feelings. It proved to her that life is unjust and that things never go right, so why bother?

They each experienced their partners having an affair, but since they each had made a different agreement about life, the conclusions they each came to were totally different. To each person the affair proved that a different thing was "true" about life.

> **Impeccable Words**
>
> "As human beings, our greatness lies not so much in being able to remake the world—that is the myth of the atomic age—as in being able to remake ourselves."
> —Mahatma Gandhi

Remarkable Realizations

Frank realized that people simply are the way they are. It wasn't that his wife had hidden her true personality; it was that he never saw her the way she really was. He also saw where his agreement originated from. When he was little, his dad left home, and his mom always used to say, "Your dad lied to me. You can never trust that people are who you

> **Warrior Warnings**
>
> A Warrior never plays the blame game. The key is to see the repetitive patterns, reveal the truth, take responsibility for our half of the creation, forgive all parties involved, and love ourselves for taking the time to uncover these sabotaging behaviors.

think they are." After that, he always saw people and situations from that suspicious point of view. His revelation set him free from carrying around his mother's wound and living his life through her eyes.

Sharon saw that her husband left the marriage, but he never really "abandoned" her. That was just the way she chose to see what happened. When she was young, her parents had to give her to an aunt to be raised. As a little girl she felt alone and abandoned. As a result, anytime a person left her in life, whether it was a girlfriend moving away, or her dog running away, it was abandonment. From this revelation she was able to forgive her parents and her ex-husband and put that point of view behind her. She also forgave herself for victimizing her life with this unhealthy agreement.

> **CAUTION**
>
> **Warrior Warnings**
>
> By using concepts to describe our experiences that are emotionally charged, we open ourselves up to having an emotional reaction to both the word we are using and our experience. This is a double whammy! When you use the words "abandoned me" rather than "our relationship ended," before you even know what happened, you already have a judgment and an uncomfortable feeling about it.

Anna realized that she had a habit of seeing everything in her life as being unjust; her friends used to make fun of her for constantly whining, "It's not fair!" She finally realized why she always reacted to life in that way. When she was little her mom used to hit Anna but never punished her sister. Her sister was the golden child. She had a lot of resentment toward her sister and felt that everything about her existence was unfair. She realized now that it wasn't that her sister wanted to be good, it was just that she was scared to death to be bad! Her sister had made an agreement about life that was much different than Anna's. This revelation enabled Anna to stop her whining, forgive her sister and herself, and start enjoying life.

What was so great about this exercise was that all three participants could clearly see the repetition of these patterns in their lives. The revelation enabled them to become free from the fear-based beliefs that they had subscribed to for most of their lives.

Next time you have a quiet night with your dearest friends, pick an experience that you have all had, and each share your own version of what happened.

- ◆ Can each of you comprehend the point of view you've chosen to see life from?

- ◆ What are the exact agreements that you made?

- ◆ What is the truth of what happened to you, both in your shared situation and in your past?

The Strategies of the Mind

Our minds are such incredible strategists; I am in constant awe of the ability we have to hurt ourselves without even realizing it! I personally feel that my mind is brilliant; after all, it got away with 40 years of self-deprecating behaviors committed right under my own nose! I would like to share the experiences of two people whose minds trapped them in their own stories. See if you can relate to either of these situations.

Brilliant Logic

Genna was a brilliant and successful doctor specializing in plastic surgery (working 60-hour weeks). She always gave off the perfect outer image, with only occasional anger in her personality when things were not going her way. When I learned more about her, I found out that she was in a lackluster marriage with a man who lived in another city. In addition, she had no hobbies, few personal friends, and did very little for fun. On her hard-earned vacations, she spent time with the husband she didn't even enjoy being with, instead of venturing out on a fun vacation of her own. As a child, Genna was brought up by a cousin who never was thrilled about her presence in her home. She treated Genna like a stepdaughter or second-class citizen who didn't deserve anything.

Genna wanted to make changes in her life and be happier, but every time I approached her about taking action to make those changes she would get angry. With the most brilliant logic of her well-educated mind, she said that her life was okay; certainly it wasn't as bad as some of her friends'. She said she had to work hard to keep her practice going the way it was; there was no other way to do it. Of course it did not leave her any time to do other fun activities, as she was exhausted when she did have time off. Regarding her husband, she would say it was the perfect situation to be in; she had the house to herself and could do what she wanted. It was apparent that although she said she wanted to change, she had no intention of changing. Or better said, her mind knew all the right things to say to maintain her current situation.

> **Warrior Warnings**
>
> Toltecs advise us not to believe ourselves, or anything our minds are telling us. This is an important tool that we have to stop these types of logical assaults from our minds.

Deep inside she wanted to be free, but her mind had it all worked out so that no matter what you said to her she had the perfect answer back. There was no way to penetrate the wall that her mind's belief system created for her. She declined to see that her lack of self-love, self-worth, and self-respect had her in a marriage that was not a marriage, but an excuse to avoid experiencing true love and opening her heart. Genna would not admit her fear of taking a vacation by herself and having to experience the adventure of life at its fullest. She ignored her fear of being in a relationship that might involve making passionate love and letting go. Genna was afraid of everything, and she worked herself like a dog to justify escaping from her fears and to avoid confronting them.

As we can see, it is important to witness the logical excuses our mind makes, and not to fall prey to this kind of sneaky strategy. It's so easy to use your life circumstances as an excuse not to actually get out there and live your life!

Exiled from Life

Thomas was a very quiet and hardworking man who lived a busy and seemingly successful life. He never got involved with much of anything; he had no hobbies, but he did have a couple of friends that he saw at times, and a cat. He had had three serious relationships in his life, none of which led to marriage. We spoke quite a bit about his life and he shared with me that it had always been this way, that he never had many friends even when he was young. His father was in the military and they traveled much of his youth. Each time they moved to another place he would have to make friends all over again. When he was a teen, his father thought karate would be a good sport for his shy son to get into. Once in the class, though, Thomas found he was so shy that his nervousness made him uncoordinated and he was made fun of. After that he stayed away from any group activities and sports.

Thomas knew that he needed to have more fun in life and increase his happiness. When I suggested that he get involved with more people though different activities—the local Sierra Club, a wine-tasting class, a singles trip, or a book-discussion club—he became irritated and said he had already tried socializing and it was useless. He said that if I was going to suggest something to him, I should at least suggest something he could do. Of course I knew that would happen, because it was obvious from the start that he liked things just as they were. His setup was perfect for him to victimize himself and feel bad about his lonely life. It didn't matter what anyone said; his program had the perfect response ready to refute any suggestion made.

Warrior Wisdom

How many ways do you have to say "I can't"? Each way is another chain you place upon yourself and your freedom.

Thomas was afraid of the judgment of others, and his own judgment of himself was monumental. He made himself an outsider simply by putting himself on the outside of his life. By telling himself he never fit, he rationalized and justified his not fitting in. Everything was perfect for things to remain just as they were. Just like Genna, he wanted to be free, but his program and what he believed about himself were strong and blinding. He created himself to be like a shadow, to fade into the background in any social situation. And that was how he lived, gliding though life, enjoying nothing, watching others have fun, like the walking dead.

Here are a few thoughts to consider:

◆ Using your imagination, name some of the agreements these two adults might have made when they were children. Take some time to meditate on this. Understanding the human mind will help you to have better interactions with people in your life.

◆ Using your own life's experiences, what do you see as your main fears? Do you see what situations caused them?

◆ If you could name your mind's main strategies, what would you call them? (For example, I named Genna and Thomas's strategies, "Brilliant logic" and "Exiled from life.")

◆ Do you see how successful these patterns are in keeping your life exactly as it is? What actions would you have to take to thwart those strategies?

The Enemy Is Undermining Our Life

Sometimes the strategies of the mind are so successful that it can actually get the body to harm itself to the point of death. In other words, the mind can tell us that our life is so terrible that there is no way out, propelling us in extreme cases to commit suicide or at least live in severe depression.

I'm going to share two different situations that could take us in that direction, and I would ask you to see if you have ever felt like this. If you have never felt this way, perhaps you know someone who has felt very depressed at some time as a result of what their mind told them about their life. Perhaps reading this will help you understand why people can feel this way, and how certain kinds of depression can occur.

Loves Me Not

Catherine was a quiet and kindly woman who grew up in New York in a family with two alcoholic parents and an older sister. Her older sister ran away from the household as soon as she could, never to be heard from again. That left Catherine to manage the home to the best of her abilities. Instead of her parents feeling grateful for her help, they were mean and caustic to her. No matter what she did or how much she helped, she could never earn her parents' love. The truth was that their first love was alcohol and their daughter was a distant second. In the end they both passed away in a car accident and Catherine could not remember them telling her once that they loved her. Catherine never drank herself, but was instead addicted to men who would tell her they needed her, and later would leave her.

Catherine was always finding needy people just like her parents, putting her heart and soul into trying to make others happy and "earning" their love. Unfortunately, the people she chose would use her until they could not stand her kindness anymore and then they would dump her. She spent her life looking for men to need her, passing up many opportunities to be with healthy men. The last fellow she tangled with drained her financially, and on top of that, she ended up losing her job due to his demands on her time, which of course she gave in to. In addition, she ended up pregnant by him, and when she told him about it, he proceeded to call her names and hit her.

She felt trapped and cornered, with no one to turn to and no place to go. One night her mind told her that no one loved her and she was not worth loving. How would she be able to love a child or take care of it? It would end up hating her, too. She was a failure, doomed to a life of pain and misery. Her mind insulted her until she could take it no longer and she tried to end her life. Fortunately she was not successful, and was able to receive help. In retrospect she realized that the only person who could ever love her completely was herself. Once she had self-esteem and self-love, she wouldn't pull needy, destructive men into her life. She also saw that she didn't need to prove her worthiness to anyone. She was perfect the way she was and didn't need for people to need her or validate her existence. As a result of her breaking her fear-based beliefs, she was able to start her life again with new friends and healthier situations, along with a beautiful baby.

Impeccable Words

"Man stands in his own shadow and wonders why it's dark."

—Zen saying

Weight of the World

As a child, Sylvia was always a little overweight. Her mom, on the other hand, was one of those women who always looked beautiful, even if she was wearing a rag. Growing up, Sylvia felt uncomfortable and ugly. In truth, Sylvia was a beautiful girl, but she only saw herself compared to her mother, and in her eyes her mom was a princess. Since she couldn't compete with her mom, she made the agreement to stop caring about herself, and she let her appearance go. From the time she was around 13 her weight went up steadily until she reached 250 pounds at age 18. Sylvia put all of her passion into school and ended up in a wonderful career in cancer research. She earned a great salary but never treated herself to lovely vacations or a beautiful home. Everything was utilitarian, including her appearance.

Sylvia hated herself and her body. She felt it was a curse and that no man would want to be with someone as disgusting as her. Life went on this way until she was involved in a study that required her to go out into the field and work with cancer patients. She befriended a woman who was part of the study; this patient intrigued her with her courage. The woman felt that her beliefs about herself caused her disease to a certain extent, and that if she was going to heal, she first needed to heal her mind. Sylvia, for the first time in her life, looked at what she believed about herself. She started to see that the agreements she adopted were lies, and she realized that there was nothing wrong with herself other than her self-image. She stopped believing those horrible things her mind was telling her about herself. Spurred on by this new attitude, she started to lose weight; she changed her clothes, hairstyle, and makeup, and started enjoying life. She ended up dating a co-worker whom she eventually married. Her gratitude for her new friend's wisdom was immense.

> **Warrior Wisdom**
>
> Our body is the vehicle that takes us through life. Whatever we have been given must be good enough because that is all we have. Gratitude and love is the kindest thing we can have for our bodies.

Ask yourself these questions:

◆ Do you dislike any part of your physical body? If so, what do you say to yourself about those parts?

◆ Since this is the body you have for life, do you feel that being mean to it will change anything? If not, what effect do you think your thoughts are having toward your body?

♦ What concrete actions could you take so that it's possible to come to a place where you can have absolute gratitude for your body and love it (and yourself) just the way it is?

♦ Do you feel you're worthy of love? How is that reflected in your life, or not?

♦ If you love yourself 100 percent, why do you allow yourself to do things that go against yourself (like working long hours, being in the company of people who aren't doing you any good, or allowing yourself to argue with the people you supposedly love)?

I think we can see that no matter what life confronts us with, the way we choose to see things and the agreements we make about our circumstances make or break us. They propel us to make certain choices in our lives that can either help or hurt us. This is why a Warrior is ruthless in looking at the past and at what he or she believes. We recognize that we can have a challenging life, but we don't have to suffer.

The Least You Need to Know

♦ Toltecs split their mind into two so that they can observe their mind with their mind.

♦ Searching for the repetitive patterns in our life will lead to powerful revelations about our agreements and beliefs.

♦ The mind uses logic, justification, and rationalization to keep us living fear-based and limited lives.

♦ Careful observation will enable us to see how our mind's programming is trying to undermine our life.

Chapter 14

Resistance Is Not Futile

In This Chapter

- Using denial to prevent ourselves from seeing our self-sabotaging behaviors

- Acting defensively toward others

- How we have been trained to take things personally and to be offended by the actions, words, and deeds of others

- The only thing we can control

In Chapter 13 we touched upon some clever strategies that our minds use to keep us locked into repeating the same behavior patterns in our lives. We spoke briefly about denial and the use of justifications; in this chapter we will expand on exactly how we use them. Denial is the number-one way that we avoid looking at ourselves and our issues; therefore, it's important that we understand its place in our growth process. We'll also get to know denial's best buddies: blame, rationalization, and justification. These are the tools we use to resist life and create conflict within us.

Once we can get past our denial system, everything changes and we are well on our way to the Mastery of Awareness. Remember how we said that we cannot change what we are not aware of? Well, denial is the best way to prevent us from ever knowing anything about ourselves. Let's see if together we can slay this enemy of the Warrior. With this expanded awareness, we'll then be on our way to learning how to make those changes in Part 5, "Mastery of Transformation"!

Denial Ain't a River

Nope, *denial* isn't a river, but the more you stay in denial of your life circumstances, the further up the river you will be from your goal. Denial enables us to avoid looking at the characteristics of ourselves that are not working. All of us have mastered this technique to varying degrees. From the time we were little, we watched our family interactions carefully and learned from them. (We may have watched our parents lie to get out of situations or place blame on others, for example.)

> **Toltec Topography**
>
> **Denial** is an unconscious defense mechanism characterized by our refusal to acknowledge painful realities, thoughts, or feelings. When we are in denial, we can disown or disavow our own acts and blame them on others.

Some of us are humble and accept responsibility for our acts, but the majority of us indulge quite a bit in denial and its counterpart, blame, which enables us to project everything onto another person. This takes an issue from a perspective of "it's all about me" to one that's all about the other person and his or her faults. Of course, a warrior never plays with denial and blame because he knows that he is responsible for co-creating everything he gets himself into. Let's look at three stories that illustrate how blame and denial work.

Selfish Situations

Hannah and Franny used to be roommates at a time when they were both going through life changes and toiling at new jobs. By joining forces they were able to find a nice home to share while their new businesses were growing and finances were lean. Hannah, though, always felt that Franny was manipulative. So when the time came when Hannah could afford her own place, she made the decision to move out. Franny was upset about this, telling Hannah how selfish she was, and that she only thought about her own welfare.

Franny was so belligerent that instead of talking to her, Hannah wrote her a letter to explain why she needed to move. She reminded Franny that she had made no guarantees that they would live together forever; Hannah had thought both women understood that they were only co-habitating until each of them got on their feet. Hannah pointed out that she was not responsible for Franny taking her move personally and using it to make herself angry. After seeing this in writing, Franny got the message. Once Hannah was away from Franny, she felt better not being in an environment where she was constantly being emotionally manipulated.

Consider these questions:

◆ Can you see how Franny used the concept of friendship to try to manipulate Hannah into staying?

◆ Do you see that Franny was actually the selfish one? And do you see how Franny projected her selfishness onto Hannah?

◆ Can you see how needy Franny was, and how she had no respect for Hannah's choices?

Used and Abused

Once they were in their respective homes, Hannah mentioned to Franny that she was going to start painting her bedrooms. Franny, who loved to paint, wanted to come over and help, but previous experience told Hannah that Franny would later hold that "favor" over her head. Franny insisted, though, and Hannah was not brave enough to say no. Hannah's parents were helping out, too, and when the painting was done for the day, they offered to take both girls out for Sushi.

When Hannah told her about her parents' generous offer, Franny blew up, screaming at Hannah, "You know I hate raw fish! You're so selfish, always doing things like this! It's always what you want, never what I want!" Hannah replied, "You don't have to get raw fish there. They have other food that I know you like. And besides, my parents are the ones who suggested it and they're paying. We can ask them to pick someplace else if you're that upset about it." Franny wouldn't hear it and stormed out with her righteous indignation, projecting her own selfishness onto Hannah.

> **Impeccable Words**
>
> "The hardest thing in the world is to assume the mood of a warrior. It is of no use to be sad and complain and feel justified in doing so, believing that someone is always doing something to us. Nobody is doing anything to anybody, much less to a warrior."
>
> Carlos Castaneda, *Journey to Ixtlan* (as quoted in *The Wheel of Time*)

Stopping Denial in Its Tracks

Franny and Hannah had a mutual friend, Linda, who would often mediate arguments between the two of them. Franny called Linda to complain again about how rude Hannah had been not to consider her preferences in food when she had worked all day long painting. Linda asked, "Don't you think that you were being a bit unreasonable, taking nothing and making it into a big deal?" Franny denied this vehemently and said, "It's obvious that Hannah only thinks of herself. I don't know why I keep putting myself into these kinds of situations. I guess I am a sucker for getting used."

Shocked, Linda said, "Franny, you are the one who offered to paint, and you are the one who created the resulting drama. Hannah told me that she offered to switch restaurants. And besides, you and I ate at that restaurant before and you had the teriyaki chicken, which you loved. So don't tell me that you couldn't find something to eat there. What I see is that you like to create drama for the heck of it and at the expense of your friends. It isn't Hannah who's selfish; it's you. When you're ready to take responsibility for your garbage, let me know and we can talk about it!"

Now ask yourself this:

◆ Are you able to see how Franny was in total denial of the situation she was creating? Do you see any of Franny's behavior within yourself? If so, how?

◆ Do you see how Hannah co-created this situation because she was afraid to say no to Franny's offer of help in the first place? When have you said "yes" when you meant "no," or said "no" when you meant "yes"?

◆ Can you see Franny's repetitive behavior pattern? What agreement has she made with herself that drives her behavior? This is an important question, so see if you can take a guess.

◆ Are you able to see that when we do not take responsibility for our issues, we end up projecting them onto others, making our issue all about them? Can you give one example of a time when you have done the same thing?

◆ Do you see how you could easily live your whole life in denial of your issues, always blaming them on others and feeling totally self-righteous about it?

Beware of the Victim Trap!

Perhaps you feel like siding with Franny here. It's important to make it clear again that life does not always conform to our expectations. We cannot have expectations of other people or their lives. They need to do what they need to do. Hannah, for example, needed to move out, whether it was the best thing for Franny or not. Franny took Hannah's decision personally and assigned blame to it. She did the same thing with the dinner issue, expecting everyone else to cater to her preferences, and taking it personally when they didn't.

A Warrior would never turn herself into a victim to satisfy the needs of her mind's programming. It is important for us to have the awareness to catch ourselves perpetuating the pattern of using the people we supposedly love to hurt ourselves and create drama. Since Franny believes that people use and abuse her, she will do anything to create situations in her life that prove that belief to be true. If she could move beyond her denial, she could stop justifying her behavior and end her pattern of blaming others for situations that she herself has created.

Defenses, Justifications, and Rationalizations

The human mind is extremely creative. The amount of *justifications* and *rationalizations* we invent for our actions and behaviors is astounding! I myself have been responsible for some incredible excuses that in retrospect I find extremely amusing. Of course we've all done this, and there is no reason for judging ourselves for things we have not been aware of or were unwilling to take responsibility for at the time. Let's take a look at some examples of how we do this and what exactly this strategy looks like.

Sticky Fingers

Stephan had been working for a mid-size corporation for approximately six years. He had been climbing the typical corporate ladder to success until he reached his current position. He was uncertain as to whether he or another co-worker would advance to the next step. To his dismay, the other person received the promotion. Stephan was infuriated at the perceived injustice of the situation. He felt that he was better than his colleague, and he wanted revenge (remember self-importance?). He started doing something he had never done before: stealing. He figured that if he couldn't have the raise, he was going to make up for it in what he called "benefits."

> **Toltec Topography**
>
> A **justification** is when we create an explanation for ourselves or another person (using the contents of our belief system) to make our actions appear right, reasonable, or necessary.
>
> A **rationalization** is when we make something that we are doing or saying seem consistent with reason (the reason of our faulty programming, that is!) or to devise self-satisfying but incorrect reasons for our behavior.

The first "benefits" he took were legal pads and pens. After that, coffee packets and sugars traveled home, followed by markers, toilet paper, paper clips, folders, rolls of calculator paper, and discs. Thousands of dollars of supplies ended up leaving the office with Stephan. When one of his friends questioned his actions, he said he was totally justified in taking the stuff because he should have gotten that position. He got defensive with his friend and said, "If it were you, you would have done the same thing." His friend replied, "Stephan, I would not. I don't care how you choose to justify or rationalize it, stealing is stealing."

Does this type of behavior sound familiar to you? Have you ever found yourself in a similar situation? Maybe you did not steal, but found yourself rationalizing some other action. If so, how did you rationalize your behavior? This story about Stephan illustrates a common way we justify and rationalize our actions. As Warriors we must always watch for this kind of behavior and do our best to nip it in the bud.

A Shopping Obsession

Sally and John had been married for one year. During that time it became apparent to John that Sally had a shopping habit that she had never revealed to him. When John approached Sally about her credit-card bills, she said she did not understand what was wrong; she had always spent that much on clothes. John suggested that allocating such an extreme amount of their income to her shopping habit did not fit into their joint financial saving plan, and that if they wanted to retire in 15 years she had to cut down. Finally she said okay.

But Sally kept shopping. Whenever John would question her about it, she had an excuse. She explained, "Honey, that shirt was on sale. How can you expect me to pass up that kind of discount?" John pointed out that it didn't matter if it was on sale or not, she didn't need it. This bickering went on for another six months until Sally changed her strategy to "If you loved me you would let me enjoy myself" and "How dare you tell me what to do and try to run my life! All of my friends' husbands let them shop!" John tried his best to refute her argument, but Sally had already decided that their issues were all about her husband, his stinginess, his self-centeredness, and his lack of love for her. No matter what he said, she had the perfect rationalization and justification for her behavior.

> **" "** **Impeccable Words**
>
> "We are so clothed in rationalization and dissemblance that we can recognize but dimly the deep primal impulses that motivate us."
>
> —James Ramsey Ullman

Up in Smoke

Jennifer and Nora were partners for five years, and both of them were smokers. When Nora started developing problems with her lungs, they both became frightened and made a pact to stop smoking. It seemed that they were doing really well, until Jennifer noticed that Nora had a pack of cigarettes in her purse. She was upset because she had quit for Nora, yet Nora was the one with the lung condition who was smoking against doctor's orders. When confronted by Jennifer, Nora said, "I'm only having one or two cigarettes a day. Not enough to cause any problems. I feel great." Jennifer replied, "Nora, it doesn't matter if you have only half a cigarette a day, it still isn't quitting. The doctor told you specifically you could not smoke anymore or you could end up with emphysema like your aunt. I was there with you, so you can't lie about what he said."

"Oh, Jennifer," Nora said. "You're so dramatic. How does the doctor know how I'm feeling? I'm fine, and if you hadn't seen those cigarettes in my bag, you would have never known I was smoking. Besides, what gives you the right to go into my bag? I think you just don't trust that I'm mature enough to take care of myself. How dare you treat me like that?"

Jennifer was shocked that Nora could take her concern for her and twist it around into making *her* the demon! She was surprised by the level of denial of her health condition and by Nora's willingness to blame something she was doing on her partner.

We can see how someone in each of these stories was in complete denial of what he or she was doing. In addition, these folks indulged in all kinds of rationalizations and justifications for their behavior and were defensive in the face of the truth. None of these people took responsibility for the drama they were creating or their actions.

Knowing this, consider the following:

- ◆ Can you give three examples of situations where you blamed, rationalized, or justified your actions?

- ◆ How did you turn around what you were doing and put it onto someone else?

- ◆ Are you able to see how many times you have actually created the drama in your life (as opposed to the drama already being present around you)? And can you see how ignorance is not bliss?

- ◆ Will reading this inspire you to take more responsibility for the life you're creating for yourself? In what ways?

Being Offended Is Just a Choice

If we frequently take things personally and blame what's happening in our lives on others, we'll live in a state of being offended. In the preceding stories, can you see how each of the people indulged in feeling offended by another person or situation?

Being offended or angry is not something that happens of its own accord. We have to decide to feel that way. When we were little, we got upset when we didn't get what we wanted, but we forgot about it right away. Then our parents taught us the art of taking things personally and getting offended. No use blaming them for their nonawareness! What is important is to take our newfound awareness of this process and stop this behavior before it happens. Let's look at two situations that illustrate these concepts.

> **Warrior Wisdom**
>
> We have been trained to enjoy the angry emotions that we generate when we are offended. It's like being addicted to the chemicals that rush through our bloodstream when we are upset. Warriors work at breaking the addiction to those angry emotions and start becoming addicted to joy.

Don't Tell Me What to Do!

I met Kathy on a spiritual journey to Guatemala some five years ago. She was a very angry and resentful woman whose family was always against her, or so it seemed from her point of view. As a result she was a needy person, feeling that everyone owed her, always victimizing herself to prove her own beliefs to be true. Kathy always pictured herself as the black sheep of her family, never seeing that her agreements about her family were causing so much of the conflict in her personal relationships.

On this trip we specifically advised the women to avoid taking baths, because the water was not safe. She had a "don't tell me what to do" attitude that was a reflection of her anger, rebellion, and resentment. Sure enough, she ended up very ill, with a high fever, vomiting, and diarrhea. Because of her illness, she was unable to participate in the journey for three days until she recovered. Rather than taking responsibility for not following instructions, she got furious and blamed what happened on the group leaders.

Kathy went into denial and spent the rest of the trip offended by the horrible injustice dealt to her. She was rude to the group leaders and to everyone on the trip. She never apologized for her behavior and left the journey further convinced that what she believed about life and people was true. When asked by friends how the trip was, she said it stunk, the leadership was terrible, she learned nothing, and *they* made her get sick by taking her to a place that was unhealthy. Kathy got to be comfortable feeling offended, spending most of her life in that state of being, never realizing that *she* was the one choosing to feel that way.

Do unto Others?

Loretta was a woman whom I met on a spiritual journey to Central America many years ago. Now, Loretta came on this trip not to improve herself, but because her friend Laura was joining us and she wanted to know what was making Laura so happy. I suspect that she was jealous of Laura's happiness and wanted to find a way to stop Laura's joy; she did not want to be alone in her misery.

From the very beginning of the trip, Loretta commented on how everyone on the journey had issues except for her. Loretta had judgments about everyone and everything, and constantly let all of us know that she didn't need to work on herself like *we* did. Laura, meanwhile, was having a great time making new friends whom she started to spend more and more time with. Loretta began to feel slighted by Laura's enjoyment and told her that she was being rude by ignoring her. Laura told Loretta there was no reason why she had to hang out with her all the time or baby-sit her. She reminded Loretta that she came on the trip for her own personal growth, and that she had never asked Loretta to come.

Loretta became furious, telling Laura that she spent a lot of money to be with her. She said she had come along to make sure Laura would be okay, and that if Laura weren't so self-centered she would be able to see what a good friend Loretta was. Laura, in turn, told Loretta that she was not being truthful, that she only came along because she wanted to see why she didn't need Loretta the way she used to. Upon hearing this, Loretta stormed out of the room.

When we arrived in one of the big cities, we were instructed by our tour guide not to travel the streets alone, especially at night. But that night Loretta had the fight with Laura, and in her anger, she disobeyed the instructions by going out at night by herself.

> **Warrior Warnings**
>
> It is rare that we do something for another person without hope of reward or payback at some time, or even the desire to feel good inside. The ultimate way of giving is with complete detachment and total compassion for the other person. Only then are you not being selfish, and your actions are truly for them.

She ended up being robbed at knifepoint. Thankfully, she managed to get back to the hotel, shaken but unhurt. Loretta turned all of her anger, resentment, and wrath upon Laura. She placed all the blame on Laura and took no responsibility for what happened and what she created. She was happy to fall back into her lifetime pattern of being offended by everyone and everything.

Drying Up Denial

In the stories in this section, we can see how Kathy and Loretta created the perfect situations to fulfill their behavior patterns and confirm what they believed about people and the world. Denial is a powerful thing, isn't it?

- Can you see how each of the people in these illustrations chose to be offended, and how they created the perfect scenarios to do so? Take the time to remember three situations when you did something similar.

- Can you see why each of these people did what they did? Are you able to see what possessed you to take the actions that you did?

- Can you see how addressing your denial would give you the power to change your life? How so?

Your Control Is an Illusion

The last part of this process is understanding that we do not have control over what is happening outside of ourselves. I know this might sound like it contradicts what I said about us co-creating our reality all the time, but it does not. Each person has free will and is contributing his or her part of the kaleidoscope of creation. We are only responsible for our side of the creation, our actions and reactions. Everyone else is responsible for the same. We know that we can only change our side, our beliefs, and our agreements about the way we see life.

CAUTION

Warrior Warnings _____

Have you ever looked into a kaleidoscope? Each time you turn the dial, all the pieces inside move simultaneously in their own way to contribute to a new and beautiful reality. It is the same in life. In each moment, every sentient being takes an action and the reality changes. How can you possibly be in control of the actions of those other beings as life is moving through them?

How Control Hurts Us

As humans, we like being in control. We get scared when things are not the way we want them to be. The gap between what is and the way we wish things were is responsible for our misery and disappointment. Rarely do things turn out exactly the way we want them to be in life, and yet, we still do our best to assert our control over people and situations. This act of assertion causes conflict between people, disagreements, and friction. No one wants to be bossed around, manipulated, or told what to do. We can always ask to get what we think we need, but we cannot force people to comply. Besides, the universe may have better plans for us, plans that we are fighting, which are trying to manifest through the actions of another person!

In each of the situations we talked about in this chapter, the only thing these people had control over was the way they chose to see their reality, and how they chose to react to it. This is very powerful! As humans we are always trying to control what is outside of us, giving our personal power away in the process. That power would be better directed inwardly to give us the strength to change what we can, and not to try to change what we cannot. It is a Warrior's task to change our own behavior patterns and to look for those hidden agreements that drive us to take selfish and self-centered actions.

Fighting Our Resistance

The key to not getting into the types of situations we described in this chapter is to become as aware as possible of what you are doing (doings yet again!). As soon as you notice friction between what you want and what is, pay attention to what you're feeling and what your mind is telling you. Life can be effortless, and that means without friction.

This quote by Chuang Tzu asks us to stop fighting life and stop listening to the mind when it tells us things that are not truth. Acceptance and surrender to what *is* will make our lives easy and delightful, no matter what is happening. This is the ultimate way of living, going through life without conflict, friction, arguments, and frustrations.

Impeccable Words

"Flow with whatever is happening and let your mind be free. Stay centered by accepting whatever you are doing. This is the ultimate."

—Chuang Tzu

Now I am going to share with you one of the most important tools you can have to increase the level of your awareness: If you *feel* resistance in your body to anyone or any situation, pay attention to your body and emotions (we will learn more about emotions in Chapter 18). Resistance is the rebellion of the mind and the belief system to the flow of life as it is. The only conflict that exists in life is within your own mind. There is no resistance outside of you. All living beings submit to life. Only humans engage in denial, blame, rationalizations, and justifications, and the end result of those actions is resistance. The reason I called this chapter "Resistance Is Not Futile" is because your resistance keeps you locked into your self-sabotaging patterns. And that is not futile from the point of view of the mind. Your resistance keeps you right where it wants you to be: unhappy. Focus on your resistance and you can transcend anything!

Based on this information, ask yourself the following:

♦ What situation are you in now that you are trying to make into something else, or that you are fighting? Is your control getting you anywhere?

♦ What would happen if you changed your point of view about it and stopped trying to control it? Would it be that terrible?

♦ What would happen if you had the serenity to know what you could change and the wisdom to know what you could not?

The Least You Need to Know

♦ By being aware of our tendency to go into denial, we can focus our attention on all of our unhealthy behavior patterns.

♦ There is nothing to defend in life, no rationalizations or justifications that we need to make to anyone once we have clarity about our actions.

♦ Once we understand that we have been taught to be offended, we can stop that behavior as we witness it within ourselves.

♦ Concentrating on taking control of the way we choose to react to life will have us using our personal power in the most uplifting and useful way.

15

Personal Power in Action

In This Chapter

- ◆ Understanding our relationship with energy and personal power
- ◆ Giving away personal power and energy through nonawareness
- ◆ Making serious changes in our lives by obtaining more personal power
- ◆ Resisting the temptation to abuse power

When we want to make changes in our lives, we usually have the best of intentions to follow through on them. But the way we have been trained to interface with our life puts us in an energy deficit almost every day. Under these circumstances, it's a miracle that we end up with enough extra energy to do anything other than deal with the drama of our normal lives. Warriors know that everything we do in life is based on our personal power and energy, so it's important that we have a solid understanding of what it is.

There are all kinds of mysterious writings about personal power. Most of it ends up sounding like a lot of voodoo and witchcraft. But truly, personal power is a very practical issue, and that is how we are going to approach the subject here. In this chapter we discuss personal power, what it is, how we give it away willingly, and how we can get it back.

Once we have more clarity about personal power, I think that we will be less tempted to give it away under any circumstances.

The Truth About Personal Power

Everything in this universe is *energy*. As you may remember from your high school science class, energy can never be lost within the closed system of our universe.

> **Toltec Topography**
>
> **Energy** is our ability to do work (physical or mental effort or activity). We cannot see it, taste it, or touch it, but we can clearly feel the results of it in our bodies. Energy can neither be created nor destroyed. It can only be converted or transformed from one form to another.

Although the totality of energy remains constant, the balance of it can shift in any direction. Humans are also energy; remember when we spoke about how the Toltecs *saw* that people were luminous eggs (Chapter 3)? As humans we have been gifted by Spirit with a certain amount of energy that we have available to us each day. How we use this allotment in life determines whether we use all that we have and go into deficit, or are thrifty and create a savings account. Warriors understand how important it is to not deplete one's energy supply, as everything we do depends on how much energy we have available.

The Particulars of Power

Toltec Warriors are interested in how we use energy because they are most concerned with *power* (the result of energy transformed over time). There is power in the universe at large and personal power as it relates to human life. From now on, when I speak of power, unless I specify otherwise, I mean power as it relates to us personally. (It is also important to know that we have the ability to store energy. This is known as potential power, which we can use at any time as needed.)

> **Toltec Topography**
>
> **Power,** for you physics addicts, is defined as $p = w/t$, where w = work and t = time. You may also remember that work equals force times distance. For those of us who are physics-challenged, here is an easier way to word this: power is energy transformed over time.

The reason we are so concerned with power is because we need it to create the dream of our life, to shift levels of awareness, and to align with Intent (the force that life uses to manifest creation). We also need power to break from our fear-based agreements and to make changes in life. We know that when we feel exhausted and drained, it is unlikely that we are going to attempt any major life changes. But if we had more energy and power, we would feel like we could accomplish anything!

Forms of Power

So, as we can see, energy and power are intricately linked. The key is to learn to use our energy and personal power as carefully and as wisely as possible. Power can come in many forms; for example, money is power. As we all know, when we have money, we have the means to accomplish many things. Other objects can also represent power, such as a diamond, which has monetary value. This is one reason why Toltecs spend their money wisely, as they do not want to waste this form of personal power.

Another form of power is wisdom. We use our life force and energy learning and experiencing life. The wisdom we gain through our hard work can be translated into power: we can use that wisdom in many ways in our life—for example, to uplift others, or to manipulate others with evil Intent.

One's position in life also holds power, as there is potential to do many things as a result. For example, Donald Trump is a powerful man because of his position, holdings, and money.

Power-Efficient Lives

Power can be wasted. A car uses gas to run the engine, but not all the gas is converted into the acceleration of the car. A large amount of power is wasted in friction, heat, and exhaust. A Warrior does his best to make sure that whatever energy and power he possesses is converted as efficiently as possible. This is why he would never get involved in an argument with another person, because the friction involved would drain his power, which could be better used for something else.

Toltecs are very energy-thrifty people, because they know if they want their freedom and a happy, centered, and peaceful life, it's going to take all their power to create that. After all, we have a lot of habitual behavior patterns to break, and we would be hard-pressed to accomplish that task without energy.

Another way we drain our power is by investing it in our belief system and concepts. When we defend our belief system to others, or when we get involved in denial, justifications, and rationalizations, we waste our energy. I know that we do not want to fight with our beloved or our parents, but we may be doing it anyway. If we want to stop this pattern, why can't we? Simple. We can't break the habit or addiction to drama without more personal power, and our power is tied up in maintaining what we already believe!

Another way of looking at this would be to say that our faith is invested in our programmed beliefs, concepts, and point of view about ourselves and life. If our faith is invested in this direction, we drain all of our personal power in maintaining the structure of our minds' programming. But if we truly see that what we believe is not absolute truth, then we can detach from those beliefs and put our faith in our Spirit, or Nagual, rather than in the mind and our Tonal. If you no longer have anything to defend, then you are free to use your faith to believe in yourself and whatever your heart directs you to create. The choice here is whether you are going to invest your energy and personal power in your limiting beliefs or in your infinite Spirit.

> **Impeccable Words**
>
> "It doesn't matter how one was brought up. What determines the way one does anything is personal power. A man is only the sum of his personal power, and that sum determines how he lives and how he dies."
>
> —Carlos Castaneda, *Journey to Ixtlan* (as quoted in *The Wheel of Time*)

> **Impeccable Words**
>
> "Our personal power is dissipated by all the agreements we have created, and the result is that we feel powerless. We have just enough power to survive each day, because most of it is used to keep the agreements that trap us in the dream of the planet. How can we change the entire dream of our life when we have no power to change even the smallest agreement?"
>
> —don Miguel Ruiz, *The Four Agreements*

Giving Away Your Personal Power

So now that we've started talking about how we give away our personal power, let's get a little more specific. If we can clearly define all the ways in which we give away our power, we can plug up those leaks and start saving the energy to make the changes we're so excited about.

One of the most common ways we drain ourselves is by letting others upset us. We talked about how Warriors do not take anything personally (in Chapter 10) and how they aren't offended by others or victimized by themselves (Chapter 14). Now that you have a better understanding of power, you can see why this is so critical. When someone says something that we take offense to, what is really happening is that one of our beliefs is getting tweaked, right? Then we react emotionally to what we are hearing by getting upset. Our anger is draining us of energy that is better used to address the belief that got us upset in the first place, rather than in arguing with that other person.

Draining Agreements

Let's look at a practical example of this in action.

Al has been working on a project at work for two months now. He put his heart into this presentation and feels really good about what he has created. On the day that he makes his presentation, his boss tells him that his work lacks the quality and depth of imagination that he is looking for. Al manages to hold his tongue in front of his boss, but afterward he is seething. He calls his wife, screeching about how hard he worked on the project and what an ingrate his boss is. He is so upset at how much time he wasted, how he is not appreciated or valued, and how his boss made him feel worthless.

What we can see here is that it is not Al's boss who has made him angry, but instead what Al believes about what just transpired. Rather than using his personal power to rage for days about the perceived injustice about this situation, it would be better to put his energy into breaking his beliefs. What beliefs could he change? The ones that are making him upset!

♦ Al believes that he is not appreciated or valued. This is a lie. His boss felt that the *project* did not meet his needs. This is not personal; it is business. His boss never said he was not valued, just that he did not get what he wanted and that his expectations as a boss were not met. The fact that the *project* was not useful does not mean that *Al* is not useful.

♦ Al believes that he wasted his time, which is another lie. You cannot waste time, you can only experience time and learn in life. There are no guarantees regarding anything we do, and just because something does not go our way doesn't mean that we should judge that time as wasted. That is a victim's point of view, a creative strategy that Al's mind is using to make him feel bad.

♦ Al believes his boss made him feel useless. This is not truth, either. Al has linked his self-worth and self-esteem to what others feel about him. No one has the power to make Al feel bad except himself. Just because his project was not accepted does not mean Al is not a worthy person.

If Al used his personal power to get rid of those lies or fear-based beliefs, he would not have to drain himself emotionally for days. All of us have been in situations like this, where we make what has happened all about the other person rather than taking responsibility for what we have created with our agreements.

Circular Thinking

Another way we drain our personal power is by thinking too much and then questioning our decisions. We know when we have to make an important decision; we may mull over it and agonize over it for days. We've discussed this concept before, but I just wanted to include this as a reminder of how our power is drained in this way. Rather than getting caught wasting energy in circular thought, take that energy and put it into getting clarity on the conflicting beliefs that are causing this type of thinking in the first place. Let's not feed the judge our personal power! Let's make a choice, be done with it, and live in peace.

Power Donations

Giving away our power to others is another way we drain ourselves of energy. When we abdicate control over our lives to others, let others make choices for us, or allow them to act on our behalf, we are doing just that. For example, we may have a husband who makes all the choices in the household. In this case we would be abdicating our power to him, especially if he makes choices that go against what is best for us. When someone tells us that we are not good enough to accomplish our goals, and we believe him, then we give him our power. When we feel afraid to do something and we get someone else to do it for us, we give that person our power. When we submit ourselves physically to others when we really do not want to, we give them our power. If we want to say "no" in a situation and instead we say "yes" out of fear, we are again giving away our power.

I am sure we have a good idea now of how easy it is to drain our power without even realizing it. With awareness we can keep an eye out for power leaks, and repair them right away.

Obtaining More Personal Power

So now that we know how we lose our power, let's spend some time looking at how we can get our power back and obtain more energy.

The more energy we possess, the more power we have to change the things that are not working for us, along with those feisty behavior patterns. One of the most obvious ways of obtaining more power is by not wasting it in the first place! We spoke about how we drain our power by arguing with others, defending our points of view, and engaging in emotional outbursts. This is by far the number-one way we waste our energy. If we can get a grip on this power drain, we will increase our power considerably.

Each belief that we have in the mind's programming requires energy to maintain its position there. Every time we make the effort to say "I refuse to support this belief that is causing me pain," we free up some energy. If Al, for example, gives up his beliefs about being underappreciated, about having wasted his time on this project, and about his boss's motivations, he will free up an enormous amount of energy. He will also save energy by not getting emotional and not having to defend his point of view, especially since those beliefs are not even truth.

We also free up energy when we break the agreements we have made in our childhood that are the cause of all those unhealthy behavior patterns. We will be talking more about that in Part 5.

> **Warrior Warnings**
>
> One of the mind's best strategies for keeping our life exactly as is, is to make sure that we drain all our personal power by the end of each day. That way we'll have no energy to change anything even if we want to. Let's remember this when we're tempted to argue with someone.

A Battle for Power

Every time we face a challenge in our life and move through it with grace and ease, we gain personal power. Remember when we said that a Warrior looks at everything that happens in her life as a challenge (Chapter 9)? Now we can expand on that to say that each and every challenge is a battle for power, and that with each challenge, we either win or lose power. I'm not talking about whether the situation works out to our liking or not, but about whether we have drained our energy in the challenge.

For example, let's say a loved one becomes very ill. We could spend all our energy worrying, getting angry at the doctors or our spouse, and being frustrated with Spirit for giving us this challenge. If we do, this situation will suck us dry energetically. On the other hand, we could face the challenge with an open heart, with calmness, and with the understanding that this is just a challenge and not a personal assault on us by life or Spirit. In this way, we will grow from the experience and gain wisdom (power). In addition, since we will not become emotional due to our fear-based beliefs, we will not drain the power we already have.

If we can take a Warrior's stance and face life's challenges with detachment and clarity, we will automatically be calm and not drain ourselves emotionally. That will enable us to move through what is happening with less effort. This is a powerful tool, and if we can put it into practice, our personal power will grow considerably.

Tone Your Tonal

Another way to boost our power supply is by maintaining a healthy Tonal by taking good care of our physical body and general living circumstances. It's important to eat in a healthy way, exercise, stop drinking or partying too much, and watch the number of hours we work. All of these things affect the condition of the Tonal. When our body's energy is drained, we must deploy power needed to make any changes in life into maintaining our physical being. We only have so much energy each day, so getting proper sleep to rejuvenate ourselves is important. We can work really hard on our mind and behavior patterns, but if the body is a mess, we will have no balance in the trinity of the body, mind, and Spirit. This is a holistic process, and sometimes we have a tendency to focus in one direction to the exclusion of others.

> **Warrior Warnings**
>
> In the martial arts, students know that the condition of the physical body is very important for success on one's spiritual path. That is why this mind, body, Spirit training is such a large part of all Warrior traditions.

Our Powerful Planet

We can also obtain energy and power from our mother earth. Since all creation is part of the one life, we can use the energy from the earth to help us break our agreements and beliefs. When we go on our spiritual journeys, or *power journeys*, we address our inner issues in places that are energetically powerful. (More about this in Chapter 23.) Through ceremony and ritual we can connect with mother earth and make use of her energy. I have had some of my most powerful experiences while I was away on these journeys, and I am in debt to the earth for her kind assistance in my process.

> **Toltec Topography**
>
> A **Power Journey** is when we travel to avail ourselves of the energy that our mother earth holds, for the specific purpose of enhancing our process of personal growth and enlightenment.

There are places all over the world that have been built by humans with the specific Intent to help facilitate the evolution of enlightenment. In many places it is said that the earth herself instructed the humans on what to build and how to build it. Of course, Teotihuacán is one of those places, but so are Macchu Picchu in Peru, Angkor Wat in Cambodia, and

Taktsang in Bhutan. There are so many that I could never write them all down here. These are powerful and mystical places where space between realities is thin, and magic can happen at any time. But even if we can't journey to these powerful places, we can take advantage of the earth's energy in our own area simply by spending some time in nature—even if it's in our own backyard.

Every time we have a shift of awareness, as on a power journey, or we make a major change in our process of personal growth, we gain wisdom, and therefore power. This is a slow and steady buildup of power that will always be with us and is hard earned. Wisdom born of experience on the Warrior's path is an excellent way to boost power. Each time we gain more wisdom it helps us get to the next plateau, which leads to the next boost. It is a self-perpetuating and healthy way to gain power.

> **CAUTION**
>
> **Warrior Warnings**
>
> Obtaining more power by taking others' power is an absolute no-no. This is considered an abuse of power, which we will talk about in the next section. It is important for us to do our work step by step and advance by our own hard work and determination. This is not about taking what is not ours, or trying to take shortcuts where none really exist.

Abusing Power and Other Temptations

There comes a point on every Warrior's path where he must make some important choices. With greater awareness comes greater responsibility. As we have a better understanding of how our own mind works, we also have a better understanding of how other minds work. With this knowledge comes the ability to manipulate the awareness of others and use one's knowledge for personal gain rather than for the happiness of humanity. In the end, nothing good can come out of this type of behavior, as it certainly doesn't promote love and the uplifting of those around us.

Manipulating Awareness

When they are not aware, people can be susceptible to the whims of others. They are easily swayed by the opinions and points of view of those with more personal power. All we have to do is look at human history to see that this is so. How did millions of people become swayed to participate in the mass extermination of people in World War II? Or how was it possible to get thousands to participate in bringing millions of

Africans to the United States for the slave trade? Simply appeal to people's fears and desires, and it is possible to get them to do anything. Adolph Hitler, a master of manipulation, understood this when he said, "The broad masses of a population are more amenable to the appeal of rhetoric than to any other force."

A person who is totally aware cannot be manipulated under any circumstances, but she can manipulate others. So for the Toltecs it became necessary to present these teachings in such a way that the teachings would not be abused. How could they get their apprentices to detach from the wants and needs of their egos before they had enough personal power and awareness to misuse them?

In my lineage, we work hard with our apprentices so they can see that they are not their mind or their beliefs, but instead are the Infinite within them. We teach them to slowly detach from their mind so that they do not act from an egocentric place of self-gain. In the end they let go of everything they believe about themselves, their resentments and anger, and their fear-based beliefs. We call this "losing the human form." Once this happens they have no desire to harm anyone or to manipulate others; these kinds of behaviors are meaningless for them. Their personal power is very strong, but they use it only in service of the higher good of humanity. (More about this in Chapter 22.)

Transcending Temptation

Attaining this level of awareness is exciting for us, but it takes years of letting go of our attachment to the mind and its agreements. It is definitely worth it, and although we are an "I want it now" kind of society, as Warriors we learn patience, and we understand that the process will simply take however long it takes. Be cautious when searching for a teacher; make sure that they are not operating from the place of egotistical mind. If a teacher asks an apprentice to give him his power, or promises the apprentice his freedom, this is not acceptable or even possible. (We'll talk more about teachers in Chapter 23.)

Once we've reached a place of detaching from our mind and ego, the only thing we desire is to be happy, to channel the Infinite through us, and to be in service to life. But before that happens, every Warrior must be on guard at all times for the temptation to use one's knowledge for personal gain and benefit. Every human is a divine entity, but we all have minds that contain corrupted beliefs and concepts. And until those are all addressed, we (the personality-ego) cannot be trusted. The ability of humans to behave in evil ways is simply the reflection of the amount of corruption in our programming and our ability to justify evil actions (the result of believing in lies). I have faith that the force of the Infinite within all of us will eventually compel us to transcend our minds and find the totality of ourselves and our freedom.

Here are some questions to ponder:

- Can you think of some beliefs that have been draining your energy?

- Can you identify some behaviors that are sucking you dry?

- Do you see any ways that you have been giving away your power to others?

The Least You Need to Know

- Everything in the universe is energy. Power is simply the result of energy being transformed over time.

- We give away our personal power by supporting our fear-based beliefs and agreements, our unhealthy behavior patterns, our emotional reactions, our circular thinking, and our tendency to abdicate control of our lives to others.

- We can obtain more personal power in life by maintaining a healthy Tonal, by breaking with unhealthy beliefs, agreements, and behavior patterns, and by facing our challenges like a Warrior.

- Personal power and energy can be gained from our mother earth.

- As long as we are still in our ego-mind, we must be careful to avoid the temptation to abuse power for our personal gain or to hurt others.

Part **5**

Mastery of Transformation

We've spent a lot of time working on Mastery of Awareness, and at this point we will focus on Mastery of Transformation. Now that we have the awareness about what we would like to change in our lives, we will learn how to transcend the patterns and beliefs that are limiting our full expression in life. I love taking action, and Part 5 of this book is all about shaking things up and breaking routines. In these four chapters, we focus on the Toltec technique of Stalking, which consists of a wonderful set of practices and tools we can use for evaluating our fear-based agreements, beliefs, and doings.

Chapter 16

The Art of Stalking

In This Chapter

♦ Hunting for the aspects of our minds that are not serving our happiness

♦ Learning the steps to a clear understanding of Stalking

♦ Applying the techniques of Stalking to the minds of others

♦ Five elements, four moods, seven principles, and six results

Stalking and Dreaming are the two keystones of the Toltec tradition. By using both techniques we can free ourselves from the mind and its fear-based beliefs and agreements. We cover Dreaming in Chapter 21, as it is better aligned with our discussion of Mastery of Intent. We will explore Stalking now, as it is the definitive tool for learning Mastery of Awareness and Transformation.

The most important suggestion I can make about Stalking is to have fun with it! This process enables us to learn about many hidden aspects of ourselves. If we can enjoy this process, our path will be easy; but if we take ourselves and our doings too seriously and with judgment, it will make the process more difficult and painful. In this chapter I out-line the basics of Stalking and everything we need to know to begin to incorporate this practice into our lives.

Hunting the Mind with the Mind

A Warrior is an excellent hunter. His many qualities resemble a cat's: patience, discipline, focus, detachment, readiness, presence, and watchfulness. The Toltecs had enormous admiration for the large cats that roamed Mexico, such as the jaguar. They modeled the Warrior's attributes after this animal; we often see images of the jaguar at the pyramids and ruins throughout Central America. As a tribute to the amazing hunting skills of the jaguar, Toltecs called the process of hunting the mind with the mind *Stalking*.

> **Toltec Topography**
>
> **Stalking** is the process of hunting, following, and observing our habits, beliefs, and weaknesses for the purpose of transforming them into our strengths. A Warrior will Stalk her own mind to break her obsession with the rational mind, with thinking, and with the Tonal.

The Toltec term "Stalking" has nothing to do with the way we use this word in modern life. I wanted to make this clear, lest you think we Toltecs spend our time peeking into bedroom windows! Nope, what we enjoy peering into are our own minds so that we can have clarity and understanding of our programming.

The Unbiased Witness

In Chapter 13 we talked about the many strategies of the mind and how we can use the mind to observe the mind. I mentioned that the way to do this is to take the point of view of a *witness* who is impartial and without judgment. A jaguar, as an impeccable hunter, will Stalk his prey without opinion. In other words, a jaguar will not say to himself, "Oh, that rabbit sure is dumb." This is an important point to remember when we start Stalking our own minds. If we watch ourselves and get upset because we're finally seeing our unhealthy behavior or how our beliefs have hurt us, we won't be encouraged to go on. Instead, it will make the process of revelation upsetting.

> **Toltec Topography**
>
> A Toltec **witness** is one who can give a firsthand account of something seen, heard, or experienced. He sees exactly what is, without judgment or opinion.

It does us no good to call ourselves names, or to insult or condemn ourselves for our lack of awareness. This is why we Stalk like the cat, with absolute impartiality. When we are emotional, we have no clarity. If we become emotional as a result of our Stalking, we will not gain any wisdom from our observations. Instead of gaining power, we will be wasting our time and actually draining our personal power. (And we know from Chapter 15 how thrifty

Warriors are about personal power and energy!) It is imperative that we take the position of a neutral witness, someone who watches without opinion or point of view. I hope that we can now see how all of the concepts I shared earlier in the book are coming together in a comprehensive way.

Hunting Agreements and Beliefs

In Chapters 11, 13, 14, and 15, I shared stories of people looking at their fear-based beliefs and unhealthy behavior patterns. These were actually stories of people Stalking their own behaviors and what their minds were telling them. This is part of the Mastery of Transformation, which we will be focusing on over the course of Chapters 17, 18, and 19.

Stalking is the key to gaining clarity of our dream of the first attention (the Tonal), the dream we created as children when we learned to use our attention for the first time. Once we make a thorough *inventory* of our mind and the contents of our programming, we will have the opportunity to break down that structure of beliefs and rebuild a new dream, the dream of the second attention (Chapter 22). Then we will use our attention for the second time to create a masterpiece of life.

Toltec Topography

The **inventory** is the totality of the contents of the human mind: all its concepts, beliefs, judgments, agreements, points of view, and experiences.

An Internal Inventory

The inventory is an important part of Stalking. It's like a complete download of all our beliefs and agreements. Once we know what's in our minds, we can choose what's working for us and what's not. Then we can reprogram ourselves to behave calmly, with kindness, compassion, and love. We will not be driven to create life in ways that sabotage ourselves, or that set ourselves up to fail or to be hurt by others. This is because we will no longer be possessed by all those agreements we made when we were young, which have caused us to see the world in such a distorted way. Since we are only in control of what we do or think, it would be more accurate to say that this is mastery of our own mind, rather than the mind being the master of us! (Now *that's* a switch worth looking forward to.)

When a Warrior has taken a complete inventory of her mind, she is in a position to see the nontruth of her human concepts. Then she can make the choice to either continue to be attached to what she believes, investing her personal power in maintaining that illusionary structure, or she can detach from it and be free. In life we are always adding information to our inventory. The mind is a fragile entity, and in order to keep itself safe and intact it carefully chooses what to add to the inventory and what to ditch. If someone says something to us that does not match what we believe, we discard it. If the information fits into our inventory, we agree with it and download it into our program.

Impeccable Words

"Warriors, because they are stalkers, understand human behavior to perfection. They understand, for instance, that human beings are creatures of inventory. Knowing the ins and outs of a particular inventory is what makes a man a scholar or an expert in his field."

—Carlos Castaneda, *The Power of Silence* (as quoted in *The Wheel of Time*)

We have all had the experience of someone trying to put something into our inventory that we don't agree with. This immediately upsets us and we start defending our point of view and rejecting the other person's. Their information is shaking the foundation of our inventory, and that is frightening to the mind. To be free, a Warrior slowly and gently adds truth and love-based information to his inventory (which can be quite contrary to what is currently in his program). This acts as a "good" virus, transforming his programming and breaking his fixation on his mind without upsetting the mind too much. The key is to break the inventory gently. (We'll address this in Chapter 22.)

The Ten Steps of Stalking

Stalking is meant to be a practical way to observe and watch ourselves. I have created a basic outline of the process of Stalking to give you a birds-eye view of this unique method of personal inquiry. It essentially involves two levels of investigation containing five steps each. This should make it easy to follow in a linear and logical fashion. I have also made references as to which chapters discuss which steps, so that you can refer to any part of the book that you are specifically interested in. We will refer back to these 10 steps many times as we move through the next three chapters, and this outline will act as our guiding light.

Level One: See It, Hear It, Write It!

In level one, we Stalk what we are doing now (in our present-day lives) to see which actions we have been taking and why. This enables us to take responsibility for our unhealthy behavior patterns and to change them. But the Toltecs recognized that this isn't enough, as it only constitutes behavior modification. This doesn't enable us to get to the root of our behavior patterns, where our personal power is locked up in maintaining our fear-based beliefs and programming. The second level of Stalking, then, involves taking what we are doing now into the past to determine the cause(s) of our programmed reactions and self-sabotaging behaviors. So let's start!

Step 1.   In the first step of Stalking, **we watch ourselves with absolute objectivity, observing how people behave in our presence and how they react to our actions.** (Remember doings from Chapter 7 and the examples I gave in Chapters 13 and 14? There is more to come in Chapter 17!) We then journal exactly what we see—not what we *think* we see, our assumptions about what we see, or what we would like to see!

Step 2.   The second step involves **creating an inventory, through journaling, of what we believe about what is happening to us, noting our judgments, opinions, and points of view.** We write down any justifications and rationalizations that we hear coming from the mind, as well as our internal dialogue (Chapters 6 and 14).

Step 3.   In the third step, **we examine our emotional reactions and journal what we believe about each of the emotions we have listed.** Our emotions are very important in this process, since they come from our integrity. We make a list of all the emotions we are experiencing in reference to any given situation. We then journal all the beliefs we can identify associated with each individual emotion (more on this in Chapter 18).

Step 4.   In step four **we look at everything we have journaled to date, and ask ourselves if our journaled beliefs reflect the truth.** Now is the time to take stock

CAUTION

Warrior Warnings

You may need an objective person to help you with figuring out what is truth. After all, you obviously think your beliefs are true or you wouldn't have adopted them in the first place!

of what we believe and the contents of our programming (we'll go deeper into what truth is in Chapter 18). Is what we believe about everything true, or are these just concepts that were downloaded into our program that we decided to adopt as valid?

Step 5. In the fifth step, **we acknowledge the truth of what is happening in our lives, and accept responsibility for our half of making it happen.** (I gave examples of accepting responsibility in most of the stories I have shared so far, plus there are more in Chapter 18.) Taking responsibility for half is an action that leads to change, resolution, and forgiveness.

Level Two: Recapitulate, Forgive, and Forget It!

Okay, now we are going to reach into our past, into the storage closet of our mind, and clean out all those unhealthy cobwebs. Let's get rid of all those old beliefs, resentments, and grudges and be happy and free.

Step 6. In step six, **we recapitulate our lives by going back in time and seeing where our beliefs and agreements originated from.** (We will be focusing on this in Chapter 18.) Without this part of the process, we would never understand why we do the things we do, and we would never truly understand ourselves as having a programmed mind.

Step 7. In step seven, **we release all of the expectations we have in life about everything and everyone** by detaching from our rigid points of view, making the choice to let go of those fear-based beliefs, agreements, and concepts. In doing this we let go of all of our "it should be this way" beliefs (more on this in Chapter 19). As a result, all the personal power we have invested in maintaining and supporting these beliefs will come back to us. Maintaining lies only drains our personal power and life energy.

Step 8. **We forgive and let go** in step 8. Without forgiveness we will not be able to let go of the past. To be free, it is necessary for us to hold no grudges, resentments, or dislike for anyone. Forgiveness is the actual process of letting go of these old harmful judgments. It involves not only forgiving others in your life but forgiving yourself, too (Chapter 19). This in turn is the way we heal our wounds and our hearts.

Step 9. In step 9, **we erase our personal history.** Once we have broken our fear-based beliefs and agreements, forgiven others, and let go of everything that is not serving us, we are on our way to a newly groomed island of the Tonal. Without a past history to hook us, we can live in the moment, not ruled by things that are not truth. (We will learn about this in Chapter 19.) When we accomplish this we can take action in life rather than being in a reactive state, because we are detached and have absolute clarity.

> **Warrior Wisdom**
>
> Warriors know that Stalking takes them from a place where the world revolves around them ("It's all about me") to a place where the world is impersonal ("Nothing is about me").

Step 10. **We become impersonal by totally detaching from the egotistical mind** in step 10. When a Warrior has totally detached from his past, he does not take anything personally. This is because he's finally able to see that nothing in life is personal or about him. He's no longer being tyrannized by the mind! Freedom and unconditional love, along with living one's life in bliss, are the results of all of the hard work contained in this 10-step process. (This process is also known as losing the human form—see Chapters 19 and 22.)

Having this outline should make it easier to follow the process of Stalking. You can also go back to some of the previous stories if you'd like to see the different steps of this process within each one.

Stalking in Here and out There

Stalking is a way to not only observe the mind, but also to observe our behaviors and the behaviors of others. Since everyone is a mirror for us to see our own behavior and habits reflected back to us (more on this in Chapter 17), it is useful to apply the Stalking principles to everyone we meet. We are going to go a little deeper within the doctrine of Stalking to investigate the ways that these techniques can be employed.

Calculated Control

Warriors saw that by systematically controlling their behavior they were able to accomplish a couple of things. First, they could uncover all the aspects of their own personalities and the masks that they presented to the world. Second, they found that by taking unusual actions and behaving in ways that were foreign to them (not-doings), they were able to move their assemblage points in subtle ways, therefore changing their points of view about life. The Toltecs realized that people were slaves to their personalities and that what prevented them from having an effortless life was their need to be "themselves" (which, in reality, was only a program).

> **Warrior Wisdom**
>
> When a Warrior is fluid and can be "no-thing" in any situation, she is no longer attached to personality. For the first time, a Warrior feels her integrity come out and take over her life, rather than her "self." Her integrity represents the divine aspect of herself that has been under wraps her whole life. And the integrity of the Infinite is very powerful.

We are in so many situations in life that require us to assess what is happening and then take an appropriate action. What sometimes prevents us from making good choices during these times is our need to approach new situations in the same way we have always dealt with similar situations in the past—even when those actions are not necessarily the best solution for the present-day dilemma. If we could be anything we wanted and morph ourself according to what was needed in any moment, we could address life on *its* terms and not on the terms of our domestication and programming. Once we stop seeing ourself as a "self" and instead see ourself as the "no-thing" of the Infinite (Chapter 11), this is easy to do.

Land Mines of the Mind

Once we become extremely adept at Stalking our own minds, it becomes easy to understand the minds of others. After all, we are fairly similar to each other in our domestication processes, our wounds, and our painful experiences. Once we comprehend these similarities, we can live our lives while having a better understanding of how to communicate with people and work with them to accomplish our common goals. Once we stop taking things personally, we can focus our attention outside of ourselves and be able to interact with people without pushing their buttons, because we are able to *see* those buttons. As a result, our lives become easier, because it is so simple to get along with others.

I like to imagine life as a video game where I must cross a minefield without being destroyed. In my game, the land mines represent people's buttons or wounds. When you are a good Stalker, you can see those land mines within people and avoid them. A great Stalker will never get into arguments with another person, because he sees where that person is coming from and how the other person's mind is working. The Warrior just steps around those mines.

I am sure you have had the experience of getting angry with a loved one and purposely saying something that you knew would upset her. When you choose not to get upset at people because of their words and actions, then you won't want to step on *their* land mines, either. Before studying the Toltec path, I was great at stepping on people's land mines, creating huge dramas and conflicts. Thankfully, for everyone's sake, I gave up that self-sabotaging addiction!

Tenets of Stalking

The tenets of Stalking include the principles of Stalking, the moods of a Stalker, the qualities that a Stalker must possess, and the results of Stalking. This information will form a foundation for the next three chapters.

Five Elements Useful for Stalking

I mentioned in Part 3 the qualities a Warrior possesses that make her successful in life. I can't imagine practicing Stalking without them. There are five specific elements that are extremely useful when practicing Stalking:

1. First, one must obtain *control*. As you can see, to be able to engage in actions different from what we normally would do, we need to be in control of ourselves.

2. Second, we need to have *discipline*. Stalking as a discipline is a self-imposed training that Warriors use to produce specific changes in their patterns of behavior, which leads to an expansion of possibilities in life.

3. Third, we utilize *forbearance*. Tolerance and restraint in the face of provocation is what we need to deal with petty tyrants (whom we will learn about in Chapter 17) or people whom we tend to take very personally.

4. *Timing* is the fourth quality. A Warrior always waits for the suitable or opportune moment to take whatever actions are necessary in life. He never allows himself to feel rushed or impatient, as timing is often critical to an outcome.

5. Engaging our *will* is number five. A Warrior's will is a reflection of her Intent, desire, purpose, and determination to manifest in this reality those things that will lead her to freedom.

Four Moods to Cultivate

Since Stalkers are in control of their behavior, they are aware of four moods that they can cultivate to accomplish anything in life. Do your best to imagine these four moods as something you could choose to experience in your daily life, a state of being within yourself that you purposely encourage.

1. The first mood is *ruthlessness*. We talked about this when we discussed the way a Warrior sees life in Chapter 10. In the context of Stalking it means that we have no pity for ourselves or others, which enables us to do what we need to do in life. But it never means that we are nasty or cruel to others.

2. The second mood is *patience*. As we just said, Warriors never feel hurried, and their timing is impeccable. Yet we will never find them procrastinating, negligent, or dawdling. They are always calm and collected, just waiting to do what they need to do.

> **Warrior Wisdom** ___
>
> When we combine these five elements and four moods, they create a shield to protect us in our battles for power and to move us through any situation in life with grace and ease. This shield protects us from the unknown we face on our path to freedom.

3. The third mood is *cunning*. A Warrior is given to the art of subtlety, which he executes with ingenuity, skill, and inventiveness. This is definitely not about being deceptive or manipulative.

4. The fourth mood of a Warrior is *sweetness*. We aim to have a pleasing disposition to move though life with. As we all know, we catch more flies in life with honey than with vinegar, and this applies in Stalking, too. It doesn't mean that a Warrior is silly, spacey, or foolish.

Seven Principles That Guide Us as Stalkers

These seven principles guide us in facing life as Stalkers and Warriors in the most impeccable way. By applying these seven rules to whatever we do (from the simplest situations to the most life-threatening), we can reach the six results of Stalking (which will be discussed in the next section of this chapter). Truly, this all boils down to common sense when we look at it closely.

1. A Warrior always chooses her battleground. *We* choose when and where to take on a particular challenge. It is always best to face challenges on our own turf if

we can. If we are going to engage in a discussion with our partner, for example, we will not be goaded into arguing; rather, we will discuss the issue when we are feeling calm, rested, and nonemotional.

2. Stalkers know that it is important to get rid of any unnecessary baggage in life. Carrying stuff around just weighs on us and slows us down. We need to let go of old possessions, relationships that are not serving us, beliefs that are not truth, resentments and grudges, and old agreements that no longer are serving us well.

3. A Warrior knows that every choice he makes could be his last. As a result, he stands by his decisions 100 percent. Once a decision is made, he lets go, detaches, and accepts the consequences of his choices. A Stalker will never mull over his choices for weeks on end or beat himself up about them *after* the fact.

4. Stalkers know that they must be calm, collected, and nonemotional to be able to make clear, concise choices. To do this, they are relaxed and totally present. They abandon themselves to the moment and live each minute to the fullest, never allowing fear to immobilize them.

5. No matter what the circumstances, a Warrior is always optimistic and confident. This is because he has total faith in himself and in his resources rather than in his programming. If he is unable to ascertain his next move, he retreats and relaxes, and lets what he needs to know come to him.

6. Stalkers use time to their advantage. When most people are stressed about something, they can't think clearly; as a result, they use time unwisely, and time appears to move quickly. Conversely, by being calm, collected, and in the moment, time expands as Stalkers need it to, and a moment can feel like an hour. As a result, they have the time to make their choices and accomplish what needs to be done.

7. On the battlefield, a Stalker will never put herself on the front line. She will do her best to arrange things so that she is working behind the scenes and has a team of people handling any matters that involve confrontation.

Anyone can apply these seven principles to his or her life and notice a change immediately. All of these steps result in a Warrior conserving a huge amount of energy. It is not necessary to make things complicated, as the seven principles are relatively easy to enact and practical to follow.

Six Results of Stalking

If a Warrior follows the seven principles, utilizes the four moods, and possesses the five elements, he will surely come to realize the six results of Stalking:

1. First and foremost, a Warrior gains faith in himself and his ability to do anything his heart directs him to create. By practicing Stalking, his faith is transferred from his mind and beliefs to his heart and his Nagual.

> **Toltec Topography**
>
> A **dream of heaven** for a Toltec does not refer to the religious concept of the place of reward in the afterlife. It means heaven on earth for a Warrior; a life of beauty, unconditional love, grace, self-acceptance, inner peace, and happiness.

2. The second result of Stalking is that a Warrior learns to stop the world and break her fixation on the first attention and the Tonal. Anything is possible at this point, and she begins to assemble the world of the second attention and her *dream of heaven*.

3. Third, a Warrior stops taking herself seriously or personally because she doesn't believe herself, and she has the capacity to laugh at herself with abandon. Her laughter comes from self-love and respect, not from self-deprecating humor.

4. Fourth, a Warrior attains patience, which enables him to be centered and at peace. He never needs to worry or feel like he is stressed or pressured.

5. The fifth result of Stalking is that a Warrior obtains the ability to improvise and be truly creative in life. Most humans can't do this because they can only execute the will of their programming, which is not original at all. True creation comes from the Infinite being channeled through us.

6. The sixth and last result is that a Warrior gains the capacity to enjoy life to the fullest, never disturbed by the normal ups and downs of the manifest world. She knows that she is a mystery in a most mysterious universe and embraces that knowledge. Fear no longer stops her, and she lives her life in bliss, gratitude, and unconditional love.

As we can see, it is worth the effort to be able to live our life in this way, enjoying life to the utmost, free and in love with life, but most of all with ourselves!

The Least You Need to Know

◆ Stalking constitutes the heart of Mastery of Awareness and Transformation.

◆ The practice of Stalking is used specifically to hunt all those beliefs and agreements that cause unhealthy repetitive behaviors and self-sabotaging actions in our lives.

◆ Stalking can be used to hunt beliefs in our own minds and also in the minds of others, so that we might have clarity and understanding in our human interactions.

◆ The tenets of Stalking give us guidelines for an impeccable way to conduct ourselves, leading us to freedom and happiness.

Chapter 17

Simple Tricks for Transformation

In This Chapter

- Not-doings as a way to see and change the behavior patterns in our life
- The Warrior's use of petty tyrants
- Death as an advisor
- Mirrors for us to see ourselves, our wounds, and our issues clearly

As we learned in Chapter 16, Stalking is a wonderful way to practice watching our own mind and the minds of others and our habitual behaviors. It can be entertaining to use these techniques to illuminate the actions we take that cause issues in our life.

In this chapter I share four excellent tools of Stalking that we can use to change our life. These are some of my favorites; I have personally used them to make a huge difference in my life, especially in my interpersonal relationships. Using not-doings, petty tyrants, death as an advisor, and the technique of mirroring will beef up your toolbox of tricks for transformation. These are practical exercises that anyone can do and even make into fun activities to share with friends.

Not-Doings Breaking Routines

Not-doings are my very favorite tool for identifying and eliminating limiting behavior patterns and beliefs. If you remember, in Chapter 7 we defined "doings" as activities we engage in that are directed by our mind's programming to create our world exactly as our mind wants it to be, confirming our fear-based agreements and beliefs. Since not-doings are unfamiliar acts to our "self" (the ego, personality, or program), they engage all of our attention so that we can see our "self" more clearly. It is a Warrior's challenge to see what the ego has been doing, because we are often blinded to our own programming. Not-doings are activities designed to put our doings in the spotlight and make them obvious to us, so that we can change them. Let's spend some time looking at some examples so we can feel comfortable with this technique.

Doing the Opposite

For every doing we have, there is a not-doing that we can create. For example, the not-doing of internal dialogue and thinking would be inner silence. Dreaming and engaging our second attention is the not-doing of being in the first attention. On a more practical note, public speaking would be a not-doing for shyness. Putting oneself into silence for a day would be the not-doing for a chatty Cathy. Calling up our sister whom we have not talked to in 10 years is a not-doing for our habits of holding resentments and grudges and exhibiting our self-importance and pride. Leaving dishes in the sink or not folding our underwear before putting them in our drawer is a not-doing for our obsessive-compulsive behaviors and routines.

Now that we have a general idea of what not-doings are all about, let's look at a specific example.

Doings Aren't Always Logical

When asked, Francine would always tell you that she was a natural, down-to-earth kind of girl. She would never wear makeup or anything flashy that might attract attention to herself. She would say that people who dress themselves up do so for show and aren't genuine. Her argument sounded logical enough, but as we know, programs always have ulterior motives and things are rarely what they seem.

Upon talking with Francine, I learned that when she was a teenager she had a best friend who was extremely stylish and pretty. Francine, meanwhile, had always been a little pudgy and had low self-esteem and self-worth compared to her pretty and outgoing friend. Well, this friend started dating the one boy Francine had a crush on. Francine was so angry and hurt by this that she made an agreement that girls like her supposed friend were fake and that she would never behave in a similar way. Instead of acknowledging her lack of self-esteem and self-worth, taking responsibility for her own fears, Francine focused her attention outwardly and blamed everything on her girlfriend. Her attachment to her logic in turn supported her hidden fear-based beliefs, which locked her into portraying herself in a way that was not really truth.

Warrior Warnings

Humans are great at justifying their actions and deeds with convincing logic. Don't be afraid to challenge your own logic. Just because it sounds good doesn't mean it's the truth. Always look for the hidden motivations behind your reason.

Undoing Those Doings

After Francine had chatted with me, she decided to address her issues and take responsibility for her agreements and behaviors. Her not-doings consisted of getting a fashionable haircut and meeting with a makeup artist. She also made major changes to her wardrobe. Francine was terribly uncomfortable at first and felt like she was trying to be something she was not. Perfect! This is exactly what this exercise is all about. We are not the "self" that we think we are (the one we've created according to the agreements we've made). Freedom means never having to be any way at all, never having to be our personality or what we believe about ourselves. Our personality and its rules limit our self-expression and our possibilities in life.

People started perceiving Francine differently just from these changes in her external appearance, and her life began to shift in surprising ways. She was able to forgive her girlfriend and break that agreement she had made as a teen. By addressing her self-esteem issues, she saw that she was a beautiful woman at size 14, just the way she was. There was no need to hide herself behind plain clothes because of her self-judgment, and she began to love herself in a way she never had before.

In the end, Francine realized that her not-doings weren't about dressing differently to please others or to look like a model, but instead about having the freedom to do whatever she wanted, without fear of judgment from others or from her own judge. She also saw that to be successful in the world, it's necessary to be able to be a fluid Warrior, with no fear and no self-imposed limitations.

Doing the Not-Doings

Have fun creating not-doings for yourself. If you have trouble thinking of what to do (or what *not* to do), engage some of your friends and do this as a group. I bet they will be able to find something you will feel uncomfortable doing! This is because they see aspects of you that you may not see in yourself. Remember, though, that if you're *really* uncomfortable doing something, then you're not ready yet. Have respect for yourself. Pick something that you feel uncomfortable doing, but not something that's going to make you feel sick. With each not-doing, you will free up personal power that will enable you to pick a more difficult not-doing next time.

Before engaging in a not-doing, make sure to identify the agreements and beliefs that created your doings in the first place. You'll forever free yourself from this behavior pattern, and you'll take your power back from having to maintain that part of your mind's programming.

> **Toltec Topography**
>
> A **petty tyrant** is a person who has the ability to drive us crazy, irritate us endlessly, get us frustrated, and drive us to distraction. They are the best tool for making us face our own self-importance and self-centeredness.

The Petty Tyrants in Our Lives

The Toltecs knew that the most difficult task on their path was giving up their self-importance and ego-centric point of view. Remember that self-importance is one of the enemies of a Warrior (Chapter 11)? Creating not-doings was one way to address this issue, but they discovered an even better, more effective way, using what they called *petty tyrants*.

Petty Tyrants as Tools

Simply put, a petty tyrant is someone who has the ability to irritate and annoy us to distraction. For example, our mother-in-law could be a petty tyrant in our life because she's family and we cannot get rid of her. We could allow her to annoy us until she dies, or we could get over ourselves, stop judging her and trying to make her wrong, and love her just the way she is.

A petty tyrant can also be someone who holds our very life in his or her hands. Imagine if we were in jail and we needed to kiss up to one of the guards just to survive. That person could mean the difference between our life and death, and it doesn't matter what we think of him, or what our judgment of that person is, or how much pride we have; we have to eat humble pie in order to survive in this person's presence.

Petty tyrants are tormentors, and usually end up in positions of power where they can flourish in their environment. They are great at pushing our buttons (more land mines), which is actually useful, because when this happens, we can examine our wounds. If we *can* argue with petty tyrants, we *will* argue with them, as they *really* get our self-importance and ego going. Petty tyrants will have us arguing to prove them wrong so that we can make ourselves right. But as a result, the beliefs and judgments that are causing us to drain our personal power will be clearly illuminated. All in all, believe it or not, they are blessings in our lives—at least from a Warrior's point of view (we love a challenge because we grow and learn)! The key is to recognize these people for what they are, and then to use them as part of our training to deal with our self-importance. Let's look at an example of this tool.

Petty Ty-rantings

Federico, or Cobra as his friends call him, currently works at the premier car-customizing shop owned by his father-in-law, Alberto. Although Cobra was not the best student back in school, he excelled in art and design classes. It was a miracle when he met Alma and married her, and her father offered him a job in his shop. He loved the opportunity to design the most outrageous car interiors and to use his creative abilities in such a cool way. Even better, Alma's dad wanted to retire in the next few years and was looking for someone to take over his business, his "baby." The only glitch was that Alberto was no average petty tyrant; he was the devil incarnate, at least from Cobra's point of view.

Alberto was constantly yelling at Cobra, telling him his work stunk, that he was lazy, and that he didn't follow instructions. Alberto would chastise Cobra in front of the other employees and say things like, "I can't believe my daughter married a bum like you," or "I'll never retire if I have to trust my business to you." Cobra, who had a tendency to lose his temper, loved his wife and his job very much; otherwise, he would have beat his father-in-law to a pulp and walked out. He wanted a better life for himself and Alma, and was willing to use this situation as an opportunity to address his own issues.

It took a lot of help from his wife to see that the issue was not with her father (even though he was a challenging man to deal with), but with Cobra's way of seeing the man. Cobra

Warrior Warnings

People who are unable to transcend the power of a petty tyrant sometimes end up becoming one themselves. Someone who was abused as a child, for example, may grow up to be an abuser as an adult.

realized that Alberto really did want to retire, but that the business was his creation and he wanted to make sure that Cobra was responsible enough to take it over. Cobra was taking Alberto's insults personally when they weren't personal at all. He saw that he was turning Alberto into his *own* father, when the truth was, the two men were not alike at all.

Transcending Our Tyrant

When Cobra was a teen his father left his mom. That never bothered him since his relationship with his dad was terrible. He hated his father for yelling and for hitting his mom, and for constantly telling him that he was stupid and would never amount to anything. Since Cobra was not the best student, he took his father's comments to heart, which wounded him inside. His anger and quick temper were a front for his lack of self-esteem and self-confidence.

He made the agreement that men like his dad were trash, and as soon as he met Alberto, he could only see him through the eyes of his beliefs and agreements. In turn, he projected what he believed about his father onto Alberto. Alberto, of course, didn't know that Cobra felt self-conscious about his poor grades, so when he insulted him it re-opened Cobra's old wounds.

Cobra and his wife designed a set of not-doings to change the way he acted in Alberto's presence. But first Cobra needed to forgive his own father and break his agreement that men like his dad and his father-in-law weren't worth respecting. He realized that his father had had deep physiological issues, and although hurting his mom was not appropriate behavior, Cobra could understand what had possessed him to behave that way. He had compassion for his dad's difficult life and let go of his anger toward his father. He saw that Alberto also had his own issues that made him rage the way he did, but that he wasn't a bad man, even though his behavior was not always appropriate, either.

Once Cobra could see his father-in-law's issues, he could use them to get him to have trust and appreciation for his work. He let go of his self-importance and his need to be right about everything with Alberto. He answered with "You are right, sir," and "I appreciate your comments, sir." He would say things to Alberto like "I'm so lucky to be working for you. I know you're working hard to train me to be the best manager I can be. I'll always be able to provide for your daughter and our children because of you." At first it made him sick to say these things, but later, when his self-importance started to decrease, he realized how much gratitude he had and actually started to mean what he said. As a result, Alberto started to change, too, and they developed a decent relationship.

Cobra also forgave himself for not getting good grades in school. He realized that not all kids are successful in the traditional classroom setting, especially if they are artistic. That didn't make him less than anyone else, unless *he* made it that way. He realized how easy it was to make life pleasant when he no longer had anything to defend or to prove.

Based on Cobra's story, consider the following:

◆ Who is the number-one petty tyrant in your life, and why?

◆ How does your self-importance and need to be right contribute to the friction in that relationship?

◆ In what ways do you purposely feed the fire in that relationship? In other words, how do you make the conflict worse?

◆ What actions could you design in the form of not-doings that would help shift the balance of power in the relationship?

Death as a Personal Advisor

One of the reasons that humans can be so self-centered and egotistical is because they function under the idea that they will live forever. But when we know that we only have a short time to live, every one of our acts are of the utmost importance and become absolutely impeccable. In general, people are cavalier about their actions because they believe that there's always tomorrow to change, fix, or repair their doings. The Toltecs knew this was not true, and decided to use this knowledge of death to help them address their self-importance issues. By seeing death as an angel who is always with us, watching us and waiting, we can constantly be reminded to be impeccable in our words and deeds.

> **Impeccable Words**
>
> "We say that the hour of death cannot be forecast, but when we say this, we imagine that hour as placed in an obscure and distant future. It never occurs to us that it has any connection with the day already begun or that death could arrive this same afternoon, this afternoon which is so certain and which has every hour filled in advance."
>
> —Marcel Proust

Savoring Life in the Face of Death

I see death as a little angel who sits on my shoulder and whispers in my ear, advising me what to do and what not to do. Death asks me, "If you knew you would be dead tomorrow, would you do what you are about to do?" This is an extremely powerful question to ask yourself. For example, if we're about to argue with our beloved, let's ask ourselves: What if she died in the night and we couldn't apologize to her? What if we said something we weren't able to take back or repair in the morning? Then it's best not to say it in the first place, right?

If we only had 24 more hours, would we use it fighting with people, gossiping, or talking about nonsense? I doubt it. We would probably make sure everything in our life was in order, and do whatever we could to enjoy ourselves within the available time frame. Death gives our everyday lives perspective. Knowing that we are being Stalked by death is an excellent way to temper ourselves into becoming great Warriors.

There are many people in the public eye who have shared their stories about using death as their advisor. Lance Armstrong, the cyclist who fought cancer (I quoted him at the end of Chapter 10), used his experience to make himself a stronger athlete, especially mentally. Most people who have faced death or who have an ongoing relationship with death live their lives intensely and with no regrets. They are truly impeccable Warriors.

Detaching or Suffering

Death not only helps us become impeccable in our word and communications, it also assists us in detaching from things that we believe are ours. Our reality is populated by people and things, and we are under the illusion that we own these things. But this is not truth. Our reality is transient and not absolute. Death claims everything sooner or later, and if we are clear about that, we do not have to lose our happiness when death takes back what is hers. Thinking otherwise just promotes a false sense of safety and security.

For example, if a fire burns down our home, we can understand that we never really owned it anyway. The same applies if our business folds, we lose our job, our husband leaves us, or someone we love passes away. All of these situations and things are transient, including our own bodies. Allowing death to do her job helps us detach from people and things, and to make room for all that is new and exciting in life.

Life is like a clothes closet. If we don't clean it out and get rid of things on a regular basis, we will be locked into the past, and we will have no room for new stuff! Let's look at an example of how death can be used as an advisor and helper on our path to freedom.

Killing Pride

Karen had just come through an encounter with death, as her sister had recently passed away from ovarian cancer. During her illness, Karen's sister taught her so much about bravery and about what's truly important in life. When Karen and her husband Doug were going through a divorce a year after her sister's death, the situation started to get ugly. There was a lot of fighting about the children, the house, and the things they had accumulated during their years together. Doug always had a way of getting on Karen's nerves, pushing all of her buttons (more land mines!). Their arguing was starting to affect the children and the emotional state of their family.

Just when things looked like they were about to enter a major battle state, Karen had a dream about her sister. In the dream, her sister told her that nothing was worth fighting about and that life was never what anyone expected it to be. She begged Karen to not forget what she taught her about life. Karen was pretty shaken up by this, since she had not dreamt of her sister since her death. She took the dream seriously and decided that she was not respecting herself or her life by playing these games with her husband.

Warrior Warnings

Often life will teach us a very intense lesson that shatters our life and belief system. What is amazing is how quickly the mind will try to make everything go back to "normal" when, in truth, nothing can ever be the same. If life is pushing you to change and learn something, resist your mind's tendency to go back to your old ways.

She told Doug about the dream and that she was not going to argue with him anymore. She said life was too short to be creating conflict and drama where they didn't have to exist. Surely they could find a way to divide things fairly and civilly, with respect for each other and the children. Of all things in life, love was the most important, and she was not willing to compromise that for self-importance and pride. (She saw that her fighting was not about love—it was about her need to be right, and if she really loved her family she would "walk her talk.")

Although her husband tried to push her a bit afterward to see if he could manipulate her, she was firm. This became the turning point in the proceedings, and in the end, they were able to resolve things to everyone's satisfaction. She felt it was because of her sister's death that she was able to see her life from a healthy perspective again.

Based on Karen's story, consider the following:

♦ If you died tomorrow, what circumstances would be left unresolved in your life? How would you feel about that?

♦ If you knew that you only had one week to live, what situations in your life would you want to bring to resolution?

♦ If death were sitting on your shoulder every day, what behaviors would you stop perpetuating? In what ways would you conduct yourself differently?

♦ How could this idea of the angel of death encourage you to start living the life of your dreams?

Mirrors Are Everywhere

One of the most powerful techniques for revealing our unhealthy behavior patterns and fear-based beliefs is mirroring. Everyone we see and meet is a mirror for us. What we cannot clearly see within ourselves we most often see in others. The problem is that we normally don't take responsibility for what is inside of us, and instead project our behavior onto others and make it all about them. We dislike and judge the aspects in others that we dislike and judge the most in ourselves.

We also tend to draw into our lives the very people who most support and perpetuate our wounds and issues. If we know this, the concept of mirroring becomes a powerful tool to break our beliefs and unhealthy behavior patterns, and to draw new and healthier people into our lives. The best way to understand the practicalities of mirroring is through example, so let's look at a situation where we can see the process more clearly.

What We See Is What We Project

I had the opportunity on a power journey to spend time with a woman named Kenisha. She came to me to complain about how rude and nasty so many of the people on the journey were to her, and proceeded to give me a blow-by-blow description of the personality defects of each of the people in question. After about 15 minutes of listening to her vent, I asked her about her side of each of these interactions. She immediately became defensive and said that it had nothing to do with her; hadn't I heard what she was just trying to explain to me? I said I absolutely had heard what she said, and that it clearly indicated to me that something was going on with her, not necessarily with them.

We spent some time discussing the idea of mirroring, and I explained to her that I rarely encounter rude and nasty people because I am not rude and nasty. I do not see the world that way. I perceive everyone as lovely even when they are unhappy. Since I do not believe anyone can do anything to me, I never take others' behavior personally and so they never upset me.

I shared with Kenisha that I had not received any complaints from anyone else regarding these people. I asked her if she was willing to go into silence for two days and hang around those same people and see what happened. Kenisha agreed to do so. After the two days she came back to me and said that she really enjoyed being with these people, and she realized that it was only when she talked to them that conflict occurred. Being in silence gave her the opportunity to observe others interact with the people in question. Kenisha saw that no one else had trouble with them being nasty or rude, and realized it was something that *she* was doing or saying that was creating this reaction from them. They were mirroring her own behavior back to her without realizing it.

Unpleasant Reflections

Later, we all got together and talked about this exercise. The other folks saw how they went into reaction to Kenisha, and how they had taken her actions personally. They acknowledged their judgments and beliefs about her. Kenisha was able to see the agreement she made from her childhood that people were always out to get her and take advantage of her. It was clear

> **Warrior Wisdom**
>
> Have fun with mirroring. If you are dealing with an angry sales- or waitperson, rather than reacting to the person because of your judgment about his behavior, try something different. Be nice to him and see if you can shift his point of view, rather than allowing him to take you down and drain your personal power.

> **Warrior Wisdom**
>
> Remember how the universe works on the principle of action-reaction? What we project will be mirrored back to us. If we want our life to be lovely, let's use our personal power to be impeccable in our words and deeds. Consistency on our part will make the process more effective. And be patient—the reaction is sometimes not instantaneous.

why Kenisha was defensive and how her fear-based beliefs drove her to be nasty with people. Her rudeness triggered the same behavior in others. Kenisha decided to break that agreement. For the rest of the trip she had the most amazing time with everyone, and took home with her a most useful tool.

Based on the above situations, consider the following:

- Name five people around you who irritate you with their behaviors.

- For each of those people listed, what are they doing that you find annoying? Why is that behavior bad?

- Can you see that the way you judge them is the way you judge yourself? In other words, that what you don't like in them are aspects that you don't like in yourself?

- Look at your best friends and your spouse or partner. Why have you pulled these people into your life? What characteristics within you are they reflecting?

- Look at your boss and the people in your work environment. Why have you pulled these people into your life? What characteristics within you are they reflecting?

- Next time you're about to get mad at someone for her behavior, take a look at how you were behaving first, and ask yourself what she is mirroring back to you.

The Least You Need to Know

- By creating not-doings for all of our limiting and unhealthy behavior patterns, we can break them for good and take back the personal power we had invested in them.

- We can use the challenging people in our lives, our petty tyrants, as a means for getting over our self-importance and egocentric behavior.

- By truly understanding that any moment could be our last, we can be impeccable in our words and actions and put into perspective what is truly important in life.

- We can use the technique of mirroring to become more aware of what we are projecting into the universe, so that we can take control of our projections and who we pull into our lives.

Chapter 18

Getting "Waste" Deep in Transformation

In This Chapter

 ◆ Illuminating the hidden beliefs and agreements in our programming

 ◆ Using emotions to identify fear-based beliefs

 ◆ Identifying the truth: the Warrior's challenge

 ◆ Taking responsibility for our doings and their resulting folly

 ◆ Recapitulation: the highlight of Stalking

Now that we've had a thorough overview of the Stalking process, we will learn more about each of the 10 steps discussed in Chapter 16. In this chapter we will focus on the first five steps, which constitute level one. We'll also discuss step six, which is the beginning of level two. I will share examples of how each of these steps work and, more importantly, how they all function together.

Stalking truly is a comprehensive exercise, with all of the components coming together for maximum benefit and awareness. As we move along, let's bear in mind that events are happening in our life right now that we could apply this method to. Let's use our imagination and have some fun!

An Impressive Inventory

To this point I have put forth many questions in this book for us to consider. They've had us focusing on what we believe about ourselves, situations we have personally experienced, the world in general, and the other people in our lives. Whether you realized it or not, we've already started the process of creating a Stalking inventory, and are well on our way to beginning this illuminating exercise! It's best to have a journal for this inventory process so that we can see on paper all the beliefs, judgments, and agreements we have in our minds.

A Solid Start

A good inventory consists of a hefty list of all our judgments, fear-based beliefs, and agreements. Combining the first three steps of the Stalking process makes it easy to see the interrelationship between our beliefs, judgments, emotions, and doings when we create our inventory. Recall the first three steps from Chapter 16:

Step 1. Watch ourselves with absolute objectivity, observing how people behave in our presence and how they react to our actions.

Step 2. Create an inventory, through journaling, of what we believe about what is happening to us, noting our judgments, opinions, and points of view.

Step 3. Examine our emotional reactions and journal what we believe about each of the emotions we have listed. For instance, let's say we just got off the phone with our mother, and as we hung up we said, "Gosh, Mom is so stubborn, and old-fashioned, and she always insists that we wear a dress to church." This constitutes our judgment of our mother, a reflection of our book of law and the inventory of beliefs in our mind. Next, we can note the emotions generated as a result of our judgment. So we might jot down that we are *irritated* and *frustrated* with Mom. To finish the process we would add the beliefs that are responsible for our fear-based emotions and judgments toward our mom, knowing it is not our mom who is irritating us, but instead what we believe about her! We might write in our journal, "I am feeling irritated and frustrated with my mom because I believe she doesn't have the right to tell me how to dress, and there is nothing wrong with wearing a pantsuit to church. She never takes what *I* think or feel into consideration." By writing this, we can see this is only our point of view based on our judgment and is not necessarily truth, especially not from Mom's point of view!

We can also note our reactions to Mom in our journal so that we are aware of our behavior, or doings, in this scenario. So if we were snippy and argumentative with our mom on the phone, we will want to make note of that, too.

Okay, so that's all it takes to start an inventory! As we can see, we have just completed steps 1, 2, and 3 of our 10-step Stalking process.

Judgmental Programs

Let's practice this some more so that we make sure we have a clear understanding of the inventory process.

Hal works at a computer software company in a position that he really enjoys, but he doesn't like one of his co-workers. Eddie is one of those people who talks a lot to anyone willing to listen. Hal, on the other hand, is a quiet fellow. Every time Eddie comes over to Hal's desk to chat, Hal first answers his questions curtly, and if that doesn't end the conversation, Hal gets a bit snippy. Eddie then makes comments to Hal like "Maybe if you had a little fun, Hal, you'd lighten up!" This irritates Hal since he feels that he's not the issue—Eddie and his chattiness are.

When Hal put this situation into his inventory journal it looked like this:

- (Step 1) My doings are that I can be a bit short with Eddie and, as a result, my co-workers have told me I am rude. I do not believe I am mean; I believe that Eddie is the rude and inconsiderate one.

- (Steps 2 and 3) I *feel* irritated by Eddie because I *believe* he talks too much. People should keep their mouths shut if they have nothing useful to say. It is impolite to chatter away with no point.

- (Steps 2 and 3) I *feel* inconvenienced by Eddie *because* I believe he is wasting my valuable time. Doesn't he see I am busy?

- (Steps 2 and 3) I *feel* annoyed by Eddie *because* I believe his talking is hurtful. He is giving me a headache!

- (Steps 2 and 3) I *feel* frustrated by Eddie *because* I do not know how to shut him up. I don't want to be rude but he needs to stop talking.

In his inventory, we can clearly see the emotions that Hal is feeling *and* the fear-based beliefs that caused those emotions. Hal has stated what he is doing (according to his point of view and that of his co-workers), along with listing his judgments of Eddie (rude and inconsiderate). He has completed the first three steps of our Stalking process.

Let's not forget about Hal and Eddie since we're going to revisit this scenario when we get deeper into the Stalking process later in this chapter.

Emotions Are the Key to Our Freedom

As we can see, our emotions are extremely important in the Stalking process since we use them to identify our judgments and beliefs. We can depend on our emotions for information because they come directly from our integrity and are the truth. In other words, what we feel is authentic even though the reason for our emotions may not be truthful. What do I mean by that? Simply that our emotions come from our body and are a reflection of the level of love or meanness contained within the messages that we give to ourselves. When we believe things that are fear-based, they can only result in us experiencing fear-based emotions.

In other words, any belief that reflects the programmed mind or ego's *perceived state of lack or need* will create a fear-based emotion within us. For example, when Hal says he feels "inconvenienced" by Eddie, it's because he believes his time is being wasted, which is a fear-based belief on his part. The truth is that time cannot be wasted, only passed, but the silent agreement behind this statement is that we will lose valuable time in our life or that someone or some activity can steal our time from us. No person or activity can waste our time, since this would mean that we are at the mercy of other people or situations—victims of our life circumstances. The programmed mind perceives its own proposals in our internal dialog and then gets upset about them, feeling lack and need, and this creates fear within our bodies. Believing in concepts that are not truth will cause our physical body to react accordingly.

A Pity Party

For example, if we were sitting home by ourselves on Christmas (or some other holiday that's significant to us), our mind could tell us that our life is terrible, no one loves us, and we will never have anyone who cares for us. (If my mind told me those things, I would cry for sure!) The emotional response to that kind of mental self-abuse is to feel sad and to throw ourselves a pity party.

We can clearly see that the emotions of sadness and loneliness are appropriate upon hearing such a story, but the statements causing those emotions are lies. Just because we are by ourselves doesn't mean that no one loves us or that we will never have any-one in our life. Since we co-create our lives (we are never victims), all we have to do is look for the obvious solutions to this crisis, which may be getting out and having fun, volunteering at Christmastime, meeting new people, and being in service to life, instead of sitting at home and telling ourselves lies that hurt us emotionally. Toltecs knew that the way we feel is a choice and that the choice comes from deciding whether we are going to listen to what our minds tell us. The question is, do we allow our minds to abuse us, and if so, why?

Warrior Wisdom

Warriors avoid indulging themselves in personal sad stories because they don't want to drain their personal power in sad emotions. When they accept life on life's terms, then there is nothing to be sad about. Life just is what it is. And it's not personal.

Fear-Based Emotions

It's important to be clear on what these *fear-based emotions* are. Since in the Toltec tradition we prefer not to use the words "negative' and "positive," I have chosen instead to define fear-based emotions as the physical reaction that results within the body from the perception of the fear-based beliefs contained within the internal dia-log of the programmed mind.

Let's make a list of some of these emotions. Perhaps you can add some words to the list that I haven't mentioned. (After all, I don't want to give them all away!) It's fun if you can see which emotions you experience in your everyday life, since figuring it out for yourself will help to increase your awareness level.

Toltec Topography

Fear-based emotions are the result of believing in con-cepts that are not truth, and are not in accordance with love.

Abandonment	Anger
Anguish	Annoyance
Anxiousness	Appalled
Apprehensiveness	Betrayal
Bitterness	Cheated
Competitiveness	Compulsiveness

Confusion

Contempt

Control

Crankiness

Defeat

Defensiveness

Defiance

Denial

Depression

Desire

Despair

Disappointment

Disgust

Dislike

Dismay

Doom

Envy

Failure

Fear

Foolishness

Frustration

Greed

Grief

Guilt

Hatred

Helplessness

Hopelessness

Humiliation

Impatience

Inadequacy

Indifference

Inferiority

Injustice

Insecurity

Insignificance

Irritation

Jealousy

Laziness

Loneliness

Lust

Malice

Neediness

Nervousness

Numbness

Obsessiveness

Overwhelmed

Pain

Panic

Perfectionism

Persecuted

Pride

Rage

Rebelliousness

Rejection

Remorse	Repulsion
Resentment	Resistance
Righteous indignation	Sadness
Self-consciousness	Self-importance
Selfishness	Self-pity
Self-rejection	Shame
Shyness	Smothered
Stress	Stubbornness
Stupid	Superior
Tension	Threatened
Unloved	Vanity
Vengeance	

It's too easy to default to the most basic of all fear-based emotions: anger. To have clarity about what you are experiencing, it is important to know *exactly* which emotion you are feeling, as each fear-based emotion stems from a specific fear-based belief. Now you can take this list and apply it to your inventory process. Simply write what you're feeling, like "I am feeling stupid," and follow it with what you believe, a statement such as "because I believe that other people are more educated than me," just like Hal did in the earlier example. It's that easy!

It's important to note that if you have beliefs that are bringing joy into your life (that originate from love-based truths), great; keep your faith and personal power in them for now. Just watch out and make sure that you are not obtaining happiness at the cost of others. For example, some people may rob banks because it gives them a rush and makes them "happy." But clearly this is not coming from a belief that is uplifting to humanity, nor is that really happiness. Instead it is a corrupt and distorted version of happiness.

> **Warrior Wisdom**
>
> Warriors know that the inventory is a maze in the mind that has our attention trapped. Once we can see the contents clearly, we can re-arrange our inventory to our liking. Instead of us being the slave to our inventory, we become the master of it. The result is the cultivation of love, wonderful relationships, and peaceful lives.

The bottom line here is that when we take the point of view of the Nagual, we are never in lack or need; we see the perfection of life and have faith in our creation and live in bliss. But when we take the point of view of the ego or programmed mind, we can only see what we have in relation to others and constantly feel victimized or judged. We never have enough, we are never happy or satisfied, and we live our lives in fear coveting what others have.

Better to Tell the Truth Now Than Later

Back in Chapter 6 we talked about how concepts, beliefs, and opinions are not necessarily truth. We can understand this statement intellectually and agree with it, but when it comes to challenging something that we believe to be true, that all goes out the proverbial window! If we are having a fear-based emotional reaction, we're having it because we obviously believe what our mind is telling us, or we wouldn't be reacting in the first place.

We write down all our judgments, emotions, and beliefs in our journal so that we can look at them objectively, challenge their validity, and see them for what they are. Sometimes by simply writing it down on paper, the absurdity of what we believe becomes crystal clear. Now we will begin step 4 of the stalking process:

> **Step 4.** Look at everything we have journaled to date, and ask ourselves if our journaled beliefs reflect the truth.

Impeccable Words

"There are truths covering lies, and lies covering truth. Like peeling an onion, you uncover the truth little by little until in the end, you open your eyes to find out that everyone around you, including yourself, is lying all the time."

—don Miguel Ruiz, *The Mastery of Love*

Truth or Consequences

Remember the story I shared with you earlier about Hal and Eddie? Let's revisit that now. As we know, the next step in Hal's process is for him to look at his beliefs and see what's truth and what's not. Based on careful consideration of the situation we discussed earlier, ask yourself the following:

- Is Eddie the root of this conflict, or is Hal, or is it both of them?

- Is it truth that people should not talk so much, or that talking a lot is impolite? Who made that rule?

- Can Hal's time be wasted? Why?

- Can anybody give us a headache? How?

- Is Hal's inability to communicate how he feels to Eddie co-creating this issue? If so, how?

- Who is being rude or inconsiderate and why?

Have you answered these questions? Great! Let's continue.

Identifying the Truth

Hal has a belief that people should keep quiet if they have nothing useful to say. But what constitutes useful? And who decides what is useful? There is no absolute truth to this comment. Hal realized that there is nothing wrong with someone being extremely talkative as long as another person is willing to listen. Upon recapitulating his past (something we briefly discussed in Chapter 16 and we'll also discuss in more detail in the next section of this chapter), Hal found that his parents used to say "If you don't have anything good to say, keep your mouth shut." As a result he became quiet as a child and adopted his parent's judgments as his own. Now he judges others and himself with that belief, which is preventing and limiting his ability to express himself in life.

Indeed, he doesn't even feel capable of expressing himself when it's appropriate to do so, such as by asking Eddie to please visit him when he is not busy. Upon seeing the nontruth of his agreements, Hal decided that if he *was* busy, he would simply tell Eddie that he prefers not to be interrupted when he's "on a roll" at work, and that they could catch up at lunch. The same thing applies for his belief that his time is being wasted by Eddie, and that Eddie is giving him headaches. Of course, the truth is that no one can waste our time and no one can make us physically ill; we do that to ourselves.

We don't want to make Hal right and Eddie wrong, or vice-versa; we want to see what *is* so that we can become free of the judgments and beliefs that are causing our fear-based emotions. The truth is that they each have their own beliefs, however valid or invalid they may be. The bottom line is their *beliefs* are in conflict—not Hal and Eddie.

Seeing the truth can be more complicated than we think. We often need someone who doesn't share our beliefs to be able to reflect back to us the nontruth of what our mind is telling us! Once we have clarity, everything shifts and we are in a position to make choices and take action rather than be in reaction.

There Is No Right or Wrong

When we have compassion and respect for one another, we don't have to get upset about or judge others' behaviors and beliefs (or judge *them*). And if we can let go of our own beliefs and agreements that we have adopted over the years, we won't be motivated to be at odds with people. Instead we can live from our integrity and communicate clearly and lovingly with people. My guess is that you either sided with Hal's or Eddie's point of view, depending on your personal beliefs, when actually neither set of concepts is right or wrong; they only represent points of view. Neither set of beliefs represent absolute truth, which as we have said before is transcendent to concepts.

The Toltecs realized that there is no right or wrong when we see with the eyes of the Infinite. These dualities exist only in the world of concepts, which in turn exist only in the virtual reality of the mind. Resolution lies in the revelation of the truth and the concepts that are creating discord and varying points of view. By recapitulating our past, we can see where those beliefs and agreements came from and who gave them to us. Then we can finally break the unhealthy behavior patterns that result from our attachment to those beliefs.

Impeccable Words

"Ultimately there are no dualities—neither black nor white, neither oppressor nor victim. We are all connected in a journey toward the happiness that is labeled enlightenment."

—The Dalai Lama

As the Dalai Lama alludes to in the accompanying "Impeccable Words" quote, true happiness results when we reach enlightenment, or when we learn to see as light (the Infinite or Nagual). At that time we will have transcended the duality of our concepts and are able to see the absolute truth of life rather than getting caught in the limited points of view of the programmed mind. In that place we can only spend our time judging, making things right or wrong, and suffering from our own fear-based emotional reactions.

Assuming Responsibility

The first thing we normally do when things are not going well in our lives is to project outside of ourselves. We immediately blame our circumstances on whatever is happening around us. When we make the choice to become a Warrior, we decide that we are going to take responsibility for our co-creation, which is the fifth step in the Stalking process:

> **Step 5.** Acknowledge the truth of what is happening in our lives, and accept responsibility for our half of making it happen.

By doing this, we can get clarity on what the truth is so that we can address the real issues inside us. Truly, steps 4 and 5 go hand-in-hand with each other.

In taking responsibility, it's important to make sure that we don't take responsibility for other people's issues. In every co-creation, there are two sides. We are only responsible for our own doings. Following this logic, it's important that we don't point our fingers at others for their doings.

Impeccable Words

"Responsibility: A detachable burden easily shifted to the shoulders of God, Fate, Fortune, Luck, or one's neighbor. In the days of astrology it was customary to unload it upon a star."

—Ambrose Bierce, *The Devil's Dictionary*

Controlled or Uncontrolled Folly?

As we know, our doings are executed without our awareness, driven solely by our programming. Toltecs say that our actions in life constitute our *folly*, because our actions are taken without consideration, and are based on information in our minds that is not necessarily truth. We then engage in repetitive actions that often lead to self-sabotaging outcomes.

Warriors know that there are no right or wrong actions in life, only actions taken with or without awareness and clarity. (Of course, Warriors don't engage in acts that harm the one life that we are all part of.) That means we can play in this reality without having any attachment to anything or caring about the outcome of our actions. This doesn't mean we can do a shoddy job at work; of course we do our best. But we know we are living and working in a virtual reality that has no absolute truth to it. As a result, a Warrior (who is in a state of expanded awareness) uses controlled folly to function in the dream of the planet where so much unawareness exists. Toltecs call this way of living *controlled folly*.

> ### Toltec Topography
>
> **Folly** is a lack of good sense, understanding, or foresight, leading to foolish or senseless behavior as a result of putting one's life on autopilot and having no awareness.
>
> **Controlled folly** is a Stalker's greatest accomplishment. It is playing in this reality with no attachment, no expectations, and absolute awareness of one's choices and actions.

Let's take a look at a situation where we can see one person's folly and how he takes responsibility for his creation. I added little parenthetical notes throughout this story so that you can see which of the first six steps of the Stalking process we are dealing with.

A Scientific Experiment

Donald was a caring and dedicated physician with a successful practice. One of the issues he dealt with was a high rate of turnover of office employees; he was always wasting time and energy training new assistants (his folly and doings). Since Donald was a solo practitioner, without partners to lean on, this was challenging because the burden of the practice was on him. He shared with me that there were not enough good workers out there. People were lazy these days, he said. They couldn't think for themselves and were not self-motivated. His other complaints were that his employees wanted more money than they were worth and were often rude and ornery (his judgments and beliefs).

I suggested that Donald try Stalking himself so that he could identify the reasons for his issues with his employees. We put a small tape recorder in his coat pocket. After a couple of days, we sat down and listened to what he had recorded. Donald never realized how condescending he sounded when he spoke to his staff, both in his office and in the hospital. He snapped at people and wanted certain tasks completed *right now*, without any consideration for what others were in the middle of doing. He wanted respect from his employees, but he was not willing to respect them in return (his expectations based on his beliefs). He wanted his staff to take responsibility for initiating things, but when they did, it was never the way he wanted it done and he would insult them (more doings). Because of this, the staff stopped doing anything but what they were directly asked to do (the reaction to his actions).

As I was listening to his story, I could see that Donald was projecting his issues out onto everyone else (not taking responsibility). As we know, it is never what is happening out there that is the issue, but instead, it's what we believe about what is happening based on our judgments, our point of view, and our agreements.

Warrior Wisdom

Warriors never assume that the results of their interpretive processing are truth. They understand that the conclusions they come to can be varied, depending on what point of view they choose once they have awareness. A new choice can be made in any moment based on their desire to be happy, not aggravated.

A Successful Self-Diagnosis

Donald never realized that his behavior was sabotaging the very things he wanted to get done. By recording himself speaking to his staff, he realized that the reason for his high turnover rate was not a lack of qualified employees in town. The word was out in the medical community that although Donald was a good physician and kind to his patients, he was not an easy man to work for.

Donald saw that he was unreasonable in his demands of others because he did not comprehend his employees' workload. His concept of their job was that any idiot could do it, but when his office manager sat with him and explained the series of tasks they completed day after day, he was quite surprised (seeing the truth). He realized that all his judgments and opinions about the staff and the way things *should* be were creating unreasonable expectations, projected anger, and righteous indignation (taking responsibility and challenging his beliefs). He obviously believed what he was telling himself, and he let those beliefs make him miserable, which empowered him to treat others rudely. This revelation led to him investigating his need to be in control of everything and everyone, and he decided to make the effort to end this behavior pattern (recapitulating his childhood to locate his fear-based agreements and beliefs—see "Recapitulation Creates Clarity," which follows).

In the end he hired a part-time nurse, ended his habit of raising his voice to others, and listened to what his staff was saying without judgment. Last, he apologized to the nurses and staff he worked closely with, and worked to cultivate healthier relationships with them (taking responsibility for his creation and forgiveness). The result of these changes was a more relaxed workday for everyone and less personal power being drained in the fear-based emotions of anger and frustration.

Donald had always wanted everyone and everything around him to change. Can you see how changing ourselves causes everything around us to change (rather than the other way around)? As you can see in this example, it's important to take responsibility for our part of our co-creation. By doing so, can you see how all the other parts of the process fall into place?

Recapitulation Creates Clarity

The most basic of all the Toltec tools of transformation is the process of *recapitulation*, which is step 6 in the Stalking process:

> **Step 6.** Recapitulate our lives by going back in time and seeing where our beliefs and agreements originated.

Toltec Topography

Recapitulation is a summary or concise review of the supposed repetition in the evolutionary development of an individual's life history.

Basically what this process involves is a systematic reviewing of our life until we have totally detached from our life story. This process requires that we view our life and watch for the repetitive actions we have taken throughout, due to being in reaction to all our fear-based agreements and beliefs. The key is to identify those aspects, have clarity regarding their origin, and change them.

Radical Recapitulations

Some of us have read other Toltec teachers who state that in order to complete the process of recapitulation, it is necessary to make a huge list of every person we have ever known in our lives and remember and relive all of our interactions with them. Maybe we've read that the best way to do this is by burying ourselves underground for days or by locking ourselves into a closet, crate, or coffin. These methods work, but the truth is that most of us are not likely to be digging up the lawn anytime soon. The most practical method for engaging in the process of recapitulation is allowing it to happen spontaneously. Why? Because life is always presenting us situations that our mind wants us to believe is exactly like something that happened to us years ago.

All we have to do is see what part of our past our current situation reminds us of. We simply observe life in our mind's eye as if it were a grand movie, first as the witness (without judgment), and then by replaying the situation with ourselves in our old role (in other words, with our old judgments). Both positions are important. By being part of the movie, we can re-experience our emotions and see the beliefs behind them so that we can address them. When we watch the movie from the point of view of the witness, we see it as it is, not the way we want to see it. We see the truth, and by seeing what is, we can heal our wounds, forgive, and let go of our need to view our life from that old viewpoint.

Persistent Patterns

Since our behavior patterns repeat themselves over and over in our daily lives, it's easy to realize how programmed we really are (we discussed these repetitions and revelations in Chapter 13). What's great about this process is that it's like hitting many birds with one stone (so to speak). We can move along quickly in our process because we can heal a long strand of life incidents that are all repetitions of the same story.

For example, once Hal recapitulated his life, he was able to acknowledge the agreements that he adopted from his parents. His inability to communicate when appropriate has created deep anger and frustration within him and is responsible for his passive-aggressive behavior. This pattern of behavior in turn has affected his ability to communicate in every relationship he has had in his life.

By acknowledging his agreements and unhealthy behavior patterns, Hal totally changed his interpersonal communications. He saw himself in the context of his life's "movie," behaving curtly toward people (as he had with Eddie), making it difficult for people to be around him. In the end, he felt good about making the choice to express himself clearly to Eddie, without self-judgment. As a result, his headaches went away, too.

I am sure you can see the benefit of the first six steps of the Stalking process, especially recapitulation. By following these steps, you can break your major self-sabotaging behavior patterns just by seeing their origins and taking your personal power out of those beliefs and agreements that are not truth. Try to put these steps into practice with a situation that is happening in your life *right now*. Let's see if you can discover something about yourself that you were not aware of before!

Once you see the direction your recapitulation is going, you can use each life situation as an opportunity to further explore that particular topic. For example, if a conflict regarding your career has come up for you, then you can take the time to look at all your beliefs on that topic, not just what is coming up for you in the moment. In this way you can uncover layers of beliefs and agreements in a deeper and more compressive way. Some other topics you could explore would be: relationships/ marriage, home/environment, family/friends, heartbreak/love, physicality/exercise, spirituality/religion, politics/government. Any human concept will do.

The Least You Need to Know

♦ By creating an inventory of the contents of our rational mind, we can have awareness of the beliefs and agreements that are sabotaging our lives.

♦ Making notes about all the emotions we feel in any situation will lead us to our fear-based beliefs.

♦ Once we see a situation with the eyes of truth, we can take action based on clarity rather than being in reaction from our programming.

♦ Once we take responsibility for the folly of our doings, we are then in a position to make changes in our lives.

♦ Through the Stalking technique of recapitulation, we can transform hundreds of behavior patterns that are limiting our lives and, in turn, heal our wounds.

Chapter 19

Taking Out Your Garbage

In This Chapter

- ◆ How expectations create limitation in our lives
- ◆ Letting go of pain and resentments to heal wounds
- ◆ Emotionally unhooking ourselves from the past
- ◆ Becoming impersonal as the end result of total recapitulation, forgiveness, and self-love

In this chapter we address the second level of the Stalking process, steps 7–10. These steps constitute the more difficult part of Stalking because they involve challenging our belief system directly and changing our ideas about things that we have been attached to our whole life. But in the end, the results from these steps are incredible.

In these four steps, we are truly Stalking our mind with our mind. It takes fortitude and support to move through this aspect of the path. This is where having some good buddies to work with can make all the difference, not unlike having a workout partner to get us going when we are feeling lazy or blue. No matter what level you are at, please try the exercises and suggestions in this chapter, and enjoy!

Letting Go of Our Expectations

It didn't take the Toltecs long to figure out that their expectations of the way every-thing in their lives *should* be were causing their unhappiness. By analyzing their emo-tional reactions, they saw that they got upset whenever something didn't go their way or when they didn't get what they wanted. That led them to look at the source of their "it should be this way" patterns of thinking, which of course led them back to their programming. This part of our process constitutes step 7:

> **Step 7.** Releasing all of the expectations we have in life about everything and everyone.

During our domestication, we were taught values and concepts about the way things should be. Our minds are chock-full of ideas about the perfect relationship, work environment, friendship, family situations, and so on. But in looking at these concepts with the eyes of truth, do our ideas actually match up with what *is?* Sometimes we get lucky and they do, but for the most part they do not. The Toltecs recognized that our beliefs create our expectations, and getting emotional over our disappointments drains our personal power. Rather than wasting energy fighting life and trying to make the world fit into our mind's programmed ideas, what if we look at what is (the greater truth) and work along *with* life?

Expectations in Action

So what do our expectations look like? They manifest themselves in every aspect of our lives, from the very small to the very large. When we complain about rush-hour traffic, that's because we have an expectation that we should be able to arrive home in a timely fashion. If we are annoyed because our partner didn't take out the garbage, that's because we have an expectation that a good partner should do what we want. Maybe our secretary didn't complete the task we gave her today and we are furious; if so, that's because our expectation is that she should work at a speed that *we* think is appropriate.

As for the larger expectations in life, we may feel that if someone loves us, then he should know how we are feeling. Maybe we feel that one of our parents should apolo-gize to us, or we will never speak to him or her again. Perhaps we feel that we should get that promotion over the other people who applied for the position. If we ask for something, we may expect to receive it.

As we can see, expectations come from the specific concepts, values, and beliefs in our programming. By completing an inventory, we will have a better idea of what our expectations are, especially if we list our emotional reactions. (We always have an emotional reaction when our expectations are not met.)

Based on this, consider these questions:

♦ List four situations in which you had a fear-based emotional reaction this week.

♦ What were your expectations in those situations as opposed to what actually happened?

♦ Were the outcomes of your four situations totally surprising?

♦ If you knew there was a possibility for things to work out the way they did (however remote that possibility was), why did you allow yourself to get upset about something you knew might possibly happen and was not really a surprise?

♦ Looking at these situations with what you know now, would you be willing to change your behavior if these four scenarios occurred again? How would you choose to see those scenarios, what actions would you take, and which emotions would you choose to have?

> **Impeccable Words**
>
> "'Blessed is the man who expects nothing, for he shall never be disappointed' was the ninth beatitude."
>
> —Alexander Pope

Constricting Constructs

On an even deeper level, many of our expectations will limit which miracles can come into our lives. For example, if I believed that I couldn't write, I would have refused my publisher's offer to write this very book. As far as my programming goes, I could tell myself I am a doctor and have no formal training in writing. If my program says I can't write, then I would never expect to have this type of job offer because such a thing would not be possible for me from my program's point of view. If I lived by the expectations of my program, I would never have left medicine, nor would I have had the faith to embark on an adventure that has taken me this far out of my old comfort zone.

But I have faith in myself and the perfection of life. I have no expectations about the way things should be, and so when life presents me with an opportunity (like writing this book), my beliefs do not blind or limit me or tell me that I'm not capable. So we can see that our expectations can reflect not only the things we think *should* happen, but also the things we expect will *never* happen. These are equally dangerous sets of beliefs. If we expect nothing, then we can be open to having anything and everything in life.

So based on this, what things do you expect to never occur in your life?

- Do you expect never to be financially secure?

- Do you expect never to have a fantastic relationship?

- Do you expect never to have the job of your dreams?

- Do you expect never to live in a lovely place?

- Do you expect never to travel the world?

Warrior Wisdom

Warriors know that using "should have," "would have," and "could have" are not an impeccable use of their word and are a waste of their personal power.

Let's make an effort to quash our expectations and put them to rest. They have never served us personally and have certainly annoyed our loved ones and colleagues when we have imposed them on others. By detaching from our beliefs and concepts, we will be free from our expectations and will benefit from the surplus of energy we receive as a result of not having to defend and maintain our mental structure.

Forgiveness Breaks Energetic Ties

We can have all the awareness in the world about what we are doing, about our emotions, and about what we believe. We can even complete the most thorough recapitulation, but if we can't take the action to forgive, we will never be free. All of us have dealt with difficult situations where we have allowed people to hurt us in all kinds of ways in our nonawareness. But if we have the understanding that we all do things in nonawareness that are hurtful to others, this can enable us to come to the place of forgiveness in our own lives. Forgiveness constitutes step 8 of the Stalking process:

Step 8. We forgive and let go.

Many people have said to me, "He knew what he was doing to me, so he *was* aware. How can I forgive that?" Well, just because someone did something purposefully doesn't mean he had awareness. Awareness from my point of view is the knowledge that by hurting another human, you are hurting yourself. Most people take action without thinking about the reaction, and certainly they do not think of the greater harm to the one life that we are all a part of. Therefore, someone can do something to you purposely and still not be aware.

Why Should I?

The purpose of forgiveness is not to make the person who hurt you feel better about what she did, nor is forgiveness given because that person necessarily deserves it. The point of forgiveness is that *we* can let go of the burden of our suffering and pain. Many times we are still suffering from the memory of something that someone did to us 20 or 30 years ago. What happened is long gone, but the pain of it is still with us. Who wants to carry that around throughout life? If something happened in the past and it is not happening right now, why are we using that event to torture ourselves? Only *we* can dredge up the memory and replay that movie, resulting in the same old pain and emotions.

By forgiving, we can see that the offending person did what she did in nonawareness, and we can detach from our resentments and feelings of injustice. The result of this action is that our personal history and memories no longer rule our lives and can no longer hurt us! This is critical because all of the personal power we had tied up in maintaining the energy around that particular event is returned back to us upon forgiving it. It takes an enormous amount of power to keep our resentments and feelings of injustice alive within us.

Try this exercise as an example of practicing forgiveness. Think of one person in your life who you have anger or resentment toward. Take the time to write a letter forgiving them for what they did. Read the letter carefully. If it contains one drop of blame, anger, or justification for your personal point of view, rewrite the letter. Keep rewriting it until it is truly a letter of forgiveness and you no longer feel *any* fear-based emotion toward that person. In the end, this letter is for you alone and you are not required to send it unless you so desire.

CAUTION

Warrior Warnings

Warriors know that by not forgiving they are actually rejecting themselves rather than the other person. Warriors will never go against themselves in that way.

Oh, This Pain Feels So Good

What I noticed in myself was that I had gotten very comfortable with my judgments and feelings surrounding my painful memories. I realized that I actually felt safe with them even if they made me feel horrible, because I could not imagine what I would be like or who I would be if I let go of my anger concerning those events. (Wow!) Once I realized this, I vowed that I was not going to choose to hold on to my pain instead of being free. That would be insanity!

I forgave everyone in my life who I was angry with or had ever been angry with for any reason at all, especially my family members. You would not believe how many resentments I was holding against them; after all, we may act kindly to our family members, but inside we still have judgment about those folks festering somewhere in our program. Upon confronting these feelings, I felt like I must be the most evil person in the world, but by speaking to my fellow Toltecs I soon realized that we all harbor the same resentments.

As I worked through my inventory and recapitulation, I slowly let go of all my judgments and resentments, and forgave my way through my entire life. I am so thankful for having done this. I realized that, in the end, I was using all of those people to hang on to my anger and to hurt myself.

Impeccable Words

"You will know you have forgiven someone when you see them and you no longer have an emotional reaction. You will hear the name of the person and you will no longer have an emotional reaction. When someone can touch what used to be a wound and it no longer hurts you, then you know you have truly forgiven."

—don Miguel Ruiz, *The Four Agreements*

Think of it this way: All those resentments and judgments are in your mind, right? Well, if they are in your mind and their presence is making you feel upset, then why are you still empowering them? If we truly loved and respected ourselves, we would do whatever it takes to be happy and to feel good, including letting go of all that other stuff. I saw that by hanging on to all that pain, I was allowing my mind to hurt me years after the original situations were over. Now, why would I want to use my own memories to beat myself up? Simple! My own lack of self-love, self-worth, and self-respect was to blame. And what allowed this to happen was my own lack of awareness. (Thankfully, for all of us, it is not hard to change this situation.)

It Goes Both Ways, Baby!

We know it's a gift to forgive the others in our life, but what about forgiving ourselves? Forgiveness is a two-way street. Why? Because we are always co-creating in life. We have our side of the situation to take responsibility for, and the other person has his side to take responsibility for. I found that every time I forgave a person in my life for something he or she did to me, I was also able to forgive myself for participating in that scenario. This enabled me to take responsibility for my part of what happened instead of just blaming everything on the other person. I also saw there were many times in my life that I did unkind things to others in my nonawareness, including projecting anger, jealousy, meanness, and hate toward others. (Kind of like energetically sliming someone!) Through my recapitulation, I was able to let go of all of that, too, and forgive myself for all of my nastiness.

A Special Gift

It was also a relief to forgive myself for allowing myself to be in situations that went against my best interests because I was too afraid to open my mouth or take an action. By that I mean any situation that went against my integrity in any way, shape, or form. That even included forgiving myself for sleeping with some men who I was never really interested in. (Did I really do that? Yup!) In addition, I forgave myself for trying to control all the people in my life, especially my loved ones or people I was in close contact with. I saw that I was disrespecting them by thinking that I knew what was best for them and trying to tell them what to do. (I assure you, they all benefited from this aspect of my Toltec work!) I know now that people enjoy being with us a lot more when we aren't always telling them how to run their lives, how to dress, what to think, what to feel, and so on.

Best of all, I decided to forgive myself for not having faith in myself and for linking my self-worth to what others thought about me. I made a list of all the things I felt I needed to forgive myself for:

♦ For taking the advice of others over listening to myself.

♦ For not trusting my gut feelings and intuition.

♦ For not having faith in my abilities.

♦ For not loving my body the way it is.

♦ For loving others more than myself.

- For not loving myself 100 percent.

- For not acknowledging how powerful a woman I am.

- For giving away my personal power to others.

I am sure you can imagine that with all this forgiveness I became a very happy person. I felt like the weight of the world was off my shoulders. And to tell you the truth, it was. Forgiveness was one of the best gifts I have ever given myself. All my pain was just a result of information I had in my mind. As soon as I realized I had all the power within me to make things different, I did. And so can you!

The bottom line is that we don't know why all the things that happen in our lives happen. If we have faith that we can handle anything as a Warrior's challenge, then we can forgive and have gratitude for everything that has happened to us. And once that happens, we are *very* close to being free.

Erasing Our Personal History

Once we finally let go of the pain around our personal history and detach from all our beliefs and concepts, our past can no longer hook us. In terms of our everyday life, what this means is that we are living totally in the moment, unencumbered by our past or by what we think about ourselves or our world. This is truly a beautiful place to operate from, never being in reaction to anything, and being able to think clearly without becoming tangled in our emotions.

This is the result of no longer believing our old stories and points of view about our life. When we come to the place of no longer being victimized by our past, and instead have gratitude for all of the things that have made us who we are, we have done what the Toltecs call *erasing our personal history*. It's step 9 of the Stalking process:

Toltec Topography

Erasing our personal history is the process of detaching from what we believe (due to our past domestication, life experiences, and programming) about ourselves and our world and anything that could have any influence over the expression of our Spirit.

Step 9. We erase our personal history.

A complete recapitulation along with the steps that I have outlined here in Part 5 will bring anyone to this point. One of the delightful aspects of erasing our history is that we leave our self-importance and self-pity behind us.

Shifty Toltecs?

Interestingly, people find this to be one of the more confusing aspects of the Toltec path. Many people have interpreted erasing our personal history to mean that we can't talk about our past or that we must be evasive about it. This is far from the truth. It simply means that we cannot pin a Warrior down with her past, manipulate her with the past, or use it against her in any way. Warriors know the past is just a story of what happened to them, a compilation of points of view about events that happened in the life and virtual reality of one human. The best we can do is default to the most basic statements about what occurred to get close to the truth of "what was" in our lives.

So for example, if someone asks me about my medical-school experience, I can answer, "Sure, I went to medical school from 1978 to 1982," and this is truth. But if I say, "I had a terrible time in medical school because there were very few females in my class. We were discriminated against, and there was so much injustice," I would not be impeccable with my word, as this is lying, for a Warrior. This is simply a point of view that might have been truth for me in the past (based on my old beliefs, concepts, and judgments contained within my program), but since I no longer believe that there was any injustice in my life or that I was a victim of anything, this history can no longer be truth for me. That was some other woman's personal history, someone who linked her self-worth to others and believed that she was at the mercy of the doings of others.

As a Warrior, I have erased my history and all of the stories I had about my life, and I've rewritten them from the point of view of truth (simply what was), with none of the fear-based emotions surrounding them.

> **Impeccable Words**
>
> "Personal history must be constantly renewed by telling parents, relatives, and friends everything one does. On the other hand, for the warrior who has no personal history, no explanations are needed; nobody is angry or disillusioned with his acts. And above all, no one pins him down with their thoughts and their expectations."
>
> —Carlos Castaneda, *Journey to Ixtlan* (as quoted in *The Wheel of Time*)

Having said all this, can you think of one of your stories that you would consider rewriting from the viewpoint of truth? Take a few minutes to journal this story before moving on in this book. Write it down twice: first from your old point of view, and then by using your word impeccably (without any judgment or drama, just telling it like it was). By addressing one story at a time, you can totally rewrite your entire life so that it changes from one of a roller coaster of emotions and drama to one of gratitude and placidness. When you have accomplished this, you will have no more personal history to tie you down.

It Is What It Is

As you can see, by erasing our personal history we are not being evasive in any way. The only thing that can make erasing personal history evasive is if we have a personal agenda around our actions. By that I mean avoiding talking about ourselves because we want to manipulate someone, or because we still have judgment or shame around a part of the past. If so, that would mean we're not quite finished with our self-importance issues and probably have not finished taking responsibility for our life's doings. That's why as part of the Stalking training, Toltecs specifically use the techniques I shared with you in Chapter 17. For example, the techniques of working with petty tyrants and engaging death as an advisor can prevent us from becoming evasive and shifty by addressing our personal importance and lack of responsibility for our doings.

The last benefit of erasing our history is that we no longer have any stories to explain, defend, rationalize, or justify. We are finished with the kinds of games that require us to use our personal power to maintain those behaviors. Once we no longer care about our own story, we are no longer attached to the island of the Tonal, where our stories reside. When this occurs, we become totally impersonal, a concept that we will be speaking about in the following section. This enables us to detach from the first attention and engage our second attention, because we no longer are tethered by the emotional attachments of our Tonal's history. And that is very exciting!

Impersonality Is the Ultimate Reward

Becoming impersonal is the goal of all Toltec Warriors. We have a name for this aspect of the process: "losing the human form" (we mentioned this briefly in Chapter 15). For now, we will discuss becoming impersonal in a general way, as it relates to Stalking, knowing that we will be talking about the human form and what that means in Chapter 22. Becoming impersonal is our last of the 10 steps in the Stalking process:

> **Step 10.** We become impersonal by totally detaching from the egotistical mind.

Cold or Compassionate?

The first thing that most people think of when we mention the word "impersonal" is that we become cold and uncaring. But this is not accurate. As a result of recapitulating our entire lives and rewriting our stories from the point of view of truth, we come to realize something amazing: We live in an impersonal universe and nothing is really about us!

This is no small revelation! Earlier in this book, we talked about how we believe the world revolves around us as a result of the development of the mind and ego. This is why we take things personally, why we have self-importance and pride, and why we hold resentments and judgments against others. When we no longer have an ego running our life, and we are no longer tethered to its personal point of view, we open up to the greater truth about the universe, which is that life is happening around us all the time, regardless of our opinion or judgment. Life just *is*; it isn't personal. People aren't doing things because of us, they are doing things because of themselves. Life is not out to get us, nor is it there to make us suffer. Suffering is actually our own choice.

In the World but Not of It

When a Warrior reaches this place of attainment, you can say that he is able to live *in* the world but is no longer *of* the world, a concept common in other esoteric teachings. He can walk through his life totally open, with the words and actions of his fellow humans deflecting harmlessly off of him. In other words, nothing affects the Warrior's emotional state of being. He never gets angry, loses his temper, or feels hurt. He has absolute compassion for others and their actions, which is the result of understanding the point of view that they are operating from.

Once we become impersonal, we can open our hearts totally. This is because we no longer believe that we can be hurt. We reach a place of peace, contentment, and happiness that originates from deep within us rather than from external circumstances. This is the point where freedom begins; our expansion also originates

> **Warrior Wisdom**
>
> You might be surprised to know that many Toltecs consider Jesus Christ and Buddha beautiful examples of Warriors (there are many other masters I have not mentioned here). These great teachers were absolutely impersonal, able to live their lives in unconditional love, without judgment, and free of attachment to the egotistical mind.

here. This is the place from which we can express our unconditional love every minute of our life. Once we are no longer attached to our mind's programming, we no longer have conditions. And without conditions we have no limits, no boundaries, and no doubts.

The Seeing of Seers

No longer confined to the perceptual boundaries of the mind, the Warrior becomes a *seer*, one who sees exactly what is and has clarity about the human mind and its motivations. Once a Warrior becomes a seer, her knowing comes not from her mind (because she no longer believes herself and her stories) but from silent knowledge. You might remember from Chapter 2 that silent knowledge is a knowing that comes directly to us, the result of direct perception without the interpretative processes of the mind. This happens when our minds are quiet and there is a channel open to receive that information unobstructed by our internal dialogue. (Normally, internal dialogue hooks our attention and obstructs those channels.) When a Warrior can perceive in this way, we say that she is *seeing*.

Toltec Topography

A **seer** is a Warrior who has become totally impersonal and no longer has an attachment to any particular point of view. He sees the essence of the world as it is, with both the eyes of his Tonal (without story or judgment) and the eyes of his Nagual (as energy).

The most wonderful aspect of reaching this part of our path is that we now have choice. We can use our concepts when needed to play in the world, but totally without attachment. Or we can choose to connect with silent knowledge directly. We can function in the first attention, or we can use our Intent and shift into the second attention, or heightened awareness. When we finally have this absolute choice in our lives, we consider ourselves free.

A Practical Suggestion

I hope that in reading these four chapters on the process of Stalking you don't feel overwhelmed. The only way to walk a path is one step at a time, without feeling rushed or pressured. Truly we often have more available time than we realize. After all, we can Stalk in the car, on the toilet, and while seated on a plane. (Believe me, I've done it all!) The key is to just take action and have a heck of a time doing it. If you can get your friends involved, fabulous. Meet weekly for Stalking and do it together! Then you can mirror each other's beliefs and reflect things back and forth that perhaps you were not aware of. For years I belonged to a Stalking group, and it made a huge difference in my life. I made friends whom I love dearly and now call my family.

Try these suggestions when you get together with your friends:

♦ Tape your group one week and listen together to the results. Share your feelings about what you have heard, with kindness and love, of course (judgment not welcome).

♦ When you get together, discuss the results of your inventory, one subject at a time. For example, have everyone share his or her beliefs about love one week, and work another.

♦ Together, see if you can figure out what the truth was in situations you have all shared together. Seeing the different points of view about the same occurrences is very interesting.

♦ Practice forgiveness by pretending that your friends are your mother, father, siblings, or whoever you need to forgive. Tell them that you forgive and love them, and ask them to forgive you, too, for your nonawareness. Have your friends then forgive you as if they were the people they are representing. If your heart is in it, this exercise can be *very, very* powerful.

♦ Practice rewriting parts of your lives and see if you can help each other by removing all the judgmental and fear-based emotional words from your stories.

These practices can be very transforming, which is why we consider them part of the Mastery of Transformation. Now that you have mastered Stalking, are you ready for the third mastery?

The Least You Need to Know

♦ When we detach from our beliefs and concepts, we no longer have expectations to drain us of our personal power.

♦ By forgiving ourselves and others for acts and words said and done in nonawareness, we free ourselves of the burden of our resentments, grudges, and anger.

♦ When we rewrite our personal history from the point of view of truth, we erase all the old stories that had power over us and had caused emotional reactions in us.

♦ When a Warrior becomes impersonal, he no longer judges, and he lives his life with an open heart and in unconditional love.

Part 6

Mastery of Intent

We can say that Mastery of Intent is graduate-level Toltec study. At this point we are into the most esoteric aspects of our tradition. In Part 6, I will share with you some of the most powerful aspects of the Toltec tradition: working with Intent, losing the human form, Dreaming, and the process of using our attention for the second time. Although all of these aspects need to be understood through actual experience, my Intent is that you come away with a feeling of the magic and possibility of it all.

Chapter 20

The Power of Intent

In This Chapter

- ◆ Intent as opposed to intention
- ◆ Aligning and utilizing the Intent of the Infinite
- ◆ The Warrior's actions as acts of power
- ◆ Ritual as a way for a Warrior to gather his or her faith, personal power, and will

Intent is an important aspect of Toltec teachings, and certainly one of its more experiential subjects. Although the teacher can explain the concepts and didactic attributes of Intent to her apprentice, if the student does not put these teachings into practice, then these concepts can never really be incorporated into his daily life. In this chapter, we will discuss the meaning of Intent (as opposed to intention) and share the Toltec point of view of this powerful force.

We will also have the opportunity to talk about the ways that Warriors align with and use Intent to create their dream of life. I will be sharing some exercises and techniques that we can put into practice in our daily lives right now. These tools hone our will, build our faith, and gather our personal power—all things that we need to move us to a place of no doubt within us.

Intent Is Not Intention

I'll admit it, Intent is a challenging subject to talk about. We must use our concepts to discuss something utterly abstract, something that is not conceivable within the rational mind. But since we are Warriors now, we won't let that stop us! I only ask that you don't take my explanations too literally, but instead enjoy them and see if you can get a feeling for what I am trying to express and share.

The Basics of Intent

In Chapter 2, I introduced the Toltec concept of Intent as the force that life uses to create our world and the entire universe. Most of us think of *Intent* as *intention*, but this is not true from a Toltec viewpoint. An *intention* is something that we are aiming to do or accomplish. It is an uprising from the rational mind and involves rational thought. *Intent*, on the other hand, is a force similar to what we might imagine as volition, a conscious act involving will. So where *intention* involves thinking and not necessarily doing, *Intent* is the force that life uses to move and propel everything forward in the manifest reality and to change or reorder it.

Intent is also the force that glues the Tonal and the Nagual together in all of their perfection. It isn't up to us to question why the Infinite created manifestation the way it is, but to simply experience and appreciate the wonder of its complexity. Warriors know that Intent is constantly pushing life to express itself around us (for example, leaves falling off the trees, tigers hunting, and humans growing); life could not express in manifestation without the medium of Intent. We can also say that life creates the edifice of Intent, or the conceptual structure that orders the knowledge of our rational mind. When we become impersonal and lose the human form, that edifice no longer rules our life and we are free from its boundaries and limitations.

Commands of the Infinite

Intent can also be imagined as the executor of the commands of the Infinite, directing all creation (including us, of course!). This command tells everything in the manifest universe how to be and also how to perceive. We perceive the way we do as humans because we have been commanded to do so by the Infinite; that command is both encoded within our physical bodies (as DNA, for example) and within the possible positions of our assemblage point (on our luminous egg).

Although we can't tell Intent what to do, Warriors do invoke it and use it. I know that this seems to be a contradiction in terms. But since we are all part of the one life, if our purpose is the same as the purpose of the Infinite, then our command becomes the command of the Infinite. When this happens, a Warrior can align with Intent and utilize it in creating his dream. For most of us, our connection with Intent is weak, as we rarely exercise our use of it (or have the power to). But as Warriors, we learn to put the wants and needs of our ego aside and, instead, adopt the desire of the Infinite. As a result, we become better at channeling our true selves and become one with the force of Intent.

Impeccable Words

"Warriors have an ulterior purpose for their acts, which has nothing to do with personal gain. The average man acts only if there is the chance for profit. Warriors act not for profit, but for the spirit."

—Carlos Castaneda, *The Power of Silence* (as quoted in *The Wheel of Time*)

The Power of Faith

We can see a Warrior's absolute *faith* in herself, her Intent, and the Intent of life reflected in her impeccable acts. By expressing an exceptionally well-defined desire from the heart—with total confidence and without any conflicting thoughts from the rational mind—her unbending Intent can make anything happen. It's like experiencing single-mindedness that does not take place in (or have anything to do with) the mind. Channeling Intent is not about thinking or wishing; it is a feeling that comes from deep inside us and is so overwhelming with purpose and focus that we know there is no other possibility that could conceivably manifest in our reality.

Toltec Topography

A Warrior's **faith** has nothing to with believing in concepts or ideas that his fellow man blindly believes to be true. His faith is in himself as the Infinite because he has experienced this personally and knows it to be so with every iota of his Tonal and Nagual. His faith is absolute in this and he has no doubt.

Just Do It!

A Warrior knows he can use Intent without ever knowing or understanding how he is doing it. For instance, we may get in our car and drive to work every day. We know how to steer the car and use the gas pedal so that it gets us to the place we want to go. But do most of us truly understand the mechanics of how the car works? (I know I'm clueless!) The same phenomenon happens when turning on a light. We flip the switch, and if the lamp is plugged into the wall, it will turn on. But do we understand where our electricity is coming from, how it was created, what makes it move through the wires, and how that lamp "knows" to light up?

There are many things we use on a daily basis whose inner workings are a mystery to us. Intent is like that. We use it but have no idea how we are using it. We can only see and feel the results of it.

So why is Intent so important for a Warrior? A Warrior is interested in creating a beautiful dream, one that expresses the infinite or life moving through him. As Warriors, we are in service to the Infinite, always ready to take action. To do so, it is imperative that a Warrior co-create his dream by working with life, using Intent. Intent is how a Warrior moves his assemblage point, and Intent is how a Warrior creates his dream of the second attention. The closer we come to being in charge of our mind (rather than our mind being in charge of us), the more easily we can find our inner silence. From that place we can open a channel to silent knowledge and the Intent of life. And from there, anything is possible.

> **Warrior Warnings**
>
> Warriors don't care to know how they create acts of power. (That is a concern for the rational mind.) They realize that the explanation of these acts would only represent a point of view of what occurred rather than the truth about the occurrence.

Aligning and Utilizing Intent

So now that we have an idea of what Intent is, how can we actually make use of it in life? Well, before we can align and utilize Intent, a few qualifications must be met. First, we must have cleaned up our mind and ensured that the tyranny of our programming has ended. At this point, a different tone enters our lives. We feel at peace, like everything is perfect and we are aligned with life. It is from this place that we are able to utilize Intent.

Since Intent is the force that life uses to bring about manifestation, it is important to be aligned with life—both within us and outside of us. At this point we don't feel like we are fighting anything anymore; the battle is over. That doesn't mean our life challenges are over—no way! It simply means that we don't feel like we *have* anything to fight (inside or outside of us), nor do we feel that life is out to get us. We face our challenges and enjoy life—challenges or no challenges, it's all the same. This is acceptance of what is.

Will and Faith

Once we are no longer ruled by the mind, we have total faith in ourselves and our capabilities. We know that we can do anything. The question becomes, *What do we do?* Well, anything our heart desires to do! When we have transcended our mind, all our personal power comes back to us (we are no longer using it to maintain our belief system or fear-based emotions) and our faith and will (Chapter 9) are strong. Our internal will becomes a personalized force that we can employ in our lives.

For example, let's say we want to stop smoking, but we can't. The reason we are having trouble is because our will is not strong. That is because our personal power is invested in too many other draining things (like getting aggravated during the day, or arguing, both of which support the fear-based beliefs that are causing those emotions) and we don't have enough power to make the shift. As we begin to free up our power, our will becomes stronger. Then, if our Intent aligns with the Intent of the universe, we command it and our will is done. At that point, a Warrior's will is at her service and so is Intent, as her will *becomes* her Intent.

No Manual Needed

As to the question of how we use Intent, I have to answer that in a roundabout way. If you've reached the place we have just discussed, you will know how to align your Intent with that of the Infinite, simply because you will be able to. In other words, it's a natural side effect of having your personal power intact and your faith totally present. You don't have to think about it or have a technical manual with written instructions. By living impeccably, you will reach this point and your silent knowledge will lead the way. We really are pretty smart creatures once we focus our attention on the wise parts of ourselves! So wherever your heart directs you to go, or whatever it directs you to do, you can feel confident that you will create your dream of heaven, simply because it is your command.

I think we should take a moment to acknowledge that a Warrior doesn't use Intent to hurt others. We teach Mastery of Intent as the last mastery, knowing that the apprentice will have transcended his egotistic desires and have no more need to control people or harm them by this point. By the time we make it this far, we have absolute gratitude for our

Warrior Warnings

As Warriors, we do not use Intent to manipulate others or to satisfy the wants and needs of our program. Whenever we use our personal power in this way, it is bound to get us into trouble.

lives, no more resentments, and nothing to gain or lose from our interactions with others.

Although it might not seem like I shared anything specific with you in this section, I can assure you that it will make lots of sense once you've experienced this for yourself. (Warriors like to say that in the world of the Tonal we talk, and in the world of the Nagual we act.) Intent is one of those things you can't analyze through talk; you just have to do it! In the "Focusing Intent" section later in this chapter, I will share some practical exercises that you can experiment with, no matter where you are in your process, to begin to hone your will for when you are ready to exercise your Intent.

Acts of Power

There is quite a bit of mystery around what the Toltecs mean by *acts of power*, especially since there are so many fantastic stories about what the ancient Warriors used to do. So although a modern Warrior *might* have the personal power to make lightning come down from the sky, we might wonder why she would want to do that. We are very practical folks who are interested solely in freedom and expressing our love, not in engaging in strange and unusual acts to scare or manipulate people. So using our common sense, let's talk about what an act of power is in the simplest of terms.

> **Toltec Topography**
>
> An **act of power** is an impeccable action taken by a Warrior. It is driven by the Intent of the Infinite or life moving through him and is a result of his absolute faith and personal power.

An act of power is a Warrior's expression of the Infinite, or Nagual, moving through her, or, using the terms of this chapter, an expression of her Intent. From this point of view, we could say that every action a Warrior takes in her life that is impeccable becomes an act of power. This is because a Warrior never takes action for the heck of it; her acts are always imbued with purpose and Intent. (Because she uses death as her adviser, every act is executed as if it were her last, and that turns her simplest act into an act of power.)

The Place of No Doubt

For example, if I want to break a belief or agreement that is holding me back in life, how do I do it? We talked a lot about this when we discussed Stalking, but the bottom line is that we must have conserved enough personal power to be able to employ our will to make the break. What ultimately makes the break happen is our faith that we can do it; there is also no doubt about what we are doing. That's what I was alluding to earlier when I talked about a single-mindedness that has nothing to do with the mind: I know that no other possibility exists except that my fear-based belief or agreement will be broken, period. This constitutes an act of power, as does quitting smoking or drinking, creating a business, ending a pattern of bickering with a parent, or any other act that takes willpower.

The no-doubt part is the key. To accomplish an act of power, we must find the place of no doubt within ourselves. Unless we believe in ourselves 100 percent, how can we go beyond what the mind believes is possible in life? Most of the time we look to others for approval, but a Warrior only looks to himself and his inner resources. When we no longer doubt ourselves, we know who we really are. We recognize ourselves as the Infinite (more in Chapter 25), rather than our programming. As we continue to practice aligning with the Infinite, we master self-confidence and self-love; as a result, it gets easier and easier with time. The reason for the ease is that we are accumulating personal power as we continue to do this work.

Powerful Questions

Based on what you have learned about acts of power, consider these questions:

- What actions have you taken recently that you could consider acts of power?
- Did you break a habit or one of your doings? Which one?
- Did you break a belief or agreement? What was it?
- Did you leave a relationship that was challenging for you to let go of? Why was it challenging?
- Did you leave the safety of a situation or a long-standing job because it went against you? How did that feel?
- Did you forgive someone you never thought you could forgive? What happened when you did?
- For any of the above, what did it take to be able to finally take that action?

There are all kinds of acts of power that reflect a Warrior's level of personal power. Whether it's breaking a painful agreement, or forgiving someone we have been angry with for years, or creating an incredible business structure based on respect and happiness, everything we accomplish on our path that takes us closer to our freedom is an act of power. The more fear-based beliefs and agreements we break, the stronger our faith and will become until finally, one day, the whole structure of our mind's programming collapses and we are free. Finally, all that personal power is ours, and anything we create in our life that comes from our integrity and heart becomes the greatest act of power. For me, writing this book is an act of power. As I am sharing myself with you, Spirit is moving through me, touching all of you. I think this is very exciting!

Focusing Intent

There are many ways we can practice aligning our Intent in our everyday life. One of the most common ways we can accomplish this is through ritual, something included in every religion, philosophy, and shamanistic tradition. These rituals might include meditation practices, performing a sacred dance, spells, chanting, sacred art, or any number of specialized activities. And although other traditions may not use the word Intent as we Toltecs do, they use ritual to gather the faith and personal power needed to accomplish something they have their heart set upon doing. And this is still an act of focusing one's Intent.

> **Warrior Wisdom**
>
> Ritual can assist us in shifting our level of awareness by enabling us to detach from the Tonal. As soon as that happens, we have the opportunity to experience and focus on the Nagual within us.

At the beginning of our Toltec path, we are wishing and intending to make something happen (our personal freedom). But with time, as we temper our link with Intent, our intending becomes Intent, and ritual is one method we can use to begin refining that process. Ritual is a way that humans bypass the rational mind and reason and go directly to faith and spirit. And there is a lot to be said for anything that gets us out of our minds and into our hearts.

Daily Rituals

In my early Toltec days, I rebelled against my teacher's suggestions to incorporate ritual into my process, because my programming judged these types of activities to be stupid and akin to witchcraft. But then he asked me to make a list of all the rituals that I engaged in on a regular basis. Of course, I denied vehemently that I participated in any such activities, but in the end I was wrong (as usual!). I realized that I practiced lots of rituals every day that were mostly useless and had little meaning associated with them. I am sure you can think of hundreds of rituals that you engage in daily, including brushing your teeth and drinking Starbucks!

Before reading on, take a few moments to consider some of the rituals you engage in daily. Consider that a ritual is any procedure faithfully or regularly followed, like doing laundry every Saturday.

◆ Make a list of your most common rituals.

◆ Do your rituals increase or decrease your personal power?

◆ Do they take you out of your everyday life, or plow you deeper into it?

◆ Do your rituals increase your faith and self-confidence?

Cultivating Faith

Praying is a ritual that most of us have been taught or are familiar with in our Western culture. In this ritual, we are often asking God to help us accomplish something, heal us, or guide us through a difficult time. From a Toltec point of view, we could say that the prayer is a method of cultivating our faith until it is absolute and we reach the place of no doubt. Once that happens, we take the action in life that we originally asked God to assist us with and, as a result, our will is done. In other words, when Toltecs pray, we do so from the point of view that we are the Infinite, and so we are praying to ourselves for the purpose of gathering our faith and Intent to enact the will of the Infinite through us.

Funereal practices are rituals whose Intent is to ease both the transition of the person who has passed away (to help the deceased reach heaven) and the family's personal experience of that transition (for bereavement). These death rituals give us faith that our family member is okay and that we will also be fine. Marriage is a ritual we use to focus our Intent on the successful bonding and long-term commitment of the couple. This ceremony gives us faith that this couple will live a wonderful and happy life together. Again, none of these rituals is logical; their Intent is to get us out of our heads and into our hearts.

Creative Ritual

The most important aspect of a ritual is that it is creative and purposeful. When a ritual is repeated too many times, it loses its Intent. This is because the person is no longer focusing her attention and the ritual has become rote and meaningless. You may be able to think of many rituals currently practiced in society that have become empty for this very reason. (For example, a prayer you have been saying by rote since childhood that no longer stirs your heart.)

For a Toltec, ritual is an important tool, and so we change them as needed. You might wonder why we want to create a ritual. Let's say you just went through a divorce, and as part of your healing process you decide to create a ritual to detach from any remaining unhealthy beliefs about your partner or your split. You might create a small diorama that contains pictures of the both of you celebrating good times and little trinkets that symbolize aspects of your relationship. Then you could take your creation (which you designed with all the love in your heart as an expression of your Intent) and place it on a table surrounded by tall seven-day candles, each one representing a year you spent together. You could set your Intent to detach from any remaining resentments you might have, and to come to a place of absolute gratitude and forgiveness by the end of the seven days. This ritual is meant to align the Intent of the Infinite, which is unconditional love, forgiveness, and respect with your Intent.

> **⚠ CAUTION**
>
> **Warrior Warnings**
>
> Warriors never use their Intent to cast spells on others. That includes not using our word purposely to say something we know will hurt or upset another. Telling others that they are stupid, or insulting them in any way, are also evil spells. As Warriors, we don't want to deal with the reaction to those types of actions.

Think of something that you are challenged with right now in your life. Could creating a ritual around this event help you move through it? Use your imagination and creativity and consider what that might look like. Remember, you are the one assigning meaning to your ritual, and you are the one who is making it an act of power with your Intent and will.

Active Altars

Another great way to set your Intent is with an altar, another tradition present in many philosophies and religions. I have an altar at home that I use for this very purpose. It is something that is not a static feature of my home, but instead a living and breathing representation of my spiritual life. (The one thing it is *not* meant to be is a home fashion statement for modern spirituality!) Throughout my process, I have used my altar to focus on whatever issues or challenges I was facing. I would pick an object or symbol of whatever I was working on and place it on my altar. I would then create a ritual around that object and make it the focus of my attention until my faith was completely invested in what I was working on; then I would make it so.

For example, I might want to use my Intent to transfer my personal power from certain fear-based beliefs into my silent knowledge and inner knowing. So I might write those beliefs on a piece of paper, and with all the power of my spirit, detach from those beliefs having power over me, just because I say so. Coming to this place would be the result of a good recapitulation and revelation of the beliefs that have been sabotaging a particular aspect of my life. Burning those beliefs (now physically represented on paper) over a charcoal on my altar would be a great way to symbolize this detachment and the commitment to my freedom.

Creating Your Own

To create your own altar, set up an open and unobstructed area on a small table or on top of your dresser. My only suggestion is that you not have stuff from your daily life piled all around your altar. This is your sacred space for your communion with the Infinite. Since your altar is an expression of your spiritual life, you might consider including live things on it, like flowers. Some people put beautiful cloths on their table, others use a small rug, and some folks don't put anything down at all. This is all very personal, of course. You could even set your Intent to find the perfect altar for yourself while Dreaming, and then create it in your life (more on this in Chapter 21).

Once you have created your space, decide what you want to focus your Intent on and make it the focal point of your altar (for example, a picture of your mom if you are working on healing your relationship with her). You can also include a photo of yourself, and other people who are important to you. I used to put a picture of my teacher there, but others use pictures of Christ, Buddha, or other saints or teachers who they have respect and love for. As I said before, this must have meaning for you, and you alone. Spend time in front of your altar and make it your sanctuary.

Power Objects

You might remember that I talked a little about power objects in Chapter 1 when we spoke about the ancient Toltecs. Of course modern Toltecs don't use power objects for harm since that goes against life and doesn't lead to freedom, but there is no reason that we can't utilize these techniques to help us work with Intent and will in an uplifting way.

Anything can be a power object, especially something that you have created with your own hands. If you have carved a little object out of wood or stone, for example, and put all your desire and Intent into it as you were creating it, that could be a very powerful object. You might keep it on your altar to use in your personal ceremonies in order to focus your will and Intent. For those of us who do not choose to create an object from scratch, we can use a beautiful object that catches our attention, such as a ring, a crystal, or a sculpted stone. Of course, the amount of power that an object is imbued with is dependant on the personal power of the Warrior who created it.

Anyway, the purpose of these objects for a modern Warrior is not necessarily to use them in any particular way in the greater world, but instead, as a practice exercise in working with Intent. I have found it very helpful to create some of these pieces and have learned a great deal in the making. In the end, though, a powerful Warrior who has lost his human form has no need for such objects. His link with Intent has been forged and the objects are no longer necessary.

The concept of power objects is not just found in Toltec circles. I have recently witnessed an interesting modern adaptation of this ancient technique. When my parents were about to sell their home, they were instructed by friends to buy a little statue of

Warrior Wisdom

A Warrior is her own power object, which she can use to create in life, and every act she takes is an act of power and love.

St. Joseph and bury him upside down in the front lawn. Before doing so, they were told to talk to the saint most intently, letting him know the date that the house should sell by and for how much money. I must say, this is a fascinating use of a power object, having empowered St. Joseph with all their Intent and desire to sell their home! (Well, maybe not with the Intent of a Warrior, but this is still a great example of an everyday power object.)

I encourage you to experiment with these suggestions and to have fun with your rituals, altar, and power objects. If you have the Intent to use them to strengthen your faith in yourself and your resolve on your path, that will be a great help for you.

The Least You Need to Know

- Intent is the force that the Infinite uses to manifest in this reality; intention is something that we are wishing or hoping to do or accomplish.

- Aligning and utilizing intent is possible when we no longer have our faith invested in our programming but instead have invested it into our spirit.

- Acts of power are actions that are true expressions of the Infinite or life moving through us.

- By creating an altar and using ritual and power objects, we can practice strengthening our will, personal power, and faith in ourselves.

21

The Art of Dreaming

In This Chapter

- ◆ A pragmatic set of techniques we use to gain control over our attention

- ◆ Adhering to a consistently followed series of steps so that we can successfully enter the state of Dreaming

- ◆ Learning to access our energy body

- ◆ Passing through the gates of Dreaming

Of all the esoteric Toltec teachings, Dreaming is certainly one of the most challenging and interesting. It also is one of the most misconstrued aspects of our tradition. Please know that there isn't one all-encompassing way to teach Dreaming any more than there is one way to teach Stalking. There are many Toltec teachers and lineages, and each set of methods has its beauty and purpose. Again, as Warriors, we know that we can lose our freedom if we become dogmatic or attached to any one teaching structure. I've endeavored to present this topic in as clear and simplified a way as I can, incorporating concepts from many well-known teachers, as well as from my own personal experience of this process.

In this chapter I have capitalized the letter "D" when referring to the Toltec practice of Dreaming. I use a small "d" when talking about dreaming as what our minds naturally do when we are both awake and sleeping (what Toltecs call our daytime or nighttime dream). So let's start Dreaming!

Dreaming Is Not Necessarily Nocturnal

As we've learned, the Toltecs believed that we are dreaming all the time, both at night and during the day. They realized that what we see as we move about our daily lives is just a 3-D virtual reality made from light, a creation that our mind projects upon our world (Chapter 5). From their astute observations, they recognized that we can actually control what we dream (day or night) by using our attention.

The Toltecs saw this as a twofold process. First, they saw that we were responsible for what we dreamed in our minds and that that was dependant on where we chose to focus our attention. For example, choosing to be happy is as easy as putting our attention on what is beautiful in life, rather than putting our attention on believing our fear-based beliefs and emotions. Even more important, they saw that we could use our attention to take our focus off of the world of the first attention and Tonal and to create the dream of the second attention at will (Chapter 4).

Second, they saw that by changing the way we dream in our virtual reality (our mind), we ultimately change what we project out onto our *physical* reality. This, in turn, affects the entire way we co-create our lives (what we choose to create and manifest). For Toltecs, the goal was to be free to express their lives without the limitations of their programming. To do that, they needed to get control over their attention. This is where the practice of Dreaming came into play.

Warrior Wisdom

Morpheus was the God of Dreams in Greek mythology (son of Hypnos, God of Sleep). It was said that Morpheus was a master at mimicking any human form at will. Warriors look to lose their human form (Chapter 22) through Stalking and Dreaming in order to become free to express themselves in any way they choose to in life. They become shape-shifters (like Morpheus) in that they are free to express their artistry in any manner, no longer bound by the definition and limitations of their personality and programming.

Controlling the Attention

By using their *seeing* (Chapter 19), the Toltecs noticed that our assemblage points and our attention shifted around naturally at night. Toltecs saw that this was in direct contrast to the way humans dreamed during the day, their attention focused rigidly on their belief system (the Tonal) and their assemblage points fixed. They saw that people had no control over their attention at night when their dreams were all over the place, nor did they have control over their attention during the day when it was stuck on their program. If they couldn't control their attention and what they were dreaming—regardless of whether it was during the day or at night—how would they *ever* be in control of what they were creating in their lives?

Toltecs wondered what method they might create to help them master their attention (and move their assemblage points)—both during the daytime (when their attention was stuck on the Tonal), and at night, while sleeping (when it was floating freely without purpose). They decided to put their focus on designing something to get control of their attention in their nighttime dream, since they had the technique of Stalking to use in their daytime dream. The new set of techniques they created was called Dreaming. In the end, they realized that they could use their Dreaming techniques during their daytime dream, too, just as they could use their Stalking techniques during their nighttime dream. In other words, they could Stalk in Dreaming, and Dream in Stalking. What a winning combination it turned out to be!

Dreaming Is—?

So what's *Dreaming*? Specifically, it's a set of techniques to develop the use of our attention for the second time, after having spent our lives focused on dreaming the dream of the first attention. As a result of gaining proficiency over our second attention, we also learn to refine and control our energy, or dreaming body, which we will discuss later in this chapter.

Before we go further, it's a good idea to discuss the differences between dreams and Dreaming, and the differences in the various types of dreams we can experience.

Toltec Topography

Dreaming is a technique that enables us to change our ordinary dream of nonawareness into one of awareness by the purposeful and controlled use of our attention for the second time (second attention).

Dreaming Ain't—?

What *isn't* Dreaming? Dreaming is not the interpretation of regular or lucid dreams. Looking at nocturnal dreams can be helpful in understanding the subconscious mind's distress due to unresolved personal issues or conflict (the result of unhealthy beliefs and agreements in our program). Although learning to interpret our nighttime dreams can be enlightening and interesting, it is a totally different process from Toltec Dreaming.

Lucid dreaming, on the other hand, is the experience of feeling like we are fully awake while we are in our nighttime dream. While lucid dreaming is a type of nighttime dream that any of us can experience while we are asleep, Toltec Dreaming is a comprehensive approach to gaining awareness in every aspect of our daily lives.

Types of Dreams

Toltecs have observed that we have basically two kinds of nighttime dreams: regular dreams (whether they are lucid or not) and dreams of power. Most of us dream normal nighttime dreams our whole lives, though every once in a while we may have a dream of power. Generally speaking, we do not have enough energy to have dreams of power on a regular basis. What makes a dream of power different is that it has a quality that is very unusual, seeming even more real than our normal daytime dream. This is because it is an *energetically real world*; in other words, it is as real as our normal waking reality.

> **Warrior Wisdom**
>
> An **energetically real world** is one that is based on energy like our universe is. When we are Dreaming, we are experiencing a genuine reality, and if we used our *seeing*, we would perceive people as luminous beings. In a regular dream, on the other hand, we don't *see* people as energy. In other words, regular dreams are not energetically real worlds.

Dreams of power often teach us a significant lesson. In them, we might be faced with a serious challenge that we must overcome in order to leave the dream. For example, in a dream of power I had once, I found myself trapped in a strange gated plaza until I learned how to use my will to control and direct my energy body to fly out of there. As a result of that dream, I was able to do more in my actual Dreaming practices when I was awake. In the end, we can gain personal power and wisdom if we transcend the challenge of a power dream, in the same way that we gain personal power in our daily dream upon transcending a challenge in life.

It is possible to convert a dream of power or even a regular dream into Dreaming, if we have mastered control over our attention. So having said this, let's spend some more time discussing the basics of Dreaming.

The Energy Body

As I mentioned earlier, one of the most important aspects of Dreaming is learning to use one's *energy* or *dreaming body*. Our energy body is the energetic counterpart to our physical body and is often called *the double*. Using our Dreaming attention, we can project our energy body in any direction, and it can travel to other places if we wish. The energy body can also perceive and have experiences that the physical body cannot.

Toltec Topography

The **energy body** is also called **the dreaming body** or **the double**. It is our other self, the energetic essence of humans. It is not confined to nor does it have the limitations of our physical body.

Thankfully, our energy body knows exactly what its job is, even if we do not understand its capabilities. For example, we knew from the moment we were born how to breathe. No one had to explain it to us. Our physical body knew how to breathe regardless of whether or not we knew what we were doing. Same thing with the energy body. It knows exactly what to do even if we are clueless and have no idea how to use it. (Learning to use it is simply a matter of experience and practice.) Once we have developed our Dreaming attention and gained enough personal power, we have more awareness and control over what our energy body can do. Until then, we can have faith that our energy body does exist and that it can function without our knowledge. Eventually we find ourselves being able to do things that we were never able to do before, even if we don't understand exactly how we did it.

This very thing happened to me the first time I saw a luminous egg. I had been Dreaming approximately one year when I was on a power journey, resting at the site of some ruins. I was sitting and gazing (a Toltec technique of looking at something without staring at it) at a carved head across a plaza. All of a sudden the people in the plaza became energy and I could see them as luminous eggs moving around. As soon as I started thinking about what I was *seeing*, the luminous eggs were gone and the people were back.

In that moment I had no idea how I did what I did, and although I tried, I could not make it happen again. (We cannot make these things happen—we must Intend them!)

Because I was gazing, I had entered into inner silence and engaged my Dreaming attention and energy body. In other words, I was Dreaming while awake, with my eyes open, and I was able to *see* the people as energy without having a clue at the time how the heck I did it. Of course, our best learning occurs experientially. When it comes to Dreaming and the energy body, if we just trust ourselves, our inner resources will be happy to make themselves known.

For our energy body to move or do anything, we must Intend it, unlike the way we move our physical body. When our physical body moves, it is because we command it to do so through our brain, which directs the muscles to move. The energy body has no brain to direct it or muscles to make it move. Dreamers often want to move in Dreaming and try to do so in the same way they move their physical body, which of course does not work. The energy body can only move if we will it to do so through our Intent. When that happens, the energy body just takes off, as it doesn't have the limitations of the physical body. This is very exciting!

Dreaming Basics

To get started, we must "set up" Dreaming. By that I mean we are going to control the parameters of our Dreaming experience so that they are a constant in our process. But before we can even begin, we must have the experience that we are dreaming in the first place, day or night. Unless we truly understand that fact, it will not be possible to move beyond these beginning exercises. Most of us understand from an intellectual point of view that we are dreaming all the time, but we have not had the sensation in our bodies that what we are perceiving is not exactly what we think it is.

As an example, when I first started Dreaming I began to have the weirdest sensation that I was living in a bubble, and that if I could just pop it everything would be okay. This feeling prompted me to walk around for weeks trying to puncture the air in front of me with my finger. Needless to say, this was quite amusing to my teacher. Later, I realized that I was trying to pop my own virtual reality, the projection I was dreaming from my own mind! Of course, my experience is unique and reflective of the quirks of my rational mind; everyone else in my group had their own particular experience of this. But once I had this experience I was able to actually enter into Dreaming.

Dreaming Positions

The first step is to make sure that when we practice Dreaming we *always* put our physical bodies into the same position. This is because we want to train our body to know that as soon as we enter into that position, we want to enter into Dreaming. In Chapter 1, I shared with you that they found many bodies of Warriors in the pyramids sitting in a cross-legged position. This is an old Dreaming position that some people still utilize. We can also sit with our knees bent and our arms wrapped around them with our head resting on our knees, or sit upright in a chair with our hands in our lap, or sit with the soles of the feet touching each other and our hands on our thighs.

Warrior Wisdom

Lying down on our back is *not* a great position for Dreaming because the body thinks we want it to go to sleep instead of Dream, and that would be counterproductive to our purposes!

Beginning Dreaming

Once we have chosen a Dreaming position, the next step is to learn to enter into Dreaming. There are many ways of accomplishing this, but in the end the same advice applies: We must use only one technique and stick to it; otherwise our body will not know what we want it to do. The best way to start is to picture—in our mind's eye—a door, a tunnel, an eye, a symbol that has particular meaning to us, or even a swirling blob of color. Have patience, since it can take a long time to train our attention to focus on the image in our mind. It's important for us to be at rest—physically still and totally relaxed. If we can silence our mind during these steps it will increase our success significantly. Once we can picture our image clearly, we are ready for the next step.

Entering Dreaming

Once we can focus on our image, we then imagine being pulled into the picture in our mind's eye. This feeling, so to speak, heralds a shift in consciousness where our body is falling asleep and our mind is still absolutely present. At this point we move into Dreaming, but without falling asleep and having our consciousness degenerate into a normal dream. If we can sustain this state, we can then use this as a point of departure to do any number of activities. We simply create a picture in our mind's eye of what we want to focus our Dreaming on, and begin.

Here are some dreaming activities that you can try after you have set yourself up to Dream:

◆ Examine one incident from your life in Dreaming. This is called recapitulating in Dreaming.

◆ Focus on a task, ability, or goal that you would like to be able to do in your daily dream and Dream it into being.

◆ Find a solution to a problem or issue in your daily dream.

These are all exercises that are beginning steps for becoming comfortable in Dreaming. Once we can sustain our attention in these exercises, we can practice some other, more challenging activities, like passing the gates of Dreaming and learning how to work with our energy body. (Both are discussed in more detail later in this chapter.)

Toltec Topography

Inorganic beings are entities who possess awareness and can perceive, but who do not have bodies that are organic or carbon-based like ours or our planet's. They exist in their own reality but can also project themselves into ours, as our reality is not the only one that exists in this universe.

Inorganic Beings

One thing I don't recommend focusing our Dreaming techniques on is the realm of *inorganic entities*. Dr. Castaneda spends a lot of time talking about them in his books, and although a Warrior can pursue this, it will not take him to his personal freedom or help him in his personal life. Dreaming was designed to assist us in getting total control of our attention and the dream of our lives, in *our* reality, in *our* world. We don't need to go into other realities that could be harmful for ourselves or for others.

The Voice of Dreaming

Something that many Dreamers encounter is the *voice of Dreaming* or the *Dreaming emissary*. After a Dreamer has a basic proficiency in her Dreaming practices, she may hear someone speaking to her while she is Dreaming—and she knows the voice is not her own. This isn't anything harmful; it's just an impersonal voice originating from the realm of the inorganic beings. (It is possible to hear that same voice when we are *seeing*, since when we are using our second attention we are technically Dreaming.) Basically this voice will only recount what is happening to or around the Dreamer at the time. I personally would not give credence to that voice, as I much prefer to trust my inner resources.

In any event, hearing this voice can be somewhat disconcerting! The first time this happened to me I was riding in a car with a fellow Toltec and I felt like I was asleep, yet I could hear the music on the radio and my girlfriend singing along with it. What made me realize that I was not asleep but was Dreaming was the fact that I could not move my physical body and yet I could see my friend sitting next to me and the road in front of us. As I was perceiving this scenario, I was having a conversation in my mind about how I must be Dreaming, and I heard a male voice say to me with absolute authority, "Yes, you are Dreaming." It scared the heck out of me and I bolted upright and awake in the car. After speaking with my teacher about this experience, I realized I wasn't going crazy and that hearing the voice of Dreaming was not an unusual occurrence. If we do not want to hear it, all we have to do is voice our Intent, stating so.

> **Toltec Topography**
>
> The **voice of Dreaming** or the **Dreaming emissary** is a voice that comes from the realm of the inorganic beings. It has consciousness but no physical body in our reality.

Dreaming Together

When we become better at Dreaming, we can even Dream together with the Warriors in our group. This is a fascinating and exciting aspect of our Dreaming practices. The energy bodies of the group of Dreamers get to know one another and have no problem going off and spending time together, having adventures and playing at night. I have spent many days and nights Dreaming with my fellow Warriors, and the process has brought us closer. I know that no matter how far away they are, they are right here with me, since distance means nothing as far as our energy bodies are concerned.

It is also possible to enter another person's Dreaming if he or she invites you in. Many times I have Dreamt with my teacher in which he was instructing me on something. The way we know that we are in someone else's Dream is because we are unable to change any of the features of the Dream, since it is not ours.

> **Warrior Warnings**
>
> By the way, you cannot be dragged into someone else's Dream unless you have given your permission for this to occur. So please don't worry that someone is going to invade your dreams or hurt you. This can only happen if you *believe* it to be so (that constitutes your permission).

The Gates of Dreaming

To perfect the energy body, we must gain control of our attention in Dreaming by traveling through the gates of Dreaming, which represent energetic challenges that we must face and overcome. As we gain more personal power on our path, we can use this energy to assist us in moving forward in our Dreaming. It is important to understand that while these gates are not physically real in nature, when practicing Dreaming they are as real as anything we could ever strive to physically surmount. In dealing with the gates of dreaming, there are always two steps: reaching the gate and passing through it.

Depending on the teacher we are working with, he or she may share a different number of gates with us. Dr. Castaneda's books hold that there are seven gates of Dreaming, but in my lineage there are many more. When we are ready to make the commitment to this level of mastery on the Toltec path, this information will be revealed to us by whomever we are apprenticing with. For our general purposes, and to enable us to get a feel for this process, we will focus on the first three gates of Dreaming. They are the most practical to learn about and fun to experiment with.

The First Gate

The first gate of Dreaming involves becoming aware of the moment when we are about to transition from our normal daytime or nighttime dream into Dreaming. I gave some simple exercises earlier in this chapter that we can use to set up Dreaming. If we can focus our attention on any of those exercises (for example, recapitulating a particular incident in our life), we can use that situation to focus our Dreaming attention as we enter Dreaming. Then if our physical body goes to sleep and our mind remains alert and aware of what it is doing, we will have reached the first gate of Dreaming.

The key then is to be able to focus on any aspect of the scene we are viewing without losing control of our Dream. If we don't maintain our attention, what was Dreaming will degenerate into a regular dream and we will fall asleep. Many of us do not have enough energy present to be able to maintain this level of awareness, and we find that our mind is all over the place, or we wake up, or we start dreaming another dream of our subconscious's choice. This is why it's so important to be impeccable with our use of energy during the day. If we spend our days getting upset, it will drain us of the personal power needed to maintain our attention in our Dreaming.

So to reach the first gate of Dreaming, we must be able to maintain our awareness while we are passing into Dreaming. By developing control over our Dreaming attention and being able to sustain our

> **Impeccable Words**
>
> "In this particular instance, since we're talking about the first gate of dreaming, the goal of dreaming is to intend that your energy body becomes aware of falling asleep. Don't try to force yourself to be aware of falling asleep. Let your energy body do it. To intend is to wish without wishing, to do without doing."
>
> —Carlos Castaneda, *The Art of Dreaming*

focus on whatever we are viewing, we pass through this first gate. Let's try experimenting with these techniques, but don't be surprised if it takes a long time to be able to move past the first gate!

The Second Gate

Once we are able to maintain our Dreaming attention and keep our focus on the subject of our Dreaming without falling asleep or meandering into a regular dream, we're ready to face the second gate of Dreaming. At the second gate, we are confronted with the challenge of waking up from the Dream we are currently focused on or moving into another Dream and then another Dream after that.

Dreamers experience a distinct feeling when they reach this point. It's as if we're waking up out of our Dreaming, but instead of waking up physically, we wake up into another Dream within our Dreaming. By practicing shifting from one Dream to another, we gain more control over our energy body and strengthen our Dreaming attention, both in Dreaming and in our daytime dream.

It is our energy body that is being propelled forward when we do this, making it an important exercise. It takes setting one's Intent to be able to wake up from one Dream and go into another, using our second attention with absolute control and awareness. I know many of us have switched from one dream to another in our regular dreams, but because there is no awareness or control involved, it is not what we are talking about here.

Warrior Wisdom

Many Warriors wear a particular item when they are Dreaming. It could be a ring or necklace, a clothing item, or something they dreamed up in Dreaming. It is just a way to focus one's Dreaming attention. Creating a ritual around these procedures can make it easier to enter into Dreaming.

The second gate is quite a challenge! If you have mastered the first gate of Dreaming, give this a try and see how you fare.

The Third Gate

At the third gate of Dreaming, we face the challenge of finding our physical body asleep while we are Dreaming and having the ability to perceive ourselves using our energy body. This is an important task because it involves seeing our physical body in the real world by using our energy body and our Dreaming attention. When we can accomplish this task, we can use our Dreaming attention in our daytime dream to see the world as it is (as energy) if we choose to.

When facing the challenge of this gate, it's important to make sure that we are really seeing ourselves and not just having a dream about ourselves. There's a big difference. Making sure that we are wearing the clothes we had on before Dreaming is a good way to corroborate this. Using our *seeing* to check if we can see our luminous egg is another way to verify this, since people have luminous eggs in Dreaming, but in regular dreams, we don't perceive that they have an energetic structure. If we can accomplish this task, we can say we have passed through the third gate of Dreaming.

The Bottom Line of Dreaming

The bottom line is that the more control we develop over our attention in Dreaming, the more control we will have over the dream of our life. As I mentioned earlier, Dreaming is about learning to get total control of our attention, dream the Dream of the second attention, and be free to create anything we can dream up in our life, literally!

Dreaming is not meant to be something separate from the other activities (like Stalking) on the Toltec path. It is part and parcel of the process. If we keep this at the forefront of our minds, we will not be tempted to try to find other realities in our Dreaming. Instead, we will focus on developing control over our attention and getting our rational mind to accept servant status instead of allowing it to run our lives as a tyrant. In this way, Dreaming enables us to create beautiful lives filled with magic and mystery, and it becomes the gateway to the Infinite.

The Least You Need to Know

- Dreaming is a technique that the Toltecs use to cultivate their second or Dreaming attention and energy body.

- By creating a specific set of steps to follow, we train our body to enter into Dreaming instead of falling asleep.

- The energy body is the energetic counterpart to our physical body and is capable of feats that our physical body cannot accomplish.

- To master Dreaming we must face the energetic challenge presented at each of the gates of Dreaming.

22

The Second Attention

In This Chapter

- ◆ Losing the human form

- ◆ Detaching from the rational mind

- ◆ Building a new dream from our integrity rather than from our programming

- ◆ Making changes in our dream right now to prepare for creating our dream of the second attention

Losing the human form is one of the most significant milestones on our path to personal freedom. Once a Warrior reaches this place, anything is possible, as she has finally detached from her egotistic mind and the prison of her domestication. This is a very exciting process, resulting in the opportunity to completely restructure the dream of her life, free from any societal constraints. Instead she creates from her integrity and self-love.

In this chapter we will learn about the human form, what happens when we lose it, and how we create the dream of the second attention. We will address more aspects of the dream of the second attention in Chapters 24 and 25 when we cover the life of a Toltec master. Although we may not be at the place of creating this dream for ourselves right now, there are many things we can do to make our dream of the first attention more uplifting and supportive for us. We discuss these suggestions at the end of this chapter.

Losing the Human Form

After years of Stalking one's mind and practicing Dreaming techniques, a Warrior reaches a point in time when he *loses his human form*. Just to be clear, the human form has nothing to do with the form of your physical body. The human form is representative of the way that humans are, the way they behave, and the way they think. (We spoke briefly about this in Chapter 15.) It's the very structure of our ego and personality. We can see it as an edifice, consisting of all of the beliefs, concepts, and ideas that we have about ourselves and our world. It dictates what we think, how we judge everything, our point of view, and the way we perceive our reality.

Toltec Topography

Losing the human form is the process of losing our attachment to all the beliefs, concepts, opinions, points of view, emotional reactions, personality traits, and domesticated doings that make us who we are. We become impersonal and are in service to the Infinite.

The human form is a construct of our own making, which determines the landscape of our dream of the first attention. It exacts payment from us in the form of fear-based emotional reactions—and as a result, we have little or no power to change it. In the end, it prevents us from being free and accessing the dream of the second attention.

Confining Constructs

Toltecs believe that all humans build their constructs of the human form similarly because our assemblage points are all located in the same area on our physical bodies. Humans think alike and behave alike because this construct directs us to do so. It has us focusing endlessly upon ourselves, our creation, and our beliefs; it has us thinking that everything in life is about us. It's like living in a house of mirrors, thinking that we are looking at something outside, but seeing nothing but a set of projections from our own mind. We're being forced to constantly look at our own reflection, believing that is all there is.

When we lose the human form, the house of mirrors collapses into a million pieces and we see the world as it is, rather than the way we want it to be or choose to see it. Until we have experienced this for ourselves, it's difficult for us to imagine, as we are still filtering what we perceive through our belief system—which, as we know by now, is not an accurate or true way of seeing. We cannot become true seers until we leave the house of mirrors and are able to see what is really out there.

When Toltecs lose the human form, we are no longer "human." This means we are no longer bound by the ups and downs of the human condition, its beliefs, rules, and morals. We are free of the chains of our domestication and answer only to the Infinite. In addition, we are free from the chains of the first attention and can create our dream of the second attention at will. Truly, we are in the world but not of the world, as we are not pulled by the needs and desires of the first attention or the ego.

The Eye of the Storm

We started to discuss this state of being when we talked about becoming impersonal in Chapter 20. I mentioned that becoming impersonal simply means we understand that nothing in the universe is about us. It doesn't mean that we are cold or uncaring. It simply means we no longer have any attachments to anything in our Tonal. When we reach this place, there are no longer any conditions imposed upon us from our mind, which is why we can love unconditionally.

The result of this is that a Warrior can walk through life with his heart open and not lose his happiness under any conditions. For example, when he sees children starving and people suffering from sickness and pain, he wishes for peace for all sentient beings (as his compassion is immense), but he will not lose his happiness from seeing such situations, since his happiness is not affected by anything outside of himself. He is like a lake that is calm and perfectly smooth in the midst of a hurricane. Nothing can upset him, and nothing can ruffle his feathers unless he allows it to.

Who Am I?

We normally become free of our human form when we physically die. Participating in the Toltec process of losing the human form enables us to have the opportunity to become free *before* our death. It takes years of practicing being impeccable and saving enough personal power and energy through Dreaming and Stalking to break all the chains of our human form. But once that is accomplished, the results are wonderful.

The end result of losing the human form is no longer having to be *us* anymore. In other words, we no longer automatically react to life in the way we have been pro-grammed to. We don't have to identify with the personality that we used to be so attached to, nor are we attached to our doings. Yes, we can remember reacting from our programmed mind, but we don't *have* to be like that. Without a human form, we are free to choose who we are and how we react to each situation in every moment. As a result, it's no longer necessary to identify with any kind of limiting definition or conceptual box. So I no longer have to call myself Caucasian, a doctor, a Toltec, a daughter, a friendly person, or use any kind of adjectives to define myself. Although I understand what those words mean, I know the real me is no-thing, and those words do not express the truth of *me*. I no longer say that I am anything, nor do I want to define myself with concepts that no longer have truth for me.

I have included a lovely little poem here from the Sufi Master, Hafiz. Although he is not a Toltec, it is clear that this concept of becoming totally free from any kind of limiting thought is not uncommon in other esoteric teachings. As we can see from his poem, he has transcended his human form and is one with the truth and unconditional love of the Infinite.

> **Impeccable Words**
>
> "I have learned so much from God that I no longer call myself a Christian, a Hindu, a Muslim, a Buddhist, a Jew. The Truth has shared so much of Itself with me that I can no longer call myself a man, a woman, an angel, or even pure soul. Love has befriended Hafiz so completely, it has turned to ash and freed me of every concept and image my mind has ever known."
>
> —Hafiz

Losing Our Mind but Not Our Marbles

So now that we have a better understanding of what it means to lose the human form, let's talk a little bit about what this really looks like. From the mind's point of view, this process is often perceived as a personal assault, and in a way it is. In the beginning of our studies we believe we are our mind. But Toltecs know this is not true. Our thoughts are simply a compilation of everything we have ever downloaded into the program of our mind and they have nothing to do with us (the *real* us, that is). Just because we have decided to invest our faith into those pieces of information doesn't make them true.

We spent a lot of time discussing the nonreality of beliefs, concepts, opinions, and judgments back in Chapter 6 and now we can see where all that was leading to. Unless we truly understand that our concepts are just mental constructs and have no inherent reality to them, it is highly unlikely that we are going to be able to extricate ourselves from them. It is a challenge to not believe ourselves when we are constantly tempted to defend our point of view and give our opinions about everything.

A Calm Coup

The mind (or ego) is a fragile construct and is constantly talking to itself (internal dialogue) to bolster and uphold its existence (*I think, therefore I am*). If we stop our thinking, then as far as the mind is concerned, it no longer exists. That is why when we quiet the mind, our world falls apart and so does the ego—at least until we start talking to ourselves again!

When we let go of everything, the mind has nothing to get a grip on and can become very disorientated. That is why we must work carefully and slowly to take down the structure of the mind so that it can become used to the idea of not being in charge anymore. When we stage a coup, it usually results in a revolt of the mind, with less-than-desirable results. The safest way to make this transition is to get our mind to believe that it is in cahoots with the real self in changing the balance of power. (It definitely helps to have a teacher during this part of the process to help make this transition smoothly and monitor your progress if you have any concerns or questions at all about your well-being.)

Warrior Wisdom

Our concepts make us feel comfortable and secure. When we talk to ourselves, we are confirming that everything is exactly the way it should be from our personal point of view.

Convincing Arguments

One way Toltecs accomplish this is to get the rational mind to believe that it wants to go on this spiritual journey with us, and that it will become better for it. When I was working through this process, I would often tell my mind that I appreciated its help in my life in communicating with language, doing calculations, and resolving puzzles requiring logic. However, convincing it to stop sharing its opinions and judgments about my life and the lives of others was a challenging project, especially when I still believed that I was my mind.

It may help to talk to your mind as if it is your child. For example, you might say, "Thank you for sharing that information, Honey, but I am not interested." Listen to what your mind is saying to you and then address the lies, nonsense, and illogical logic that it is putting forth. You can even give your mind a time-out if it is behaving in a particularly unlovable manner. Praise it for what it should be doing (like being a calculator), and train it *not* to do what it should not be doing (such as telling you what to do or think).

The key is to lose your mind without losing your marbles.

It isn't about attempting to crash the mind in one fell swoop and experiencing a kind of schizophrenic event. That is not an act of self-love. The whole idea is to have respect for ourselves, for our mind, and for the way it is set up.

At first, I had so many questions for my teacher about why the mind is designed this way and why we have to work so hard to transcend it. He told me that the universe is truly a mystery and that there are things that we will never know, things that constitute the unknowable of the Infinite (Chapter 3). I realized that it was my rational mind asking him these types of questions, straining to know itself as real, when, as Toltecs, we know that it is just a virtual reality. Watching my rational mind resign itself to the unknown was a forward step in this process.

Impeccable Words

"Although you appear in earthly form, your essence is pure Consciousness. You are the fearless guardian of Divine Light. When you lose all sense of self, the bonds of a thousand chains will vanish. Lose yourself completely.

"Why are you so enchanted with this world when a gold mine lies within you? Open your eyes and come—Return to the root of the root of your own soul."

—Rumi

Restricting Structures

Many of you have read Castaneda's description of losing the human form and are probably wondering what the experience is really like. My observations of myself and others have shown me that losing one's form usually does not happen in one defining moment, but instead as a series of structural collapses.

Picture your human form as a skyscraper formed from bricks and surrounding you entirely. All of your beliefs, concepts, and agreements are the bricks, and your faith in what you believe is truth is the mortar holding the structure together. When you face your beliefs and see them as *not* truth, you blow out sections of these walls. Every time this occurs, your structure is permanently affected. Right away the mind tries to repair the structure, but it is never quite the same.

Every time you repeat this process, the structure becomes weaker and weaker until finally one day the whole thing collapses on itself. When that happens, you are sitting on a pile of bricks and you have the choice to either stay there and protect the ruins of your beliefs, or to pick yourself up and walk away toward freedom.

Rebuilding Our Devastated Creation

So once the structure of the human form is no longer present, how do we create the dream of the second attention—and what do we do with our devastated creation? Well, there is no use sitting on your pile of bricks, defending the last pieces of your belief structure! The thing to do is to get up and start from scratch, creating a new life based on integrity, love, self-respect, and the passion of life.

The tendency is to immediately be drawn into creating a life that is similar to the one we have been living our entire lives. That is to be expected, since it is all we have registered in our program, regardless of whether we believe it anymore or not. To design a dream of the second attention, it is helpful to look to someone who has already accomplished this task as an example. (I was able to use my teacher as a role model.) Not to say that your dreams must look exactly the same—they need not resemble each other's at all—it's just helpful to see what the key aspects of such a dream look like.

The most significant quality of the dream of the second attention is the lack of structure. (In the beginning, this can be disconcerting to say the least, but then we begin to get the hang of it.) By this I mean that we can make choices about what we want to do and create *in this moment*, but not feel like we must follow through if we find that what we have chosen is not suiting us. For some of us, this point is pretty hard to swallow, since we may have a belief that once we start something we have to follow through with it. Well, since we are following our *passion* at this point, it requires us to evaluate what feels good to us and to discard what doesn't, while taking *responsibility* for the consequences of what we are discarding. We will go into these ideas in great depth in Chapter 24.

> **Warrior Wisdom**
>
> When we lose the human form and our attachment to the structure of the dream of the first attention, it no longer holds interest or meaning for us. A Warrior must start from scratch, rebuilding his life based on the truth of the Infinite rather than on the lies of his programming.

Practicing Our Artistry

As I mentioned in Chapter 1, *Toltec* means "artist"; it is logical, then, that we would want to express our artistry and integrity in the very way we design our lives. It doesn't matter what we do in life; whatever we do can be done artistically. That means that we don't have to be musicians or sculptors; we can baby-sit, pick up garbage, or wash dishes—it can all can be done creatively. It is an attitude that we *choose* to cultivate and practice in our lives.

Creating for Pleasure

Consider the process of creation as a state where we are totally in the moment, enjoying our presence and being, where we are giving birth to something wonderful. The creative process can be hindered if we feel rushed, pressured, obligated, or pushed to *have* to do what we are doing.

Warrior Wisdom

Nothing stops a Toltec from doing what Spirit is directing her to do! She never asks, "Who is going to let me do what I want to do?" Instead she says, "Who can possibly stop me?" Having confidence that we are co-creating our life with the Infinite rather than with our programming is the base from which we start dreaming the dream of the second attention.

Impeccable Words

"The intuitive mind is a sacred gift; the rational mind is a faithful servant. We have created a society that honors the servant and has forgotten the gift."

—Albert Einstein

What would life would be like if we were creating all the time, just for the pleasure of it, just because it feels good? Our artistry would be coming out of us all the time, because, as Warriors, we know that this is our true nature. For example, children are constantly creating, whether making a mud pile, building a structure of Legos, or rhythmically banging pots. Kids don't have any judgment about what they are creating; they make things without caring if anyone appreciates them. They create because it brings them pleasure. When did we *stop* creating just for the heck of it? And when did we start linking our self-worth to our creations and start caring about whether other people liked them?

Once we lose the human form, we let go of our attachment to how others feel about our creations. We just don't care anymore. Once we disbar our judge, the self-imposed pressure is gone and we are free to express ourselves without restraint. We feel like we can do anything and that anything is possible. This is true because there are no longer any limitations present from our program. The feeling that results from this process is one of expansion, like we are uncontainable. It is a great gift of self-love to no longer squash our true nature and creative self.

Birthing a New Dream

Ultimately this process is about redesigning our life and the aspects of our existence in the most beautiful way. That can mean changing the way we express ourselves in the world, changing the way we look and dress, or changing our living space. It can also mean extricating from our lives people who do not radiate sunshine and joy, or changing situations that are going against us even in the subtlest ways.

By systematically addressing every quadrant of our life, we can redesign it so that it reflects our artistry and integrity, our love for life, and our love for ourselves. Let's consider the things we could change in our life that would make it lovelier. Do things have to be the way they are, really? Or are we just arguing for our limitations and siding with our program's desire to make ourselves suffering martyrs?

Only we can answer these questions with great honesty by putting our denial and ego aside. Somewhere deep inside of us, something wants to share a dream of a most beautiful life. We just have to be silent long enough to feel the message welling up within us.

Cleaning Up the Dream

There are many things that we can do right now in our daily lives to make them more pleasant. We may not be able to change the larger aspects of our lives that need addressing all at once, but we can certainly look at some of the smaller things that require less personal power and are relatively easy to modify. To do this, it is important to look objectively at the aspects of our lives that are creating more drama and pain than pleasure. In addition, if we seek out and eliminate activities that sabotage us, that alone can make a huge difference. I am going to make some suggestions of things we can pay close attention to in our lives, but ultimately it is up to you to try any of the ideas put forth here.

TV Tensions

One thing that I decided to change in my own life was the amount of time that the TV was on in my home and the types of shows I chose to watch. When I started my path, I realized that I was behaving the same way people were behaving on the shows I was watching. They were confirming that my dramatic way of acting (such as getting angry, yelling, and having self-importance) was typical. Since I did not want to act like that anymore, I decided that it would be best to stop using the TV to confirm my unhealthy behavior patterns.

Warrior Warnings

There are a lot of "toxic energy" sources in the dream of the planet, working to keep us trapped in the first attention. A Warrior will seek out, identify, and eliminate these sources from her life.

I also took a good look at the TV news and its effect on my life. I noticed that rather than the news being shared in a factual way, it seemed to be presented in a way that tried to elicit an emotional reaction from the viewer (in this case, me!). Since I was practicing saving my personal power, I chose to stop watching the news. At the time, I was not able to stop myself from becoming upset at what I was seeing. (I was still taking the news personally back then.) Instead, I stuck to listening to the 10-minute news reports on the radio (just the facts, Jack!) for a less-emotional rendering of the day's events.

Hearing the same dramatic stories over and over was not working for me, either. I found that this created an escalating kind of emotional frenzy within me and I didn't enjoy that feeling. I also found that after listening to the news, my general level of happiness went down. I was working at being happy during the course of my day, and the news was not helping me to fulfill that goal. So after I heard a piece of news once, I didn't listen to it again.

Lovely Living

Looking at our living arrangements is another good place to start making our lives more pleasant. If you have been putting off doing things around your place to make it more cheerful, what are you waiting for? (Remember that angel of death? Do it *now!*) We are the best reason to take care of ourselves, so why not begin by putting ourselves in a lovely place? I found that cleaning up my apartment, hanging pretty pictures, and having flowers or plants around is very inspiring. After a long day, it is nice to come home to a quiet and loving place that feels like a sanctuary. Adding an altar in my home was a great way to remind me to focus on my spiritual development.

A Warrior's life is never in disarray and his home will reflect that. Since there is never stuff lying around in confusion in a Warrior's mind, it is rare to find that in his home (since his inner life projects out onto his outer reality). Having a nice place is a way to express our love for ourselves. (I do want to make it clear that a "nice place" doesn't have to be expensive. This isn't about spending a lot of money. A tiny studio apartment can be a sunny, bright, inspiring, uplifting, and pleasant space to be in.)

Happy Humans

Taking more action to do kind things for our human body is a wonderful gift to ourselves. If you have always had a belief that you must take care of everyone else before yourself, start focusing your attention on yourself *now*. It is important to take time to attend your human body, and ask yourself what kind things you have done for it lately. A nice hot bath, a good skin scrubbing, even taking time to neatly trim your toenails is an act of love. This may sound trivial, but without judgment, all acts are equally important to a Warrior and she will complete each one impeccably.

As a Warrior, I know that my body is where the Nagual resides within me. Without my body, I, as the Infinite, could not be manifest here. From this point of view, we can appreciate a Warrior's respect for her physical body, for its care and its comfort. I do what I can within my means to make my body feel good. I do my best to feed my human well. I respect what my body tells me to eat and I also respect when my body tells me it is full. I take responsibility for all of my health choices. This also applies to the amount of sleep I get and how much I exercise. Since I am 100 percent responsible for my actions, I am 100 percent fine with the results of those actions. That is the Warrior's way.

Warrior Wisdom

Learning to make ourselves happy without feeling guilty about it or listening to our judge telling us that we are being selfish is an important practice. When a Warrior builds his dream of the second attention, he is doing it for himself and not because he feels obligated to live his life according to anyone else's rules or desires.

Melodious Music

The last aspect of my outer dream I initially looked at was the type of music I was listening to. I observed that the lyrics I was singing my heart out to didn't always support the message I wanted to live my life by. I decided to let go of music that supported a victim's point of view, songs with cursing (or mal-intent), or music that contained any messages that were counterproductive to my process. Later, when I moved past taking the lyrics to the songs personally (having emotional reactions to them because I still *believed* what they were saying), I was able to listen to most music with a sense of humor at what it represented. It is still a personal choice not to listen to music with cursing, as I don't enjoy the vibration and Intent of those words.

Having mentioned these suggestions, consider the following:

◆ Look objectively at your home. What would your surroundings say to a stranger? What could you change to make your home part of your dream of heaven?

◆ What things are you doing to your physical body that are going against you or are not respectful? What could you do to change that?

◆ Is the TV on in your home whenever you are there? What "toxic" influences are you inviting into your dream, and can you eliminate or at least decrease them?

As you can see, there are many things you can do to start cultivating your dream of the second attention. Please experiment with these ideas and see what works for you personally. There are no "shoulds" here, only possibilities. Feel free to do what feels right for you, taking responsibility for whatever you do.

The Least You Need to Know

◆ The human form is a structure consisting of all our knowledge, beliefs, and domesticated human responses—everything that makes us "human."

◆ Losing the human form is the culmination of mastering the Toltec techniques of Dreaming and stalking.

◆ Detaching from everything we know and believe must be done in a way that supports the rational mind.

◆ Creating the dream of the second attention is done from our integrity rather than from our programming.

◆ By addressing the aspects of our surroundings that are not healthy for us, we practice creating a loving dream for ourselves.

Chapter 23

Practice Creates Mastery!

In This Chapter

- ◆ Having patience for our personal growth, development, and spiritual expansion
- ◆ Understanding the reasons for and against having a teacher
- ◆ Participating in spiritual journeys and retreats
- ◆ Spiritual community as an important part of our path

Walking a spiritual path is a lifelong endeavor. We often feel insecure about the many choices we must make along the way. In this chapter I address some of the important issues we confront when we engage in personal growth work. For example, we have choices about how much we will study and how often, whether we need a teacher or not, whether we should study at home or participate in a spiritual journey or retreat, or if we should bother with a spiritual community.

These are all important questions that are best answered once we have awareness of what our choices are in the first place. We will address each set of questions in order to help us feel confident in deciding what is right for us!

Rome Was Not Built in a Day

Whoever said that patience is a virtue was very wise. We know that one of the most important attributes of a Warrior is patience. We've talked about it from different points of view in several chapters. Our spiritual path is something we walk on until the day we die (when our Tonal ends). We cannot speed it up in any way. Yes, we can work hard and do our best, but this is not a 10k race! Toltecs believe that the most important task in our lives is cleaning our minds and achieving our ultimate freedom. But it is disrespectful if we put unreasonable pressure upon ourselves to learn faster than we are capable of learning. Then we are actually using our path to go against ourselves, further hurting and abusing ourselves. This is certainly not the direction we want to move in.

> **Impeccable Words**
>
> "Nobody trips over mountains. It is the small pebble that causes you to stumble. Pass all the pebbles in your path and you will find you have crossed the mountain."
>
> —Author Unknown

We can only experience our life one day at a time. If we address today's issues today, that will be enough. Tomorrow will come soon enough and we will deal with that when it arrives. If we deal with events as life presents them, our journey will take on a natural rhythm and become exciting and encouraging rather than overwhelming. (Remember how we said that a Warrior lives in the moment?) Feeling overwhelmed comes from the ability of the mind to project the amount of work to be done into the future. This type of thought process is an act of sabotage. Our path, then, is the best place to practice being in the moment.

Terrible Taskmasters

Because of my programming, I approached my personal growth and spiritual development just like my years in medical school. It was as if I was constantly being tested and graded for my performance. I wanted to be the best student and to get an A. I stressed over my stalking exercises, which were supposed to be helping me see my obsessive-compulsive behavior and help me become *less* stressed. Eek! My teacher used to say that I was making it all a lot worse than it was, but I thought he was trying to sabotage my progress. Ha! My mind always came up with the perfect illogical logic, and I believed myself 100 percent. Of course, there are no grades, there's no pressure, and no stress on the Toltec path, only life. As my beloved teacher used to say, "Practice makes the master." But practice *does not* make perfect, because the way we define perfection in the dream of the planet is a big lie (we will never be nor can we *ever* be perfect according to society's definition of perfection).

It is important not to compare ourselves to those who study with us. When I started this work, I had a competitive nature and a lot of self-importance. As a result, my teacher used to purposely tell me how other people were doing in my group (he'd make up all kinds of things) because he knew I would use that information to frustrate myself. And he was right! When I stopped attaching my self-worth to the doings of other people, he stopped teasing me in this way. It was a great lesson and act of self-love.

Assault and Battery

Along with self-comparisons go self-beratings. I've mentioned before that beating ourselves up for not being "aware enough" in life situations is not self-love, but, instead, self-loathing. If we really want to judge ourselves for our behavior, there are certainly many opportunities to do that in anyone's life! But what does that accomplish from a Warrior's point of view? Is our self-judgment conserving personal power and energy? Nope, it is doing the exact opposite. Let's do our best to avoid berating ourselves for something we can no longer go back and change.

If you are a parent, you will probably remember when your kids were learning to speak. I'm guessing that you had to help them over and over again until they could be understood and speak with proper grammar. Did you yell and scream at your children, telling them they were stupid or that they should learn to speak more quickly? Of course not! You knew that it would take time and that you needed to encourage them and play games with them to get them to learn. Same thing goes for us on our spiritual path. Let's not yell at ourselves, or put ourselves down for being the way we are. Let's appreciate ourselves and do the best we can. If we have patience and compassion and play games with ourselves, we can make the work more fun. That means having a little imagination on our path and getting creative. After all, how can we have compassion for others if we don't practice it on ourselves?

Of all the activities I have ever engaged in during my life, this path has been the best. I say that because it has yielded the most amazing outcomes for me (action-reaction!).

> **Warrior Warnings**
>
> Balance is what a Warrior strives for. Doing our Toltec work 24/7 will not necessarily make things change faster. It may in fact be another way for us to sabotage ourselves by fatiguing and draining our energy.

Do You Need a Teacher?

There is so much talk about whether one should work with a teacher or not. My personal experience is that we all have the information we need to be free within us. I have no doubt about that. We have been born with incredible resources and the ability to access the silent knowledge that is present in our universe. The problem, so to speak, is that we do not know how to use what we have or how to access this information on our own. Sometimes through serendipity we touch upon this wisdom, but all in all, we are so attached to our minds and what we believe about everything that if the information smacked us right between our eyes, there is a good chance we would never notice what hit us!

Having a teacher is important for this very reason. It's not because the teacher has information that we do not. It's because he or she has more awareness and clarity than we do, having already walked this path of life. A good teacher can see what is, and he or she can see the truth. When I first started on the Toltec path, I was stubborn, selfish, disrespectful (especially to myself), short-tempered, and unaware. My teacher was a masterful Stalker and Dreamer, and he would set me up to reveal myself over and over again. But what was being revealed was all the garbage that I was holding on to and defending, including my need to be right and to make others wrong. He was a great mirror for me, and believe me, the picture was not always pretty!

Warrior Warnings

A true teacher is in service to spirit and has no personal agenda. Be cautious of any teacher expressing wants and needs from his or her ego. Avoid anyone who crosses your boundaries in an unhealthy way.

Eventually, a good teacher helps us to see our whole belief system in full regalia and to recognize that everyone is holding on to the same concepts; we just need to get over ourselves and our self-importance. This is the place where real healing begins to happen, and the place where a good teacher can make all the difference on your path.

Pass It Forward

In the beginning, I could never understand why my teacher would put so much time and effort into working with me. (I was so dense!) But now that I am where I am on my path, I understand completely. You get to the point where you want to share yourself just because you cannot think of anything else to do with your life. You are totally happy, you have absolute compassion for others, and your love is immense. What better way to share the gift you have received than to pass that gift forward? If we can find a teacher who is happy to share him- or herself with us, that is fabulous. By this I am not insinuating that a teacher should work with us for free. I do recognize that this is a touchy subject for many students out there, as there are many beliefs that suggest that spiritual work should be given for free.

I believe that teaching must involve some exchange of energy (money, services, etc.) for it to be worth anything to the student. The reason for this is that we have been so indoctrinated to believe that if something is free, then it is not worth anything. These teachings are not worthless; indeed, from my point of view, they are priceless. But it is up to us to evaluate if the price being asked is reasonable.

I realize now that no amount of money, gifts, service given, or anything I could possibly think of, could pay for what I have received from my teacher. I truly have a debt of spirit to him that I can only repay through assisting others in the same way he assisted me.

> **Warrior Wisdom**
>
> Teachers who have lost their human form will never take us personally, yell at us, disrespect us, or project their issues onto us. That's because they've finished with their issues and have no self to project. They are a clean mirror.

Efficient Energetics

A great teacher will assist us in learning how to use our energy impeccably and will not ask for our personal power (by manipulating us for their benefit, for example). This is a very important thing to be on the lookout for. No one can take our power from us unless we give it of our own free will. Please read this statement over and over again, because it is truth. If we learn how to use and deploy our energy efficiently, we will save up a lot of personal power that we can use to make great changes in our life and to get rid of all those beliefs that are not working for us. Why would we want to put out such an effort only to give our power away to another?

This is a world filled with people who believe lies that empower them to take action against others, fully justified in what they are doing. We've talked a lot about this in this book. Let's do our best not to invite these people into our lives and onto our path. There are many wonderful teachers out there, Toltec and otherwise. Let's use our intuition and feelings to assist us in making wise choices.

Walking the Talk

Most importantly, a teacher is a living and breathing example of the work he or she is sharing. There are thousands of people teaching spiritual philosophies out there today. Anyone can lecture about any of the wonderful concepts in this or any other book. But when they are in the world, handling problems and dealing with daily life, what are they like? Are they short-tempered, judgmental, impatient, self-centered, or egotistical? If this is not how we want to be, then perhaps this is not the person we want to be learning from. From the minute I met my teacher I knew he had what I wanted, even if I did not truly understand or appreciate what that was at the time. In all eight years I have known him I have never seen him be in any other way but unconditionally loving.

The only real tools a Toltec teacher possesses to assist others with are unconditional love and the ability to channel the truth. That love, constant and steady, can bore through the toughest of shields, the deepest of wounds, and the densest of scars. Lies cannot stand up to the truth, and a good teacher will endeavor to reveal that to us.

Impeccable Words

"It is no use walking anywhere to preach unless our walking is our preaching."
—St. Francis of Assisi

The bottom line is that we all want to love ourselves and others. Learning to cultivate this requires help when the road is stormy and dark. There were times when I thought my heart would be locked up in a black box forever. But my teacher kept loving me ruthlessly and pushing me until the time when I could allow myself to fall in love with myself, until the day I realized I was *worth* that kind of love.

Ruthlessness Rules

It bears repeating: A good teacher is a clean mirror. This person will not tell us what to do or give us advice of any kind. After all, how can anyone be so conceited as to know what is best for another being? As people who are often asleep in the world, we always are giving our advice to others and telling them what to do. But once we start working on ourselves, we see that it is challenging enough to figure out what to do for ourselves, never mind for another person! As we have learned, being a clean mirror is the best thing anyone can be for another person.

A good teacher will be ruthless with us and will not play into our pity parties, complaining, or whining. We may judge them to be mean in the moment (I certainly did), but we come to realize that this is the only way to shake us out of our complacency.

As I explained earlier, a Warrior can be ruthless and unconditionally loving at the same time, and in fact, that is the best combo out there for knocking a student out of his self-importance and self-pity. Truly the amount of judgment we have against our teacher is equal to the amount of judgment we have against ourselves. I finally realized that my teacher didn't give a fig for my judgment; it only made him love me more and be more ruthless with me. I learned to stop judging from his example, as I had never before in my life seen a person who did not have judgment.

Of course, I have shared my feelings about teachers based on my personal experience. There is no right way to approach this subject. It is very personal and it is up to you to determine for yourself if you want to work with a teacher or not. As long as you are aware of the dangers and benefits, then you are in a position to make this choice with clarity. Use your feelings and inner knowledge to determine if a teacher resonates with you, and if this person embodies the way you would love to express yourself in life. Have faith and trust in what your heart is whispering to you.

Power Journeys and Spiritual Travels

One of the loveliest aspects of my Toltec training has been the ability to go on what we call power journeys, something we spoke briefly about in Chapter 15. On these journeys we go to beautiful, sacred sites and energetic centers all over the world. When we are there, we use the energy of these places to assist us in transforming our self-sabotaging behavior and beliefs that are no longer serving us. When we are guided in these places by people who have been trained to work with the energy there, this process is particularly powerful. Of course there are hundreds upon hundreds of these kinds of places on our beautiful planet. Having said this, I would like to focus on some important reasons for going on these journeys.

Watching and Wanting

We are all heavily invested in the dream of this planet, so much so that we often can't imagine that there is another way to be in the world. If we look around us, most people live similar lives and behave in similarly domesticated ways. But for us to truly change, it is important to be around people who are different and are not invested in the dream of the

Warrior Wisdom

Detach from the Tonal long enough, and the mystery of the Nagual will peek through. When we leave the comfort zone of our island of safety, anything and everything is possible.

planet, but who, instead, are in their own dream of heaven. These journeys give us the opportunity to see how a Warrior lives and functions in the world, and how she deals with people, up front and personal. I have read plenty of philosophies that have taught many things that I agreed with, but in order to put them into practice, I needed to see them in action. That is how I actually made the choice to pursue this path—by watching my teacher in action, and wanting what he had.

Exit, Stage Right

Once we are out of our own life dream, away from the cell phones, faxes, e-mails, and TV set, we can focus inwardly on ourselves. The wonderful part of these trips is that our normal reality falls away and there is only us. How often do most of us carve out five to seven days in a row to spend specifically with the Intent to change ourselves? I don't know about you, but before I started walking this path, the time I devoted to this task could be summed up as zip, zero, nada! When we work really hard and have busy lives, our idea of downtime doesn't usually include tearing our belief system apart. To counteract the tendency to turn on the TV or space out, we created these journeys in order to relax and address ourselves at the same time. These trips give us a kick in the butt and encourage and inspire us to continue doing this work even when we are back in our normal dream.

This was very significant for me, especially in the beginning years. I would come home from a journey all jazzed and feeling strong. Then after about a week, my life was back to its normal drama again. Each time I returned from a power journey, though, it took longer and longer for me to get sucked back into my old dramas and patterns. And each time, it got easier and easier to resist the temptation to return to my old programmed self. It was encouraging to actually see and feel the difference within myself. Even as adults we are very much like kids, and a little positive rein-forcement goes a long way in propelling us forward.

Farewell, Rat Race

I encourage everyone who is interested, no matter what path you are on, to partici-pate in a spiritual retreat or journey, whether it is a silent Buddhist retreat, Christian monastery, or New Age meditation weekend. Every tradition offers some kind of sim-ilar experience, and the reason they do so is because it works. There is nothing like taking the time to look deeply and thoughtfully into ourselves, our doings, and our lives. It's important for us to go off autopilot so that we can take account of life and see if it is going in the direction our heart wants us to go.

Sometimes we are so caught up in life that we don't even realize we are not happy. That's why we call it the rat race: There's lot's of rushing around with no awareness, direction, or clarity, going absolutely no-where! But when we can stop for a while, quiet our minds, and come to the place of inner silence, the truth is always revealed to us. These types of spiritual retreats and jour-neys enable us to access the silent knowledge that is waiting to be known inside us.

If it is within your means, please give it a try and experience this for yourself. Take the chance to explore and expand yourself and your possibilities!

> **Warrior Wisdom**
>
> The more opportunities we have to touch the Nagual within us, the easier it becomes to not believe our own mind and the illusion-ary world of the Tonal. A spiri-tual retreat or journey is the perfect place to experience this shift.

A Gaggle of Warriors

One of the things that was most helpful to me on my path was the ability to access spiritual community. There is no doubt that we must break our agreements and beliefs alone, and that we are the ones who must assert our personal power and will and say "No more!" to our self-sabotaging behaviors. There is also no doubt that we were born into this world alone and will die alone, but there is nothing more lovely than surrounding ourselves with people who are also searching for their personal freedom during the time in between.

This is important, because when the journey through life becomes challenging, we can always ask a friend to be a mirror for us so that we can see our doings better. These are the best kinds of friends to have, because they are trained *not* to tell us what to do, or to give us advice, or to judge us, but simply to reflect back to us the things we are saying so that we can hear ourselves.

Forthright Friends

The friends I made on my first power journey in 1998 are still my dearest friends, and I would not trade them for anything in the world. They have been forthright Warriors and have never supported my pity parties, nor would they support me put-ting myself down or not loving myself 100 percent. (Now, that's what I call good friends!)

Although we do not have a traditional Warrior's party in my lineage at this time, I consider these friends part of my generation of Warriors. We all started on the Warrior's path around the same time and have progressed similarly. I know that they are there for me no matter how far away they live. I do not need to chat with them often, because as Warriors we neither speak just for the sake of making noise, nor do we gossip, but they are in my heart and I am in theirs. More important, they are ever-present for me to access in my Dreaming at any time since we have traveled with our energy bodies together.

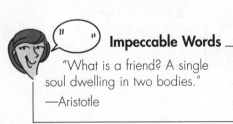

Impeccable Words

"What is a friend? A single soul dwelling in two bodies."
—Aristotle

Helpful Homies

Many of us may believe we should be stoic and not ask for help, lest other people perceive us as being wimpy. Others have beliefs about being an outsider and shy away from organizations that have a sense of community. No matter what fear-based beliefs we're sporting, community is the best way to have those limiting beliefs reflected back to us. Besides, joining a spiritual community is a fabulous not-doing for those very beliefs!

Having people to share our homework with is also powerful, because not only are we Stalking ourselves but our friends, too. In this way, we practice using our skills both internally and externally. This is great because we can then use these same techniques at home, at work, and with our family and friends. As we gain clarity about how the human mind works by understanding our own mind, we will also gain understanding about the minds of others.

As I mentioned in Chapter 19, the Stalking groups that I attended in my early years were an invaluable experience for me. We all practiced these techniques in our group before taking them out on the road, so to speak. And when we did, we came back to the group with our experiences so that we could get feedback about how we could do it better or more effectively, and how we could save more energy and personal power.

Loving Brothers and Sisters

Another powerful aspect of community for me was the opportunity to practice expressing unconditional love in a safe place. As I shared with you earlier, I had never experienced true unconditional love before in my life. As a result, I felt awkward and uncomfortable about expressing my love to others. But in my group, I felt safe and loved, and I was able to experiment with what it might feel like to open my heart and keep it open in any and all circumstances.

For me this was definitely a Warrior's challenge. With the support and love of my compatriots I was able to get out of my own way (my egotistic mind with its rules and regulations) and just go for it. And boy, did it feel good! After a while I got used to expressing my love and could take that into the world without expectations of whether or not it would be returned. And by that time, it no longer mattered.

Warrior Wisdom

Warriors know that love is the key to everything. It is the ultimate expression of the Infinite. It is without boundaries, beyond concepts, and without end. Find it within yourself and you will know it within all things.

Last of all, I have a constant resource of people with whom to engage in business projects and life adventures. What's great about this is the opportunity to work with people who are impeccable in their word, have no hidden agendas, never take anything personally or get upset, and are just a delight to be with. There is never a drama about anything, nor is there anything to get upset over or worry about. If we don't enjoy what we are doing, we all detach and create the next thing. We have all created our dream of the second attention, and these individual dreams continue to overlap in the most unexpected (of course) and delicious ways.

It's hard now to imagine that I ever lived any other way. My gratitude for these people … well, it is not possible for me to express it in words. This blessing is something I wish for all people to experience in their lives.

The Least You Need to Know

- Having patience for our progress on our spiritual path shows self-love and compassion.

- Whether we engage a teacher on our path or not is a personal choice made with clarity, trusting what our heart is telling us.

- Power journeys and spiritual retreats open our hearts and minds to experiences and possibilities outside of our normal daily dream.

- Spiritual community is something we share for our entire lives, a family we create out of love and respect.

Part 7

Living the Life of a Master

Living the life of a master is living the dream of the second attention. This is putting the Mastery of Intent into action. There are some techniques we can use to help us come to a place of living our passion, creating with abandon, and expressing ourselves in life fearlessly. This involves cultivating the ability to listen to our heart and integrity over our mind's chatter. We will also talk about spiritual journeys, community, and whether we need a teacher to guide us on our path. In Part 7, I share information that will enable you to see how a master perceives life and the things we need to do in order to achieve that point of view for ourselves. This is about living our freedom and our spiritual path.

24

The Heart of a Master

In This Chapter

- ◆ Learning to listen to the real self through our inner silence
- ◆ Using feelings and emotions with awareness
- ◆ Reaching the place of having a quiet mind and an open heart
- ◆ Expressing passion from the creative force of life

A Toltec who is a master lives his life in the most delightful way. The way he achieves this is by listening to and being guided by his heart through his inner silence. He knows how to use his feelings and emotions to his advantage and how to pay attention to them. He enjoys having an open heart and expressing it passionately through his life's creations.

In this chapter we will focus on these aspects of a master's life and how we can aspire to reach that place for ourselves. This is truly dreaming consciously and living our dream of the second attention.

Listening to the Real You

What does it mean to listen to the real us? For most of us, we already think we are listening to our real self, but from a Toltec point of view, that would not be truth. Thinking involves engaging our domesticated programming, and that is certainly not listening to the real self. Normally when we are faced with a life situation, we observe it and then think about what we would like to do about it. But listening to the real self can only occur if the mind is quiet and we are not thinking. For myself, at least, this was not an activity that came naturally. It took a lot of my personal power to overcome the tendency to analyze whatever was happening in my life in any moment.

Inner Silence or Inner Turmoil?

Instead, learning to come to the place of inner silence is key, as it's the point from which this departure takes place. Something interesting happens when we quiet our mind. As we learned earlier in Chapter 7, once we take our focus off of our mind (and Tonal), we stop the world as we know it. From that point anything is possible, as we open ourselves to the presence of something else, the real self (the Nagual). The Infinite cannot speak with concepts and language, as it is no-thing (the truth transcendent of concepts). But it can affect us deeply through our feelings and our heart. The question is, how do we access that information when we are used to thinking and mulling everything over?

One way to accomplish this is to go someplace quiet and allow your mind to settle down so you can reach inner silence. Next, visualize the situation you want answers about and watch it in your mind's eye as if it were a movie. Do not talk to yourself in your head, as that would not be inner silence; instead, put yourself into a meditative or restful state (one can even be in Dreaming to do this exercise). Watching the situation that you are questioning or confused about on the big screen of your mind's eye, and noting what you are feeling as a result, is tapping into your intuition, which is coming from the integrity of who you really are.

Impeccable Words

"The Divine Radio is always singing if we could only make ourselves ready to listen to it, but it is impossible to listen without silence."

—Mahatma Gandhi

Of course, we experience these feelings all the time, but it is rare that we trust our gut instinct alone; we usually must rationalize and justify our perceptions with whatever logic our mind proposes just to make it okay from our program's point of view. This is because the mind is afraid of being wrong, and that is why it wants to go through its thinking process rather than allowing us to follow our gut feelings. It is afraid the judge will come in later and beat it up for making a bad choice (as if there's such a thing!).

When we no longer put our faith in our judge and our programming, we no longer need to get caught up in circular thinking. We can go to the place of inner silence and meditate on what we want to do rather than mentally chewing on it. We waste a lot of personal power in circular thinking, because we get our emotions involved and they suck a lot of energy out of us. When we visualize or meditate on something in inner silence, we are not using our rational mind, so our judgment is not involved. As a result we do not engage our fear-based emotions in the process.

Integrity or Programming?

It definitely took me a while to get the hang of functioning like this, but it is a lot more effective in giving us truer answers to the questions that life presents us with. If we ponder something long enough, we may come up with some very logical and reasonable conclusions. But those answers may not be what are most aligned with our integrity; they may not be the most passionate choices, either (we'll discuss passion later in this chapter). When I recapitulated my life, I realized that my whole life was pretty much based in logic, and that the logic didn't necessarily bring me happiness. Some of my best moves in life were the ones that were absolutely devoid of any kind of logic at all (like selling my medical practice)!

This was a powerful exercise for me, and I recommend that you review your life in this way and see if this is truth for you, too. As a note of caution, some actions we take by the seat of our pants turn out quite poorly for us; I have had many such incidents in my life. But when I carefully reviewed these situations, I saw that I was not motivated by feelings coming from my integrity, but instead by my fears and the petty wants and needs of my program. These egotistic desires and fears prompted me to take drastic actions that *looked like* they were intuitive moves, but indeed they were not.

Warrior Warnings

Let's be cautious not to use these teachings to empower us to take action without consideration. A Warrior understands the ramifications of her actions and their affect on others in her life. This consideration is usually obvious if we are seeing what is, and doesn't need a lot of deliberation or thinking. No matter what kind of action a Warrior takes, it is always with total responsibility. Taking action without taking responsibility is not impeccable.

Confusion or Clarity?

Keeping that in mind, we can carefully separate the different choices we have made in life and see for ourselves what the end results were. Hindsight is always 20-20 if we are looking with the eyes of truth instead of telling ourselves a story we want to hear. Although I know many people who are not Toltecs who do trust their intuition all the time, this is not the norm. I encourage you to experiment with using your intuition and listening to what your heart is telling you when you have to make a tough life decision.

Keeping this in mind, choose four major decisions you have made in your life, and answer these questions for each one:

  ◆ How much deliberation did you go through before you reached your decision?

  ◆ What made the choice so hard? What was at stake?

  ◆ What conflicting things was your mind telling you?

  ◆ Did you expend a lot of energy in worry during the process?

  ◆ Did you have a gut feeling about what move you should make?

  ◆ After all of your thinking, was the end decision different from what your initial gut feeling was?

  ◆ Did you end up using your ability to justify and rationalize to make your choice okay?

Indecision occurs due to doubt concerning two or more alternatives, reflecting the confusion that lives within the rational mind. We already know that the mind is confused because it contains conflicting beliefs and agreements. Once we bypass this mental state of turmoil, we find that there is never anything to be confused about! The real self cannot be confused, but the mind certainly can be.

The real self knows, has always known, and will always know. It makes use of the silent knowledge that is present and has always been present in the universe. It just takes coming to the place of no doubt within ourselves and having faith in our ability to make healthy choices.

Feelings and Emotions

I've talked a lot about feelings and emotions in this chapter, but perhaps it would be a good idea to have a clearer concept of what I mean when I use those two words, as they are not necessarily interchangeable.

Remember when we spoke about our emotions back in Chapter 18? I created a list of fear-based emotions to refer to. Emotions arise as a result of perception; we perceive something and then we have an emotional reaction to it. This reaction is one that arises either from direct perception alone and/or from running that perception through our belief system and then having a second emotional reaction to what we believe about what we have perceived. Either way, emotions are our body's method of reacting to stimuli that we receive as a result of being alive and in a human body.

Impeccable Words

"Sometimes when we perceive the world, we perceive without language. We perceive spontaneously … But sometimes when we view the world, first we think a word and then we perceive. In other words, the first instance is directly feeling or perceiving the universe; the second is talking ourselves into seeing the universe. So either you look or see beyond language—as first perception—or you see the world through the filter of your thoughts, by talking to yourself."

—Chögyam Trungpa, *The Sacred Path of the Warrior*

The Facts on Feelings

Feelings, as we are referring to them in *this* chapter, are an awareness, impression, or intuitive understanding of something coming from silent knowledge. This is different from how we commonly use the word "feelings." I have listed examples of the common usage (and interpretation) of the word below so that you can clearly see the difference between these two concepts.

- When we touch something and feel it. This would be our physical body taking the action of feeling. ("I felt her smooth skin.")

- When the rational mind says that it feels something based on thinking or an assessment it made using its programmed information. ("I feel that it is not right to steal.")

- When we feel the emotions we are generating from our perception of someone or something directly *without interpretation* of the mind. ("I feel bliss from the very sight of my baby.")

- When we physically feel the emotions that are coming out of others. ("I can feel my body shaking from Tom's anger.")

◆ When we feel the emotions that we are generating as a result of our *program's interpretation* and judgment of something or someone we are perceiving. We take advantage of this aspect of feeling when we do step 3 of Stalking to reveal our beliefs and agreements. (I am feeling "x," because I believe "y.")

Feelings, as I am specifically referring to them from this point on, are a direct impression or understanding of sort that do not come from perception originating from the five senses of our physical body or our rational mind and its interpretative processes; instead, they come from direct perception by our Nagual. In other words, when Toltecs talk about feelings, we're *not* talking about any of the examples I gave previously.

When we connect with the real self or our Nagual, we do so through feeling, coming from deep within us. When we do this, we reach the place where silent knowledge resides. I shared with you earlier in the book that when I receive silent knowledge it comes to me as a blob of nonlinear knowing. It is a *feeling* of knowing that is absolute, rather than a thinking of knowing. Then I must run that *feeling* of knowing through my rational mind so that I can make "sense" out of it if I want to be able to speak about it (since speech is a linear activity). Truth is, we have all had this experience when we get a hit of intuition; we just choose to ignore it. Toltecs, on the other hand, cultivate that place of feeling within them.

What Am I Feeling?

For Toltecs, it is important to have awareness of which process we are engaged in—feeling an emotional reaction or feeling coming from intuition—because there is a big difference between the two. Both are necessary and natural aspects of our human condition, and there is no reason to change or improve upon either state. But having clarity about these processes is helpful since they both teach us a lot about ourselves.

Warrior Wisdom

Our emotions are wonderful indicators of the point of view we are choosing to perceive our life from in any moment. And our feelings (referring to inner knowing) are fabulous indicators of what the real us is attempting to tell us in any moment.

Try playing around with these questions and see if you can notice the difference between feeling coming from inner knowing and feeling coming from an emotional reaction to something you are perceiving. If you haven't had any of the experiences given, substitute a situation that you have had that is similar in nature:

◆ When you look at the person you are in a relationship with, what do you experience? Is it an emotional reaction or an intuitive feeling?

- When something inside of you says to call your mom and it turns out that she is sick, is that an emotional reaction or an intuitive feeling? Who or what knew she was sick?

- When you looked at the Grand Canyon for the first time, what did you experience? Was it an intuitive feeling or an emotional reaction?

- When you switched jobs to do something you had never done before, was that because you had an intuitive feeling or an emotional reaction about the opportunity? Or was it because you deliberated about it, weighing the pros and cons? If you experienced both a feeling and emotion about the opportunity, where did the feeling come from and what prompted the emotion?

Quiet Mind, Open Heart

A quiet mind sitting in the place of inner silence is an open channel to the silent knowledge and unconditional love of the Infinite. Reaching this place is a monumental challenge. As far as I know, the Toltec tradition doesn't include any formal meditation techniques for quieting the mind (other than using Dreaming techniques), but I don't see any reason for not borrowing techniques from other traditions for our purpose. I mentioned the use of ritual back in Chapter 20, but we can also use any Eastern meditation method or other contemplative practice to accomplish the same thing. Listening to music in a language that makes no sense to us is a method my own teacher used to quiet his mind and reach inner silence.

Don't Believe Yourself!

If I had to identify one powerful Toltec tool for accomplishing the task of quieting the mind, it would be *to not believe ourselves.* If we do not believe anything our mind is proposing to us, it will not be able to hook our attention. It would be as if we were hearing someone talking at the next table in a restaurant: If we don't focus our attention there, we will not hear it. With time, our mind will stop bothering us because we will not be paying attention to it; it will get bored and give up. But as long as we have the belief that we cannot survive without thinking, it is unlikely that our mind will give up its chatting. Even if you don't succeed in totally silencing your mind, anything that you can do to help you quiet it down a bit is a great accomplishment. No method is better than any other. The best way to figure out what works for you is by trial and error.

Warrior Warnings

If we try to use our minds and reason to figure out how to experience love and wonderful relationships, we will fail. There is nothing to figure out; instead, there is everything to experience.

The end purpose for this quieting of the mind is to get us to the place of opening our hearts. Just to clarify, you don't have to have an absolutely quiet mind to have an open heart. They are not mutually exclusive, although if you have a lot of inner dialogue (especially self-deprecating talk), your attention will be pulled to your thinking, which will take you out of the place of being and loving. But *please* do not wait to practice opening your heart until your mind is totally silent, or you may be waiting an awfully long time!

A Disheartening Agreement

For me, this process of opening the heart was a very challenging affair. Between the accumulated hurts and wounds from life and the resulting distrust of others, opening my heart was no longer a natural state. It took a lot of de-programming to turn things around. Somewhere along the line between being a loving little baby and living 40-some odd years, I had lost something essential to my very existence—the freedom to love unabashedly and open my heart just because I wanted to—and I did not know how to get it back. At first, I could not remember when I decided that it was not safe to love and that it was better to close up my heart and put it into a lock box. Worst of all, I could not remember where the heck I hid that darned key!

Through my recapitulation, I saw every little thing that had happened to me to confirm my fear-based agreement that having an open heart was not safe (an agreement I had made as a child). I was able to go back into the movie of my life, and let my inner child know that what I perceived back then was not the truth, only the point of view of a frightened little kid. This enabled me to forgive those people involved in my cementing that agreement into place, which in turn gave me the opportunity to later detach and disempower that agreement and its associated beliefs. I was left with the task of practicing doing exactly the opposite of what I had been doing my whole life. I can assure you, this was not the most comfortable exercise.

Opening Up to Love

As a not-doing, I kept putting myself into situations that required me to be present with an open heart. You could say I did a whole lot of faking it until I was making it. But one day, I was watching the most beautiful demonstration of love in action between my teacher and his mother, and the lock box fell apart. In that moment I allowed my heart to fully open because I felt safe there and I was touched by what I was witnessing. The love that those two humans were putting out in the room was like a tidal wave that my lock box could not withstand. As I sat there weeping, I felt all those old beliefs and agreements about love disintegrate (that was the lock box!), as I knew they were no longer truth for me.

From that point forward, it was just a matter of using my awareness to make sure I didn't go back to my old doings again, and instead I started practicing putting all of my focus and attention on my heart. My old way of being was much easier for me to execute, even though it really didn't *feel* so good any more (it actually went against my integrity). The end result of this was not only feeling free to love others without worrying if they would love me back, but also having the experience of falling in love with myself in a way I never had before.

> **Warrior Wisdom**
>
> Everything that exists in our reality that is illusion exists as a result of conditions. For instance, the use of money exists based on the condition that we all agreed upon its existence. What is truly real in the universe is love, and that is because it needs no conditions or agreements for it to exist.

Falling in love with ourselves is an essential part of this process. After all, if we do not love ourselves madly, it is not likely that we can do the same for another. Without having love for ourselves, what we end up sharing with others is not unconditional love, but instead conditional needs. The two are not at all alike.

Based on what we have said here, ask yourself these questions:

- What happens to your open heart when your mind starts assessing and judging someone?

- When you are upset with someone you love, which emotion is being sent out to him or her in that moment, love or anger?

- Is it really possible to have an open heart when you are angry? Can you actually send both emotions out at the same time?

- When you want something from the person you love, do you withhold your love from him or her at times? How does that feel to both you and the other person?

- As an experiment, see if you can maintain being in a loving place for one day. See if you can stop all the judging in your mind and just send love to everyone (they do not have to be aware of what you are doing).

Going through life with an open heart for both ourselves and others feels wonderful. It doesn't mean that we have to go around hugging everyone. But it does mean we have to stop *judging* everyone, which, in turn, will stop us from getting upset with people and taking them personally. (We cannot be hurt by others or suffer a broken heart from anyone—we do these things to ourselves.) It also means that we have to give up our expectations about others loving us, since a Warrior loves not because he expects something in return, but because he wants to—it is simply his nature. And if we really know in our heart that all of this is true and possible, then it is easy to walk through life with an open and loving heart.

Life Without Passion Is Death

Before I started on my Warrior's path my life was typical. I went to work in the morning, played with my friends, went to the movies, and took my yearly vacations. I visited my accountant quarterly and we discussed my newest five-year plan and I felt comfortable that my life was going exactly the way it was supposed to go. My life was one long series of doings. I was predictable. If I were a deer during hunting season, I would have been the easiest prey to hunt down!

Not so anymore. I have no clue as to what I am going to be doing with my life. Yes, I have events that I am contracted to, and I am impeccable in keeping my commitments, but outside of those types of arrangements, life is totally up in the air for me.

Warrior Wisdom

There is an old proverb that says that vision without action is a daydream, and action without vision is a nightmare. Creating a passionate dream of the second attention involves both action and vision.

I experience life in the moment, rather than planning it in five-year time bytes. This is because I do not live in the future; I live 100 percent right now. But knowing this does not stop me from dreaming about creating all kinds of things (such as this book, for example). Instead, it encourages me to experiment creatively in my life; the difference is that I am not attached to my creations anymore. I don't take it personally if people don't enjoy my creations, either. I love my creations and they bring me joy, and since this is my dream, my life, I am the only one who needs to be amused by myself.

Old Ways, New Days

In the old days, I would practically beat my head against the wall to make something happen that I wanted to happen. That is because I was living my life by what I *thought* I wanted and my mind was the whole problem. When we live through the passion and desire of the heart and Spirit, things are totally different. We can dream up something big and start moving toward that dream.

Sometimes, we may find that things are going in a direction we did not expect. I think that's fantastic! I love looking at all of the reactions to my actions and seeing what is going on. With my feelings, I evaluate if I am enjoying what is happening as a result of my actions. If not, I move in another direction. If I like what is going on, even if it is not what I originally had in mind, I continue on in that new direction.

In other words, life can often bring things to us that are so much better than we would have dreamed up on our own. The key is to be open to life and the experience of it instead of fighting it like I used to. When we live like this, life is constantly a surprise. How can it possibly be boring when our dreams can open up into all different possibilities and creations?

Getting Out of the Box!

Life becomes a trap when we put ourselves in a box. That box is formed by all of the "it must be this way" rules that we have in our programming. When I work personally with folks, they will often share with me that they are still doing what they are doing because they have no idea what they would really like to do in life. They want to do something different, but tell me that there are no opportunities present. This is a trap of their programming. Can you see it? Their program doesn't know what to do, so they do nothing. There are no opportunities present because they can't perceive in life what their program does not believe exists. Eek!

Some people are extremely lucky to know from a young age what their passion is, but for the rest of us, we need to actually experience something or taste it, so to speak, to appreciate it and know whether it is right for us. We'll either like it or we won't; it's that simple. So the key is to get out there and try different things. We are often surprised by what we find out about ourselves.

Impeccable Words

"When you are inspired by some great purpose, some extraordinary project, all your thoughts break their bonds; your mind transcends limitations, your consciousness expands in every direction, and you find yourself in a new, great, and wonderful world. Dormant forces, faculties, and talents become alive, and you discover yourself to be a greater person by far than you ever dreamed yourself to be."

—Patanjali

Faith and Passion

Again, it all boils down to having faith that you are totally capable and able to manifest whatever the Infinite is moving you to create. It is important that you *feel* and *know* in your heart what that message is, because I can assure you that you will not hear that message with words in your head. If you do, it might be an okay idea, but it is coming from your mind, not your heart. There is a huge difference!

Passion, by the way, is not something to be afraid of, and it is not sinful (this belief is not truth). Creation is a product of passion, whether the result is the birth of a baby, an incredible four-course meal, a masterpiece of art, a symphony, or a cake for a bake-sale. If we look out our window, we will see the process of creation being demonstrated everywhere. As humans, we are creating all of the time, but not always with faith, passion, or awareness. What makes our life exciting is doing it with passion, rather than doing it in a rote and uninspired way.

So let's bust open the box, forget the program, and experiment with expressing our passion and discovering ourselves in new and different ways. Opportunities are all around us. We just have to see them, take the action, and experience what the reaction is. Let's not allow our mind to eliminate possibilities strictly on the basis of whether our mind thinks they are right or not according to its limited point of view! Let's give them a try and see how they *feel* to us. If we are not passionate about life, we might as well be dead. From a Toltec point of view, when we live our lives without passion and awareness, it is a kind of death. It's time to change the paradigm we have been operating under, and take a chance on ourselves and have faith in what we can co-create with life. This is truly dreaming a dream of the second attention!

The Least You Need to Know

♦ Reaching the place of inner silence enables us to access our Nagual, our inner knowing and integrity, which is more trustworthy than our rational mind.

♦ Feelings and emotions are not the same, but they are both powerful tools we can use to better understand ourselves and the way we perceive life.

♦ Having a quiet mind and open heart means that we are an open channel for the Infinite.

♦ Unless we live passionate, exciting, and unpredictable lives, we will end up bored, predictable, and uninterested in life.

Chapter 25

The Bottom Line

In This Chapter

◆ Pursuing a path with heart

◆ The journey to self-awareness and self-acceptance

◆ A tradition based on impeccability

◆ A Warrior's expression of love

◆ Knowing yourself as the Infinite

We have come to the end of our journey together. We have learned a lot about Toltec wisdom over the course of these pages and I have done my best to leave you with all you need to know to start your adventure of self-awareness and love. In this chapter I have pulled together a few of the most important aspects and concepts of the Toltec philosophy to leave you with an overall feeling of the purpose of this path.

I have called this chapter "The Bottom Line" because I feel it encapsulates and summarizes the outstanding ideas that we as Toltec Warriors live our lives from. Although I know that we have our own language and tradition, if I leave you with anything, it would be the understanding that none of this is meant to be *memorized* as dogma, but instead *understood* as a practical, common-sense guide to *live* your life in integrity and peace.

A Path of the Heart

Toltec has been called *a path with heart* many times. As we have discussed, there are so many philosophies, spiritual paths, and religions in this world to choose from. What makes one path better than another, and how do we know which path to choose for ourselves? In my experience, the path seems to choose us rather than us choosing the path. Personally, I was drawn to the Toltec path in college after reading Dr. Castaneda's books, but never was able to find anyone teaching the work.

Years went by and I would read whatever was new on the Toltec tradition, but at the time I was caught up in my illusion, going to medical school, getting married, and doing just what was expected of me in that dream. One day I bought a Toltec paperback and noticed that this particular Toltec teacher actually gave workshops, had apprentices, and took people on journeys. Something pulled me toward this path, and that feeling was not rational or sensible at all. But off I went on a power journey, not knowing what to expect. What I experienced was my first glimpse of my true self in all its brilliance and mystery. And I wanted more!

> **Toltec Topography**
>
> A path with heart is the path we follow in life that makes our heart sing, makes our walk joyful, and strengthens our faith.

Happy Trails

You picked up this book for some reason. Maybe the title hooked you or maybe you were curious to know more about the Toltec teachings. If something I have written speaks to you, maybe this is your path. You only have to start walking it to know this for yourself. And how do you know if this is for you? Simple! If you feel an opening of your heart, if you experience a glimpse of yourself being revealed and the all beauty and majesty that entails, then this is a path with heart for you.

Many revelations will be made on our journey of self-discovery, which is why it is very important for us to feel happy on our path, to enjoy it and the changes it brings. If our chosen path has heart, it will support us when the road is bumpy, and elate us when the way is bright.

Rocky Roads

On the other hand, a path without heart will drain us of our personal power and cause the light in our life to dim. It will make us feel depressed and steal our inspiration. If our path doesn't have heart, we won't have the strength to make it through the tough times and will focus on the dark parts of ourselves. Rather than continuing to expand our possibilities, it will limit us and constantly tell us what we cannot do. A path without heart will dull our connection with the Infinite rather than encourage it, and cut us off from trusting our silent knowledge.

It is important to have faith that we have chosen a good path for ourselves despite the fact that we may not have chosen well for ourselves in our past. The difference lies in the feeling we have in our heart rather than what the mind is telling us. Our feelings, as we said in Chapter 24, will always guide us. Of course, this advice goes for any path we may choose, not just the Toltec way. Take a chance on life and go for it. What is the worst thing that can happen? We can change our choice, and change it without judging ourselves!

> **Impeccable Words**
>
> "All paths are the same: they lead nowhere. However, a path without a heart is never enjoyable. On the other hand, a path with heart is easy—it does not make a warrior work at liking it; it makes for a joyful journey; as long as a man follows it, he is one with it."
>
> —Carlos Castaneda, *The Teachings of Don Juan* (as quoted in *The Wheel of Time*)

There Is Just One Journey in Life

I think we can see that there is only one true journey in our life: the journey deep inside ourselves, into our heart; the one that leads to self-awareness and self-love, absolute self-acceptance, and, finally, total freedom. I understand that our everyday existence pulls at our attention, and it takes a great commitment to ourselves to create balance between what is really important in life and paying the bills. Yet it can be done. If we really want something with all our heart, we will find a way to make the time, to adjust our schedule, to do whatever it takes to make it happen.

Any Time, Any Place

The mistake that most people make is thinking that we need free time on the weekends to do this work. This is far from the truth. We can do it any time of day, any place, with our kids, at work, and while mowing the lawn or ironing. Our spiritual transformation is not something separate from our life; *it is* our life. Most of us haven't come to this simple awareness yet. By learning to cultivate our awareness, we will see great miracles happening every day. Our life will become easier and more delightful. And even though the self-introspection can be painful at first, we start to get used to the process and it becomes fun, because we can see the beneficial results in our daily life. How great is that?

Going for the Gold!

The question to ask ourselves is, "Are we worth this journey of self-acceptance, freedom, and, ultimately, the experience of the best life has to offer?" Most of us do not think so, and the proof of that is not in the answer that people will give you (because their programs will lie and say that they are worth it), but instead in their actions, the sum total of their lives.

If we look at our life objectively, like a stranger observing the movie of our life, what would that stranger say? Is this a life of allowing people to go against us? Is it a life of never going after the brass ring because we don't think that it's possible for us?

Warrior Wisdom

We know that we are all born and we will all die, but what happens and what we create in between makes all the difference in the kind of lives we live. Will it be a life of magic or mediocrity?

Where is the faith, passion, and desire in our lives? Only we can answer these questions with honesty, in the quiet of our own hearts.

If we believe that we deserve the very best that life has to offer, then that's great; let's make the effort in every moment to wake up in our daily life, pay attention, see where our mind is pulling us and what kind of judgments it's making. Let's make a Warriors' commitment to take actions that prove that we're worth it and to stop believing all the limitations our minds are imposing on us.

Impeccability Is a Mastery

In the beginning of this book, we said that to live impeccably means to not go against ourselves or others. Impeccability is the basis of the Toltec path. As Warriors, we know that it is the birthright of all humans to be free, and yet that freedom is not laid at our feet. We must do our part to claim it. If our actions are always impeccable, then there is no doubt that we can reach freedom.

The truth is, on the path to personal freedom, our actions and words are not always impeccable and we often hurt ourselves and others. By living impeccably, though, we can save up the personal power that it takes to break these unhealthy behavior patterns in our lives. In the end, the only thing we have is our impeccability, which, as Warriors, we depend upon until the end of our days.

Although we talked about all the ways we can be impeccable throughout this book, I would like to take a few moments for you to imagine the totality of what I have shared with you, and what life could possibly look like if we all practiced impeccability.

Impeccable Communication

Communicating impeccably means that no matter what we say or how we use our word, it is with a clear and well-defined purpose. It also means that the emotion being sent with our words is love. No personal power is wasted in judging, gossiping, useless chattering, and sending mal-intent. There is also no yelling, bickering, fighting, or arguing. A Warrior will never say anything for no reason or to just fill up time and space.

Impeccable Action

A Warrior is clear in the motivations for his actions, and doesn't drain his energy in beating around the bush. He does what he needs to in the most efficient and kind way, doing his best not to hurt others in the process. A Warrior doesn't waste time thinking too much about choices to be made, and once a choice has been made, he doesn't waste his time worrying about it. He utilizes his time well, not draining his energy trying to do more than can possibly be done in a day. By using his Stalking techniques, he knows the optimal time to say something to someone or when to take an action so that the effect is maximized.

Impeccable Livelihood

Doing what makes our heart sing is important, since we know that doing anything else will drain our energy. When a Warrior is happy doing what she enjoys in life, she is passionate, a result of the Infinite moving through her. She wouldn't work at something that goes against herself or doesn't support the higher good. This includes taking care of her physical condition, too, as a Warrior considers the body the temple for the Infinite. She balances her life and is aware of when she isn't sleeping or eating well enough. A Warrior makes sure that she starts each day with her energy reserve intact.

Impeccable Emotions

The way we choose to emote can be one of the largest wastes of our personal power. Every time we express our fear-based emotions and get ourselves upset, we weaken ourselves. When we express our joy and love, we strengthen ourselves. A Warrior makes sure that he eliminates the beliefs that do not support his happiness and soundness of mind.

Warrior Warnings

Warriors do not torture, punish, or judge themselves for not being impeccable in the beginning years of their path. They know that they have been domesticated to do everything possible to drain their energy and remain imprisoned in their dream.

Impeccable Minds

Using our program to calculate or figure out certain things in life is great. But using our minds to worry, think excessively, and carry on internal dialogue ad infinitum will drain our personal power for sure. Having conversations with ourselves in our heads that cause us to get upset is a big energy drain. Cleaning the mind of all its unhealthy beliefs and fear-based agreements is one of the most powerful ways of releasing tied-up energy and gaining power.

Impeccable Love

Living life with our heart open is the best way to resist wasting energy supporting resentments, grudges, and anger against others. Through forgiveness, large amounts of energy can be harnessed for other purposes, like opening our hearts. A Warrior's expression of his unconditional love is surely the most impeccable use of his life, as it is a living channel for the Infinite to express itself through.

These activities, if practiced impeccably every day, will have us saving enough personal power and energy to transform our entire lives. They all constitute examples of living impeccably, and they all lead to an amazing outcome: a life of heaven. Warriors know this is possible, because we are living examples of what it can be like. This is why we enjoy hanging out and working together. All it takes is *one* impeccable act followed by another one, sustained over time. The end result is freedom and paradise.

All We Need Is Love

I've mentioned love many times throughout this book, but I want to make sure we understand what a Warrior means by love. In the dream of the planet, we have a lot of ideas about what love is, but Toltecs have a much different way of perceiving it. First and foremost, when we say that all we need is love, we are talking *self-love*. A Warrior doesn't *need* anything in her life, especially anything coming from someone else. Needing, wanting, or having to have love is just an expression of the egotistic desires of our mind's programming, and has nothing to do with real love!

Love Is Kind

Above all things, a Warrior knows that love is kind and respectful. When he loves, it would never occur to him to treat another person any differently than he would treat himself. A Warrior doesn't *try* to be kind or respectful—he just *is* because it has become his nature and his pleasure. He is patient with love, never rushing it or pushing it, and never wishing or hoping it looked different. So many times we want our relationships and love to look like something we have in our imagination. We hope that the others in our lives will change or take different actions. A Warrior wishes and hopes for nothing from others but takes whatever actions he needs in order to make his side of the relationship as impeccable as possible.

Love Has No Expectations

Warriors have no expectations in life or in love; there are no "it should be this way" or "it must look this way" statements. When we do not put pressure on people to be a certain way, they can be who they are and feel good about it. Putting expectations on others just makes them feel obligated and pressured and more likely to run the other way. When we have no expectations of others, we do not feel like we have to tell them what to do or control them anymore, and that makes any relationship more comfortable. Most folks have had people trying to control them their entire lives. A loving relationship functions better when it is a sanctuary from those types of behaviors.

Love Is Not Personal

The love of a Warrior is equal, no matter who it is given to, since love is not a personal thing. By this I mean that the love that is coming out of her heart is like the light of the sun: it's always shining. When it's sunny outside, I don't think that this is a personal gift to me. The sun is shining because that's what it does. We can "shine" that way, too, with our love, except that we have been taught to mete out our love, only giving it to those we personally know, and only when someone is behaving the way we want them to. When we want something, we can withhold our love and manipulate with it. A Warrior will never do this. She will just go through life with her heart open, not caring if someone receives her love or not. She loves because she wants to, not because she has to or because she should or because anyone will notice.

Although a Warrior's love is not personal, the way she chooses to demonstrate her love might be. For example, she may choose to make love to her partner, but not to a friend. From a practical point of view, she only has the opportunity to have close relationships with some people, not with all of the 6 billion humans on this earth! Regardless of how many of those people she has time to encounter in her life, she will still send her love out to all of them (even if they have mean or violent programs). She knows that love is transformative, and it is her pleasure to uplift others with her presence and joy.

> **Warrior Warnings**
>
> Liberate your love. Holding back your expression of love is the same as stopping the flow of life moving through your body. Either way you are experiencing a slow death.

Love Is Generous

A Warrior is giving of his love and is generous, but he also respects himself enough not to let selfish people cross his boundaries. On the other hand, he doesn't clamp down on people's expression of love to him; in other words, he doesn't tell them how *their* love should look. Many times we want someone's love to *be* a certain way; we want the person to be more affectionate, perhaps, or to be more expressive, not realizing that the person may not be capable of that. A Warrior knows that others' abilities are different depending on where they are in life, and he accepts them as they are, rather than putting pressure on them to act in ways they cannot.

Love Is Gracious

Many times we enjoy giving gifts of our love to others, but we find it hard to accept when someone wants to give something to us. This is simply a reflection of our lack of self-love. Allowing people to love us and gift us keeps the energy of love moving rather than letting it get all bottled up in one place. A Warrior accepts gifts from others generously, lovingly, and with gratitude, as an expression of their love.

Love Is Unconditional

A Warrior's love is unconditional. That means it has absolutely no conditions of any kind. No matter how nasty, mean, or cruel you are to a Warrior, he will still love you.

If you act this way, he may not choose to be in your physical presence, but he will love you just the same, because love is who he is. Not being in the presence of someone nasty is simply a reflection of his self-love, which keeps him out of situations that go against him.

When I feel the presence of the Infinite, I experience the most immeasurable and vast tidal wave of unconditional love (at least, that is the best phrase I have for this feeling). Not only do I feel that presence outside of myself, but within me, too, and I am propelled to express that love in my life in order to be true to myself. Since there is only one life, I know that it is your nature, too. I encourage you to open your heart and not be afraid to be who you really are. Love hugely, passionately, and fiercely like a Warrior. I promise it feels *really* fantastic!

> **Impeccable Words**
>
> "The moment you have in your heart this extraordinary thing called love and feel the depth, the delight, the ecstasy of it, you will discover that for you the world is transformed."
>
> —J. Krishnamurti

Knowing Yourself as the Infinite

We've spent a lot of time talking about how our program sabotages our lives without our awareness. We've also spent time observing how we hurt ourselves using the fear-based beliefs and agreements we have in our minds. I introduced you to the concepts of humans being Tonal and Nagual and how as Warriors we desire to take our focus off the Tonal so that we can know ourselves as the Infinite. In looking at our beliefs, we have identified so many unhealthy behavior patterns and actions that hurt us, but there is one belief at the very root of *all* of our beliefs that is causing the most damage of all.

It's nothing I haven't mentioned throughout the book many times, but I have never written it out plainly for us to discuss. Because we've reached the end of our journey together, however, I feel that this would be the perfect time to talk about it. As humans we have been domesticated to believe we are many things, but mostly we have been taught to believe that we are our mind and our body (our Tonal). We can obviously see our body and hear our mind

> **Warrior Wisdom**
>
> Warriors know that they are not the sum total of their life experiences, but much, much more than that. They are life experiencing the mystery of itself through the point of view and awareness of the manifest.

talking, so when we are growing up we identify ourselves with them. The truth is we are not the mind or the body, they are simply our computer and physical home that enables us to move through this reality we call manifestation. Just because we cannot see or hear Spirit, it doesn't mean we are not Spirit. We've spent our lives with our Nagual (Spirit) subservient to our Tonal (mind and body), rather than the other way around. As Warriors, our challenge in life is to be free from that subservience, and to express our true selves every day of our lives. It is simply learning to change the focus of our attention from the Tonal to the Nagual. Then we know from experience itself that indeed this is true.

I Am Not

The belief that stops us from creating and being anything we desire in life is the mother of all fear-based beliefs: that *we are not* the Infinite. I hear many people who study new-thought philosophies tell me, "Oh, I believe Spirit is in all people. I know I'm that." We may understand this from an intellectual point of view, but we do not believe it. How do I know this? Simple. As a society, we are not living it! Our deeds, rather than our words, are the evidence.

If we believe that the Infinite has no limitations of any kind, and each one of us is the Infinite, then why do we argue for our limitations? How can we believe that we are not co-creating our reality? How can we blame things that are happening in our lives on others if we are the embodiment of the Infinite? Let's ask ourselves, with all honesty: If we really believe this in our hearts, then why do we persist in hurting ourselves and others?

> **Warrior Wisdom**
>
> When Warriors take total responsibility for their life, in that moment they are proclaiming that they know who they are. They know that they are the Infinite and can create anything; the Intent of the Warrior becomes the Intent of the Infinite. This is absolute and total faith in themselves.

If we say that we can't forgive someone who we are upset with, or we say that we are too shy to give that business speech, what are we really saying? We are saying *we can't*. And we say those things because we are invested in fear-based beliefs that are obviously not truth.

We can't do these things because we do not believe we are the Infinite. When we know ourselves as the Infinite, we know with every cell in our body that *we can do anything*. We stop putting our faith and personal power in what our mind is telling us—*we are not the Infinite*—and instead put our faith into what our heart is telling us—*we are*.

I Am

Believing in who we really are is very, very challenging because it goes against so much of what we have been taught to believe. For example, I grew up believing that God was something separate from me in some way, that God was somewhere above me and could possibly hurt me, judge me, or send me to hell. It wasn't easy for me to even begin exploring having the personal experience of merging with the Infinite to see for myself if these teachings were really truth. But I did, and what I found was that there is only one life, one consciousness, all equal and all-encompassing.

This experience changed my life profoundly, and from that point forward, I was able to put my faith in my Nagual rather than in all those beliefs my mind was telling me. But please, don't take my words as dogma. I encourage you all to have the experience of finding this out for yourself. Shift levels of awareness and use the Infinite within you to merge with the Infinite outside you. (And please know that what I am saying is not meant as disrespect to anyone's belief system. Everyone is welcome to believe anything that they choose.)

Impeccable Words

"When divine spirit is matter, it feels the ecstasy of God passing through it. When divine spirit is formless, it *is* that ecstasy passing through matter, giving it form. Divine spirit, the light of God, is coming and going, manifesting and unmanifesting. This is the rhythm of life, the verse of life. This interaction is how *life* creates the stars, how *life* creates matter—and matter becomes the mirror that reflects the light."

—don Miguel Ruiz, *Prayers*

A Warrior is a master when he can say that he has realized the two halves of himself as one and can move back and forth between the two aspects or points of view. Whether his focus is on the Tonal or the Nagual, he is at ease having the knowledge of who he really is. He knows he can create anything in life and chooses to create beauty, peace, and love. Even better, by focusing his attention on the Nagual within him, he can experience bliss just from the very presence of himself.

I remember the first time I experienced that feeling within me. I felt so high. I asked my teacher how that feeling could have been present within me my whole life without my ever knowing of its existence. He said to me, with all the love in his heart, "Sheri, you never put your attention on *you* [as the Infinite] before because you never believed the Infinite could possibly exist within you. You cannot experience what *you do not believe* exists." I knew then with absolute certainty that the mind creates our reality with all its inherent possibilities and limitations. Powerful, isn't it?

And this, my friends, is the result of the Toltec Masteries of Awareness, Transformation, and Intent. I appreciate your joining me on this fantastic journey, and I wish you the best, no matter what roads you choose to travel. Truly, all sentient beings live to glorify the Infinite.

As we say in our Toltec lineage: *Que tu sol sea brillante.* May your sun shine brightly! Blessings!

The Least You Need to Know

- ◆ A path with heart is the one that will bring us joy on our journey through life.

- ◆ The definitive journey for a Warrior is the one to personal freedom, self-awareness, and love.

- ◆ Impeccability is a Warrior's ticket to his personal power and freedom.

- ◆ A Warrior loves because it is her expression of who she really is: the Infinite moving through her.

Appendix A

Glossary

a path with heart   The Toltec path or any path in life that brings us joy and is uplifting to our heart.

abstract concepts   Thoughts or ideas that are conceived within the mind but have no physical or concrete existence. We use concepts to describe our personal experience so that we can communicate with one another.

act of power   An action a Warrior takes that is driven by the Intent of the Infinite or life moving through him. Since a Warrior's acts are impeccable, they are always acts of power.

assemblage point   A small area on the back of the luminous egg near the right shoulder blade. This is where the energetic patterns of light that our body is made of intersect with the energetic patterns of light of the greater universe. As a result of this alignment, perception occurs.

Atlanteans   Fierce-looking statues of Toltec Warrior women that stand 15 feet tall and are located on top of a 130-foot-tall pyramidal structure in the ancient Toltec city of Tula.

attention   Humans possess the ability to focus their attention on anything they choose to perceive. With our attention we can filter out all the perceptive input we are not interested in receiving and focus solely on what we want to hear or see.

Avenue of the Dead   The main north-south road that passes through the ancient city of Teotihuacán. According to my lineage, it is so named because the Warriors who walked down this path had to die to their old way of living before they could continue their spiritual journey toward enlightenment.

awareness   The ability to receive information about our surroundings. We attribute awareness to being alive and conscious, although that consciousness might not resemble the consciousness of humans (other forms of life have awareness, too, like plants, trees, rocks, and inorganic beings).

Aztecs   The wandering tribe of Mexican-Indians that founded the great city of Tenochtitlán (now Mexico City) around 1325 C.E.

belief   A statement that we accept as true or real. It can also be a firmly held opinion or conviction.

Chac mool   The name given to the sacrificial platform that resembles a reclining man holding a platter over his chest. We see these structures throughout central Mexico at many ancient ruins.

Cholula   A city in central Mexico founded in 600 C.E. The name comes from the Nahuatl word *Cholollan*, which means "the place of flight."

co-create   The knowing that we are conscious partners with life and that partnership is 50-50. We are responsible for our 50 percent and life is responsible for its 50 percent. In an equal relationship there can be no victims, only partnership.

compassion   A deep awareness of the suffering of humanity and our planet and the desire to heal it.

controlled folly   For Stalkers, achieving this is a great accomplishment. It means that we can play in this reality with no attachment and no expectations, and with absolute awareness of our choices and actions.

denial   An unconscious defense mechanism that humans use to ignore painful realities, thoughts, or feelings. When we are in denial we can disown or disavow our own acts and blame them on others.

doings   Actions we take that are directed by the mind's programming, usually without awareness. They cause us to create our world exactly as we want to see it according to our domestication and socialization, rather than the way it is.

domestication   The process of socialization that humans go through to learn to think, act, and see like our parents and other humans.

don Juan Matus   Carlos Castaneda's teacher, made famous in Castaneda's series of books chronicling his apprenticeship with this enigmatic and mysterious Toltec master.

dream of heaven   Refers to heaven on earth for a Warrior; a life of beauty, unconditional love, grace, self-acceptance, inner peace, and happiness.

dream of the planet   What Toltecs call the combined energetic structure of beliefs, rules, and concepts that all the humans on our planet simultaneously dream and project onto our conjoined reality.

Dreamer   A Dreamer is an expert at shifting levels of consciousness or positions of the assemblage point. A Dreamer can shift her state of consciousness to perceive any reality by the use of her attention.

Dreaming   A technique that enables us to change our ordinary dream (of nonawareness) into Dreaming (with awareness) by the purposeful and controlled use of the second attention, or Dreaming attention.

energy   The ability to do work (physical or mental effort or activity). Energy can neither be created nor destroyed. It can only be converted or transformed from one form to another.

energy body   Our other self, the energetic essence of a person. It is not confined to our physical body, nor does it have the limitations of the physical body. Also called the dreaming body, or the double.

erasing personal history   A process of detaching from what we believe about our personal life story domestication, life experiences, and programming.

faith   For a Warrior it has nothing to with believing in concepts or ideas that his fellow human blindly believes to be true. His faith is in himself as the Infinite; his faith is absolute in this and he has no doubt.

fear-based emotions   Emotions that result from our believing in concepts that are not truth or not in accordance with love.

fifty-two years   In the Toltec and Mayan calendars, the number representing one complete cycle of renewal.

first attention   When we were domesticated we learned to use our attention for the first time, and created the world of the Tonal by consensus, which put order into our chaotic universe. This order represents a point of view and is not necessarily the absolute truth.

folly   The lack of good sense, understanding, and foresight of humans, leading to foolish or senseless behavior as a result of putting one's life on autopilot and having no awareness.

grace   Not a Toltec word, but used in this book in the theological sense. When we are given divine approval, favor, and mercy, divine acceptance is bestowed upon us. Warriors strive to give themselves divine acceptance for their own folly.

heightened awareness   A state of consciousness resulting from a movement of the assemblage point, enabling us to align different energetic patterns of light outside us. The result is increased clarity and connection with silent knowledge.

impeccabilis   In Latin, the word impeccabilis means not to sin. Warriors act impeccably, meaning that they do not sin or go against themselves, and they do not go against others or our earth.

Infinite   That entity which is boundless in time or space, without beginning or end, absolute, and omnipotent. The part of us that is manifest in this reality, yet is eternal. Other terms that mean the same are Nagual, Spirit, and God.

inner silence   Absolute quietude of the mind resulting from detaching our attention from our internal dialogue. It is the gateway to the second attention and the Infinite.

inorganic beings   Entities that possess awareness and can perceive, but do not have bodies that are organic or carbon-based like ours or our planet's (our planet is also made of carbon).

integrity   The state of being whole and complete, experiencing the totality of ourselves as Tonal and Nagual. Living our lives honestly from our heart and Spirit rather than from the lies of our programming.

Intent   The force that life uses to create and manifest everything in the universe.

internal dialogue   The constant conversation that takes place within our own mind, which we call thinking. It hooks our attention by repeating the contents of our program and our beliefs and concepts. We maintain our view of the world and our personal point of view with our internal dialogue.

inventory   The totality of the contents of the human mind: all of its concepts, beliefs, judgments, agreements, points of view, and interpreted experiences.

judgment   A conclusion a person comes to based on his or her opinion.

justification   When we create an explanation for ourselves or another person (using the contents of our belief system) to make our actions appear right, reasonable, or necessary.

left-sided awareness The result of shifting our assemblage point to a place of clarity and absolute knowing (also known as heightened awareness, or a shift to the left). Complete understanding that is effortless and immediate, coming from direct knowing. When we are in this state, we are in the second attention.

lineages Groups of Toltecs descending from different teachers for the purpose of passing down the knowledge of the tradition secretly, safe from corruption and misuse for generations to come, until they could be revealed at the appropriate time.

losing the human form The process of losing our attachment to all the beliefs, concepts, opinions, points of view, emotional reactions, personality traits, and domesticated doings that make us what we are. We become impersonal, and are in service to the Infinite.

mal-intent Bad intent, or actions taken with the specific purpose of harming or hurting another.

Nagual Refers to Spirit, God, or the Infinite. It is the immensity of the unknowable, what can never be described. It can also refer to the Nagual, or leader, of a Toltec party of Warriors.

no-thing Refers to the understanding that life, the Infinite, God, the Nagual, or any term we choose to use for Spirit is not and cannot be defined or limited by any concept or idea. That would immediately make it Tonal or some-thing.

not-doings Activities that we create to illuminate and break fear-based beliefs and behavior patterns that we may not be aware of.

one life Refers to the knowledge that there is only one living being in the universe, the Infinite, and that we are all parts of this one living being. Duality is an illusion both in the concepts of the mind and in the visual illusion that we are separate from each other.

opinion A view or judgment formed that is not necessarily based on fact or knowledge.

perception The act of registering information through our five senses. This information is collected and sent to the brain for processing and to the mind for interpretation. We can also perceive directly with our Nagual and bypass the interpretation of the rational mind.

petty tyrant Any person who has the ability to drive us crazy, irritate us endlessly, get us frustrated, and drive us to distraction. Petty tyrants help us face our own self-importance and self-centeredness.

power   In the world of physics, power is defined as $p = w/t$, where w = work and t = time. In this case, work equals force times distance. For those of us who are physics-challenged, an easier way to word this is that power is energy transformed over time.

power journey   A journey for the specific purpose of enhancing our process of personal growth and enlightenment. During these trips we avail ourselves of the energy that our mother earth holds.

power objects   Items that have no use or meaning other than the Intent the Warrior gives to them. Often plain objects were used to focus a Warrior's Intent, making the item dangerous if it was imbued with malevolent desire. It can also be imbued with beautiful Intent—for example, wearing a cross your mother gave you to protect you from harm.

programming   The contents of the rational mind, ego, or the small self, which were downloaded into us during our domestication and life. It is everything we know, believe, and think, and it is the totality of all our agreements.

Quetzalcoatl   The name of the god-man that the Toltecs supposedly worshipped in their mythology.

rationalization   When we make something that we are doing or saying seem consistent with reason (the reason of our faulty programming, that is!). Or when we devise self-satisfying but untruthful reasons for our behavior.

recapitulation   A summary or concise review of the supposed repetition in the evolutionary development of an individual's life history.

revelation   An important concept in many religions. For us it is the uncovering of what is truth, an enlightening or astonishing disclosure of something not previously known or realized about oneself.

right-sided awareness   Our everyday state of consciousness that we have been taught to experience and perceive (also called the *first attention*). This state involves dependence on the rational mind and thinking.

second attention   When we focus our attention for the second time on what is, rather than on what we were taught to see.

seeing   The ability to see what is without the filtering process of the rational mind. This is how a Warrior who has lost the human form perceives; she can see what is in the world of the Tonal or see the world as it is as energy (the Nagual).

seer   A Warrior who has become totally impersonal and no longer has an attachment to any particular point of view. He sees the essence of the world as it is, without story or judgment.

shamanism   An animistic religious structure practiced throughout the world. In these traditions, a member of the society acts as a medium between the visible world and the spirit world using magic or sorcery practices for the purpose of the healing, divination, or control over natural events.

silent knowledge   The wealth of information in the universe, which we all are connected to, but which we have forgotten how to use or reach. We receive this information as a nonlinear mass of knowing.

Stalker   An expert at functioning in the realm of everyday consciousness. He can shift his behavior to become anything or anyone he wants in order to affect the best outcome in any situation.

Stalking   The process of hunting, following, and observing our weaknesses for the purpose of transforming them into our strengths. A Warrior will stalk her own mind to break her obsession with the thinking of the rational mind and the Tonal.

stopping the world   When we finally silence the mind and the world of the Tonal stops. Then we can assemble any reality we desire.

Teotihuacán   The ancient Toltec city (according to our lineage) of pyramids and ruins, located 25 miles northeast of Mexico City.

third attention   Freedom that results from the experience of the totality of you as the unknowable or the Infinite. It is absolute consciousness and presence, which spans the width and breadth of the universe.

Toltecs   An ancient society of Warriors of personal freedom. They were masters of awareness and great artists of the Spirit and anything they chose to create in their lives.

tonal   The world of reason; everything we think we know about the world, the totality of agreements we make about it and ourselves, and the linear order we put to it all.

truth   What is without conceptual interpretation, and does not need our belief in it to make it truth.

Tula   Ancient Toltec city northwest of Mexico City by about 45 miles in the state of Hidalgo.

virtual reality   The virtual reality of the rational mind is a seemingly real world created from light that totally simulates the reality outside of us.

voice of Dreaming   The voice of Dreaming, or Dreaming emissary, is a voice that comes from the realm of the inorganic beings. It has consciousness but no physical body in our reality.

void   Where the consciousness of the Infinite originates. It is connected to the manifest world through one point, which is located both everywhere and no-where.

Warrior   A Toltec who is fighting for freedom from her own domestication and social conditioning. She is free from needing to link her self-worth to the beliefs, thoughts, and wishes of her fellow human, free to be happy no matter what happens in life.

will   A force that a Warrior cultivates that is a purposefulness, determination, or deliberate desire that transcends thought or rational mind. It comes through him from the Infinite and can also be seen as the personalized force of Intent.

witness   In terms of a Toltec Warrior's party, the assistant or witness can be a man or a woman, Dreamer or Stalker; if the witness is a woman she is usually from the south. A witness can also be one who can give a firsthand account of something seen, heard, or experienced. He sees exactly what is from a neutral point of view without judgment or opinion.

wounds   Our wounds consist of all those hurts that we have accumulated in our emotional bodies over the years as a result of painful experiences that we took personally.

Further Toltec Reading

Currently Published Toltec Tomes

Abelar, Taisha. *The Sorcerer's Crossings*. New York: Viking Penguin, 1992.

Ash, Heather. *The Four Elements of Change*. Tulsa: Council Oak, 2004.

Castaneda, Carlos. *The Teachings of Don Juan: A Yaqui Way of Knowledge*. University of California Press, 1968.

————. *A Separate Reality: Further Conversations with Don Juan*. New York: Simon & Schuster, 1971.

————. *Journey to Ixtlan: The Lessons of Don Juan*. New York: Simon & Schuster, 1972.

————. *Tales of Power*. New York: Simon & Schuster, 1974.

————. *The Second Ring of Power*. New York: Simon & Schuster, 1977.

————. *The Eagle's Gift*. New York: Simon & Schuster, 1981.

————. *The Fire from Within*. New York: Simon & Schuster, 1984.

————. *The Power of Silence: Further Lessons of Don Juan*. New York: Simon & Schuster, 1987.

————. *The Art of Dreaming*. New York: HarperCollins, 1993.

————. *The Active Side of Infinity*. New York: HarperCollins, 1998.

———. *The Wheel of Time*. Los Angeles: Eidolona Press, 1998.

———. *Magical Passes*. New York: HarperCollins, 1998.

Dibble, David. *The New Agreements in the Workplace*. New York: The Emeritus Group, 2002.

Dodd, Ray. *The Power of Belief: Essential Tools for an Extraordinary Life*. Charlottesville: Hampton Roads, 2004.

Donner-Grau, Florinda. *Shabono: A Visit to a Remote and Magical World in the South American Rain Forest*. New York: HarperCollins, 1982.

———. *The Witch's Dream: A Healer's Way of Knowledge*. New York: Simon & Schuster, 1985.

———. *Being-in-Dreaming: An Initiation into the Sorcerers' World*. New York: HarperCollins, *1991*.

Eagle Feather, Ken. *Traveling with Power*. Charlottesville: Hampton Roads, 1992.

———. *A Toltec Path*. Charlottesville: Hampton Roads, 1995.

———. *Tracking Freedom*. Charlottesville: Hampton Roads, 1998.

———. *The Dream of Vixen Tor*. Tracker One Studios, 2001.

Gregg, Susan. *Dance of Power: A Shamanic Journey*. St. Paul: Llewellyn, 1993.

———. *Finding the Sacred Self: A Shamanic Workbook*. St. Paul: Llewellyn, 1995.

———. *The Toltec Way: A Guide to Personal Transformation*. New York: St Martin's Press, 2000.

———. *The Complete Idiot's Guide to Spiritual Healing*. Indianapolis: Alpha Books, 2000.

———. *Mastering the Toltec Way: A Daily Guide to Happiness, Freedom, and Joy*. York Beach: Red Wheel/Weiser, 2003.

Mares, Theun. *Return of the Warriors*. Constantia: Lionheart Publishing, 1995.

———. *Cry of the Eagle*. Constantia: Lionheart Publishing, 1997.

———. *The Mists of Dragon Lore*. Constantia: Lionheart Publishing, 1998.

———. *The Quest for Maleness*. Constantia: Lionheart Publishing, 1999.

———. *Unveil the Mysteries of the Female.* Constantia: Lionheart Publishing, 1999.

———. *This Darned Elusive Happiness.* Constantia: Lionheart Publishing, 2001.

———. *Shadows of Wolf Fire.* Constantia: Lionheart Publishing, 2002.

Nelson, Mary Carroll. *Beyond Fear.* Tulsa: Council Oak, 1997.

———. *Toltec Prophecies of Don Miguel Ruiz.* Tulsa: Council Oak, 2003.

Ruiz, Don Miguel. *The Four Agreements.* San Rafael: Amber-Allen, 1997.

———. *The Mastery of Love.* San Rafael: Amber-Allen, 1999.

———. *The Four Agreements; Companion Book.* San Rafael: Amber-Allen, 2000.

———. *Prayers; A Communion with our Creator.* San Rafael: Amber-Allen, 2001.

———. *The Voice of Knowledge.* San Rafael: Amber-Allen, 2004.

Tomas. *The Promise of Power: Reflections on the Toltec Warriors' Dialogue from the Collected Works of Carlos Castaneda.* Charlottesville: Hampton Roads, 1995.

Sanchez, Victor. *The Teachings of Don Carlos: Practical Applications of the Works of Carlos Castaneda.* Rochester: Inner Traditions, 1995.

———. *Toltecs of the New Millennium.* Rochester: Inner Traditions, 1996.

———. *The Toltec Path of Recapitulation: Healing Your Past to Free Your Soul.* Rochester: Inner Traditions, 2001.

———. *The Toltec Oracle.* Rochester: Inner Traditions, 2004.

Tunneshende, Merilyn. *Medicine Dream: A Nagual Woman's Energetic Healing.* Charlottesville: Hampton Roads, 1996.

———. *Don Juan and the Power of Medicine Dreaming: A Nagual Woman's Journey of Healing.* Rochester: Bear & Company, 1996.

———. *Don Juan and the Art of Sexual Energy: The Rainbow Serpent of the Toltec.* Rochester: Bear & Company, 2001.

———. *Twilight Knowledge of the Nagual: The Spiritual Power of Shamanic Dreaming.* Rochester: Bear & Company, 2004.

Vigil, Bernadette. *Mastery of Awareness.* Rochester: Bear & Company, 2001.

Fascinating Toltec History

Carrasco, David. *Mesoamerica's Classic Heritage: From Teotihuacán to the Aztecs (Mesoamerican Worlds)*. Boulder: University Press of Colorado, 2002.

Diaz, Frank. *The Gospel of the Toltecs: The Life and Teachings of Quetzalcoatl.* Rochester: Bear & Company, 2002.

Diehl, Richard A. *Tula: The Toltec Capital of Ancient Mexico (New Aspects of Antiquity).* New York: Thames & Hudson, 1983.

Mastache, Alba Guadalupe. *Ancient Tollan: Tula and the Toltec Heartland (Mesoamerican Worlds)*. Boulder: University Press of Colorado, 2002.

Nicholson, H. B. *Topiltzin Quetzalcoatl: The Once and Future Lord of the Toltecs (Mesoamerican Worlds)*. Boulder: University Press of Colorado, 1999.

Pasztory, Esther. *Teotihuacan: An Experiment in Living.* Norman: University of Oklahoma Press, 1997.

Sugiyama, Saburo. *Human Sacrifice, Militarism, and Rulership: Materialization of State Ideology at the Feathered Serpent Pyramid, Teotihuacán (New Studies in Archaeology).* New York: Cambridge University Press, 2005.

References

The following were referenced in the writing of Chapter 1. You may also find them helpful in exploring further the historical aspects of the Toltecs.

Baldwind, Neil. *Legends of the Plumed Serpent.* Public Affairs: a member of the Perseus Books Group, 1998.

Berrin, Kathleen & Esther Pasztory. *Teotihuacán; Art from the City of the Gods.* Thames & Hudson, 1993.

Burland, CA & Werner Forman. *Feathered Serpent and Smoking Mirror.* GP Putnam's Sons, 1975.

Carrasco, David. *Quetzalcoatl and the Irony of Empire.* Chicago: The University of Chicago Press, 1982.

Harpur, James. *The Atlas of Sacred Places: Meeting Points of Heaven and Earth.* New York: Henry Holt & Company, 1994.

Pohl, John. *Exploring Mesoamerica; Places in Time.* Oxford University Press, 1999.

Appendix C

Toltec Teachers

Published Toltec Teachers

The following Toltec teachers are published authors and have websites that will assist you on your Toltec journey.

Taisha Abelar and Florinda Donner-Grau
www.castaneda.com

Heather Ash
www.spiritweavers.com

Carlos Castaneda
www.castaneda.com

David Dibble
www.thenewagreements.com

Ray Dodd
www.everydaywisdom.us

Ken Eagle Feather
www.uazu.net/kef

Susan Gregg, DCH
www.susangregg.com

Theun Mares
www.toltec-foundation.org

Sheri Rosenthal, DPM
www.sherirosenthal.com
www.journeysofthespirit.com

Don Miguel Ruiz and Don Jose Luis Ruiz
www.miguelruiz.com

Victor Sanchez
www.toltecas.com

Nonpublished Toltec Teachers

These teachers are not currently published but have informative websites and helpful information on our tradition.

Barbara Emrys and Gene Nathan, MD
www.toltecsacredlegacies.com

Ed Fox
www.intentcoaching.com

Gini Gentry
www.nagualwoman.com

Alan Hardman
www.joydancer.com

Gloria Jean
www.toltecdream.net

Vicky Miller
www.dreamreflections.com

Luis Molinar
www.toltecheartwisdom.com/index2.html

Brandt Morgan
www.thunderheart.org

Niki Orietas and Leo Van Warmerdam
www.thedreamingmind.com

Rita Rivera
www.toltecmastery.com

Barbara Simon
www.romancingyoursoul.com

Gary Van Warmerdam
www.toltecspirit.com

Index